PARIS

Research Manager
Billy Marks

Managing Editor
Chris Kingston

Editor
Michael Goncalves

Contents

Discover Paris

Paris leaves an impression on everyone, from students perfecting their *langue française* to tourists who wonder why the French don't pronounce half the consonants in each word. This city has been home to countless films, revolutions, and kings named Louis, and, in case you hadn't heard, it's a really big deal. Nearly everyone in the world idealizes Paris, whether it's for the Eiffel Tower, the grand boulevards, or the fact that there are more miles in the Louvre than in many towns. Don't let yourself be content with ideals. If you want to know the danger of that, do some research on Paris Syndrome. This city can be rough, and, yes, the waiters are judging you. When you get Englished for the first time (when someone responds to your mangled-French inquiry with an English response), you'll realize that you maybe weren't prepared for all this. But Paris and its people pull through spectacularly for those who can appreciate the sensory experiences around every corner—the sweet tastes to be found in a patisserie, the resonating bells of Notre Dame, the spring-time greens in the Jardin des Tuileries. This city will charm and bitchslap you with equal gusto, but don't get too *le tired*—by your third or fourth sincere attempt at *s'il vous plaît,* even those waiters will soften up.

Budget Paris

CHEAP EATS

As the place where some of the world's most famous chefs learned to cook (Julia Child didn't always know the art of French cooking), Parisian food is sinfully delicious. And although you might be tempted to try renowned restaurants like Fouquet's in the 8ème (and pay an arm and a leg), there are plenty of places that offer quality cuisine at an affordable price.

► **AUGUSTE:** This small *sandwicherie* sells its signature items for only €2-4 (p. 112).

► **MASSAI MARA:** If you're in the mood for affordable African cuisine (and honestly, who can say no to that?), Massai Mara has a €5 student special (p. 121).

► **CHEZ GLADINES:** The line at this Basque cafe heads out the door as people wait to get lunch for as little as €4 (p. 115).

► **CAFÉ DES PETITS FRÈRES DES PAUVRES:** The food isn't really the draw here—this cafe serves arguably the cheapest coffee in Paris (p. 118).

► **CRÊPERIE DES CANETTES:** These crepes are not only affordable, but they're prepared in the traditional square and crispy style—no soggy pancakes here! (p. 102)

Freebies

► **MUSÉE DU LOUVRE:** If you can hold off your *Mona Lisa* cravings until Friday, the Louvre (p. 62) is free for everyone under 26 after 6pm.

► **LES DISQUAIRES:** If you don't want to pay for concert tickets, this bar hosts free live music every night at 8pm.

► **PARIS MUSEUMS:** Get ready for one seriously busy day: most of Paris's museums open their doors for free on the first Sunday of each month.

► **INVALIDES:** If you're penny-pinching, don't pay to enter the war museums—the rest of the complex is free and has samples from each collection.

BUDGET ACCOMMODATIONS

Given the variety of people who travel here, Paris needs a diverse set of accommodations. Fortunately, savvy cheapskates are covered. Don't expect to find a cheap room close to the city center; the hostels and hotels get more affordable as your travel further out.

► **PLUG-INN BOUTIQUE HOSTEL:** Located in the heart of Montmartre, this hostel gains its name from the unlimited Wi-Fi and computer usage (p. 55).

► **HÔTEL PALACE:** This newly renovated hotel charges ridiculously low prices, so book fast (p. 50).

► **OOPS!:** The only mistakes being made at this hostel are the mismatched wall colors—the young backpackers who stay here don't regret a thing (p. 52).

► **CENTRE INTERNATIONALE DE PARIS:** The clean rooms in this massive 200-bed hostel are filled with international youths, so you'll save a bundle and always find someone to spend a night out with (p. 42).

▶ **WOODSTOCK HOSTEL:** Take a trip back to the '60s at this Beatles-themed hostel (p. 49).

SIGHTSEEING ON THE CHEAP

We probably don't have to tell you that Paris is full of famous sights—there's a reason you're coming here in the first place. Luckily, the many gardens and cemeteries can be traversed for free, so you can save your money for the still-reasonable museum fees (or spend it all on chocolate crepes—we aren't judging you).

▶ **MUSÉE DELACROIX:** The mastermind behind *Liberty Leading the People* called this place home before it was converted into a museum to showcase his collection (p. 73).

▶ **LE JARDIN DU LUXEMBOURG:** This garden complex used to be exclusively for royalty, but you no longer have to be rolling in crown jewels to get in (p. 71).

▶ **MUSÉE DE LA CHASSE ET DE LA NATURE:** Be forewarned: "trophies" in here are less gold and more stuffed animal, and we don't mean teddy bears (p. 67).

▶ **ÉGLISE SAINT-EUSTACHE:** Not only is this famed church free to enter, but it even has a one up on Notre Dame: its pipe organ is the largest in France (p. 64).

▶ **MUSÉE DES ARTS DÉCORATIFS:** A ticket may cost you €9, but you gain access to three museums: Interior Design, Fashion and Fabric, and Advertisement (p. 65).

What To Do

GO FOR THE GLOBE

Everyone associates Paris with traditional French cooking, but its culinary offerings don't stop at crepes and *escargot;* this truly international city draws cuisine from around the world. **L'As du Falafel** (p. 98) is the perfect place to get an affordable taste of

the Middle East, and **Thabthim Siam** (p. 107) will transport you from the Champs-Élysées to Thailand. If you're really looking for international flair, head to **Le Jip's** (p. 96) in Châtelet—the array of flavors may be hard to understand at first, but this fusion of Cuban, African, and Brazilian cuisine is delicious.

FROM PARIS TO THE PAGE

Paris is highly romanticized as well as rich in history. It's no wonder, then, that it has served as the backdrop for many classic novels, and visitors can see for themselves the sites that these works highlight. Imagine yourself as Dr. Manette from Charles Dickens's *A Tale of Two Cities* at the **Bastille Prison** (p. 84)—though you'll also have to imagine that the structure is still standing. Or, take a trip to the **Opéra Garnier** (p. 82), which inspired Gaston Leroux to write *The Phantom of the Opera*. Then relive Victor Hugo's *The Hunchback of Notre Dame* at... actually, this one's pretty self-explanatory.

NIGHT ON THE TOWN

Paris is full of nightlife options for just about every traveler. Whether you're looking for a laid-back lounge or a rockin' dance club, this city's got you covered. For the chiller side, head to **Stolly's** (p. 126) in the Marais; when you're ready for something more lively, try Bastille's Brazilian-themed **Favela Chic** (p. 134). Almost every bar in the Latin Quarter is great, but **Le Violin Dingue** (p. 128) and **Le Fifth Bar** (p. 129) really stand out. And Paris is also famous for its GLBT nightlife—**Banana Café** (p. 123) has all-night dance parties that draw all kinds of patrons.

BEYOND TOURISM

We barely have to tell you that Paris is a popular study-abroad destination, as it's the perfect place to learn about art, cuisine, history, and just about anything else. Join the crowds by honing your French-language skills with **Alliance Française** (p. 201) or embracing your love of cooking (or the need to satisfy those late-night cravings) at the **Cordon Bleu Paris Culinary Arts Institute** (p. 202). **Volunteering** (p. 203) and **paid employment** (p. 205) are also popular options for a less-standard tourist experience.

Student Superlatives

▶ **BEST PLACE TO ASK SOMEONE TO SLEEP WITH YOU WITHOUT GETTING SLAPPED:** The Moulin Rouge (thanks, Christina Aguilera!) (p. 144).

▶ **BEST PLACE TO COMPLETE A SCHOOL PROJECT:** The Parc des Buttes-Chaumont, the birthplace of Plaster of Paris (p. 91).

▶ **BEST PLACE TO INDULGE YOUR INNER DISNEY PRINCESS:** The Palais-Royal (p. 66).

▶ **BEST PLACE TO HAVE A POLITICALLY SUBVERSIVE CONVERSATION:** The 6éme's pl. St-Michel, where the left-wing riots of 1871 and 1968 both began.

▶ **BEST PLACE FOR A NEVERENDING GAME OF DUCK, DUCK, GOOSE:** Three Ducks Hostel in Montparnasse (p. 53).

Planning Your Trip

Despite all the invasions, revolutions, and riots throughout French history, Paris was still meticulously planned. The Seine River flows from east to west through the middle of the city, splitting it into two sections. The *Rive Gauche* (Left Bank) to the south is known as the intellectual heart of Paris, while the *Rive Droite* (Right Bank) to the north is famous for banking and commerce. The two islands in the middle of the Seine, the Île de la Cité and Île St-Louis, are the geographical and historical center of the city. The rest of Paris is divided into 20 arrondissements (districts) that spiral outward from the islands. The arrondissements are numbered; for example, the Eiffel Tower is located in *le septième* (the seventh), abbreviated 7ème.

If this description sounds too good to be true, it is. Neighborhoods frequently spread over multiple arrondissements and are often referred to by name rather than number. (The Marais, for example, is in both the 3ème and the 4ème.) Neighborhood names are based on major connecting hubs of the Metro or train (Montparnasse, Bastille), or major landmarks and roads (Champs-Élysées, Invalides). Streets are marked on every corner, and numerous signs point toward train stations, landmarks, and certain *triomphant* roundabouts. You can try to walk through it all, but the size of the city is deceiving. When your feet start to fall off, buses go almost everywhere in the city, and your hostel is just a ride away.

Icons

First things first: places and things that we absolutely love, sappily cherish, generally obsess over, and wholeheartedly endorse are denoted by the all-empowering 🖾 **Let's Go thumbs-up.** In addition, the icons scattered at the end of a listing can serve as visual cues to help you navigate each listing:

🖾	Let's Go recommends	☎	Phone numbers	⇄	Directions
i	Other hard info	Ⓢ	Prices	🕐	Hours

WHEN TO GO

Spring weather in Paris is fickle and punctuated by unexpected rain. Of the summer months, June is notoriously rainy, while temperatures tend to hit their peak in July and August. Summertime is typically when the tourists move in and Parisians move out, with some smaller hotels and shops closing during August. By fall, a fantastic array of auburn foliage brightens up the parks, and the weather becomes dry and temperate. This is probably the best time to visit: airfares and hotel rates drop, travel is less congested, and the museum lines are shorter. Winters are fairly cold, with highs in the mid-40s, and there is significant precipitation, although it usually comes in the form of rain rather than snow.

NEIGHBORHOODS

Île de la Cité and Île St-Louis

Situated in the physical center of Paris, these two islands are where the French monarchy (and the country itself) grew up, sheltered by the easily defendable Seine. Some 2000 years later, after the monarchy was politely asked to step down from power, the symbolic presence still remains. Île de la Cité is the larger island, where the French officially marked *kilomètre zéro,* a circular sundial in front of **Notre Dame,** as the point from which all distances in France are measured. This island is also where you'll find the seat of government and the judicial palace. The smaller

Île St-Louis is a little more laid-back and is home to cafes and restaurants that aren't choked with tourists. We were hard pressed to find a non-uniformed French person on these islands, unless you count gypsies. You can't blame them for hanging out in this area, since the high prices guarantee that tourists will be carrying a lot of cash. When you're exploring Île St-Louis, keep one eye on the sights and the other on your wallet.

Châtelet-les Halles (1er, 2ème)

Châtelet-Les Halles is famous for the **Louvre** and the marketplace at **Les Halles.** Due to these time-honored tourist traditions, the 1er and 2ème swell beyond carrying capacity during the day. Châtelet is also the central hub of all bus and most Metro lines, but when they stop for the night the area can get a little derelict. It's often difficult to distinguish between genuinely good deals and tourist traps. The area between **rue des Halles** and **Forum des Halles** has lots of cheap brasseries that won't rip you off. The easiest way to navigate the area is to find **rue de Rivoli,** which runs parallel to the Seine and past the **Hôtel de Ville.**

The Marais (3ème, 4ème)

The Marais embodies the ultimate ugly duckling tale. Originally a bog—*marais* means "marsh"—the area became livable in the 13th century when monks drained the land to build the **Right Bank.** When Henri IV constructed the glorious **place des Vosges** in the early 17th century, the area suddenly became the city's center of fashionable living, with luxury and scandal taking hold. Royal haunts gave way to slums and tenements during the Revolution, and many of the grand *hôtels particuliers* fell into ruin or disrepair. In the 1950s, the Marais was revived and declared a historic neighborhood; since then, decades of gentrification and renovation have restored the Marais to its pre-Revolutionary glory. Once-palatial mansions have become exquisite museums, and the tiny twisting streets are covered with hip bars, avant-garde galleries, and one-of-a-kind boutiques. **Rue des Rosiers,** in the heart of the 4ème, is the center of Paris's Jewish population, though the steady influx of hyper-hip clothing stores threatens its identity. Superb kosher delicatessens neighbor Middle Eastern and Eastern European restaurants, and the Marais remains livelier on Sundays than the rest of the city. The Marais is unquestionably the GLBT center of Paris, with the community's hub at the intersection of **rue**

Sainte-Croix de la Brettonerie and **rue Vieille du Temple.** Though the steady stream of tourists has begun to wear on the Marais's eclectic personality, the district continues to be a distinctive mix of old and new, queer and straight, cheap and chic.

Latin Quarter and St-Germain (5ème, 6ème)

The Latin Quarter and St-Germain are two of Paris's primary tourist neighborhoods, playing into the hands of those who expect the romantic Paris of yesteryear. The intellectual heart of Paris, these neighborhoods are home to the **Sorbonne,** various high schools, and *les Grandes Écoles,* and they are very student- and budget-friendly. The main road that divides the 5ème and 6ème is the **boulevard Saint-Michel,** which runs along the eastern border of the **Jardins de Luxembourg.** As tempted as you may be to explore St-Germain-des-Prés, your wallet will thank you if you head to the 5ème and roam **rue Monge** and **rue Mouffetard** for food, nightlife, and accommodations.

Invalides (7ème)

With tourist attractions and museums on every corner, it can be difficult to find a deal in the 7ème. This neighborhood is spread out, so orienting yourself isn't always easy. At the center are **Tour Eiffel** and **Invalides,** each with a large grassy lawn in front, **Champ de Mars** and **Espalande des Invalides** respectively. Rue de l'Université and the quais run parallel along the Seine throughout the neighborhood, while the main roads in and out of the center are av. de Bourdonnais, which leads to quai Branly, and av. Bosquet, which leads to **Musée d'Orsay.** Travelers should take advantage of metro lines 6, 8, and 13.

Champs-Élysées (8ème)

If the Champs-Élysées were a supermodel, it would have been forced to retire for being well past its prime. This arrondissement was synonymous with fashion throughout the 19th century, and many boulevards are still lined with the vast mansions, expensive shops, and grandiose monuments that brought in tourists. But that old sense of sophistication has since been juxtaposed with charmless boutiques, office buildings, and car dealerships. Only the **Champs-Élysées** itself bustles late into the night, thanks to its unparalleled nightclubs and droves of tourists. A stroll along

avenue Montaigne, rue du Faubourg Saint-Honoré, or around the **Madeleine** will give you a taste of excessively rich life in Paris. There are fewer tourists in the northern part of the neighborhood, near the **Parc Monceau.**

Opéra (9ème) and Canal St-Martin (10ème)

The 9ème and the 10ème are the more difficult neighborhoods to wander due to their lack of tall landmarks (as opposed to, for example, the 7ème's Eiffel Tower, or the 18ème's Sacré-Cœur). Criss-crossing the 9ème are the main roads **rue la Fayette** and **rue Fontaine,** with the famous **Opéra Garnier** sitting in the southeast corner next to its appropriately named Metro stop. This is a neighborhood of extremes: the northern boundary is just before the red light district of **Pigalle,** the southern is marked by the chic shopping districts on the **Grands Boulevards,** and there is enough residential area in between to make it feel less touristy.

Right next to the 9ème, the 10ème is known (and named for) the **Canal Saint-Martin,** which runs along the eastern border of the arrondissement. Stray too far from this "mini-Seine" (i.e., anywhere west of bd de Magenta) and you'll find yourself smack in the middle of the sketchy area that surrounds the **Gare du Nord** and **Gare de l'Est.** If the gun armories and cash-for-gold stores didn't give you a hint, we'll tell you to stay clear of this area at night.

Bastille (11ème, 12ème)

The Bastille area is famous for housing the prison where the French Revolution kicked off on July 14, 1789. Hundreds of years later, Parisians still storm this neighborhood nightly in search of the latest cocktails, culinary innovations, and up-and-coming musicians. Five Metro lines converge at Ⓜ**République** and three lines at Ⓜ**Bastille,** making this district a busy transport hub. The 1989 opening of the glassy **Opéra Bastille** on the bicentennial of the Revolution was supposed to breathe new cultural life into the area, but the party atmosphere has yet to give way to galleries and string quartets. Today, with numerous bars along **rue de Lappe,** manifold dining options on **rue de la Roquette** and **rue Jean-Pierre Timbaud,** and young designer boutiques, the Bastille is a great area for unwinding after a day at the museums.

Montparnasse and Southern Paris (13ème, 14ème, 15ème)

These three arrondissements, which make up nearly one-sixth of Paris, lack the photo ops and famous sights that attract tourists elsewhere in the city. However, they do portray the local side of Paris: more laid-back, cheaper, and friendlier. The 13ème has a strange combination of characters thanks to **Chinatown,** around rue de Tolbiac, and the small hippie enclave surrounding **rue de la Butte-aux-Cailles,** which avoids the capitalist drive to overcharge for meals or entertainment. The main hub of the 13ème is **Place d'Italie,** where you can find brasseries and a huge mall. Montparnasse is more homogeneous than the 13ème and is similar to the St-Germain of the 1920s. Here you'll find bohemian Parisians whose souls have yet to harden. Markets, cemeteries, and major boulevards cater to the locals. On the border between the 14ème and 15ème, the domineering **Tour de Montparnasse** gives a point of reference and access to transport almost anywhere in the city, while **boulevard de Rennes** and **boulevard Raspail** lead to St-Germain. The 15ème is quiet and even more residential than the 13ème and 14ème; most travelers don't make it farther south than bd de Grenelle.

Slight Redistricting

Paris wasn't always divided into 20 arrondissements; strange references to *anciens* arrondissements on old churches and random street corners come from the city's old organization. While his uncle controlled most of Europe, Napoleon III conquered the internal structure of Paris, doubling the area of the city and subsequently reorganizing it all. It's no surprise Napoleon I remains the more famous of the two: as great as sensible municipal organization is, it's no match for continental domination.

Western Paris (16ème, 17ème)

These two arrondissements are almost devoid of tourists. More residential, these neighborhoods are home to ladies who lunch, their beautiful children, and their overworked husbands. The 16ème is frequented by Parisian elites who have money and are willing to spend it in the expensive boutiques and cafe lounges lining the main roads around **Trocadéro. Avenue Georges Mandel** cuts the neighborhood in two, and **avenue Kléber** will take you straight to the Arc de Triomphe in the 8ème.

The 17ème is way more relaxed in terms of residents and prices. Its sheer size and lack of notable sights make this area a retreat for the working class and overly earnest teenagers who take leisurely strolls or sit in the many cafes. Around Ⓜ**Ternes,** you'll find smaller boutique hotels and older tourists, whereas on the opposite side, around Ⓜ**Rome,** you'll get a sense of the community that exists next to Montmartre. Running through the center and connecting these two areas is **boulevard de Courcelles,** which turns into **boulevard des Batignolles.**

Montmartre (18ème)

Montmartre may just be the most eccentric of Paris's arrondissements, featuring scenic vistas at the **Basilique du Sacré-Cœur,** historic cabarets, the **Butte vineyard,** and the unsurprisingly skin-toned establishments in the **Red Light District** on the southern border. Hiking the 130m hill can be a challenge. The 18ème has recently exploded with youth hostels that keep bars full at night while simultaneously giving pickpockets an easy target.

Eastern Paris (19ème, 20ème)

This is a huge area. The lack of visible landmarks make it difficult to navigate on foot, so it's better to take the Metro during the day and a taxi at night (if for some reason you end up there after dark—trust us, you don't want to). The main places worth visiting are the **Parc des Buttes-Chaumont** (Ⓜ Buttes Chaumont, Botzaris, or Laumière) and **Cimetière du Père Lachaise** (Ⓜ Père Lachaise, Gambetta, or Philippe Auguste). Running along the northern edge of the 19ème is **avenue Jean-Jaurès,** which leads straight to the Museum of Science. From av. Jean-Jaurès any turn up the hill leads to the park. **boulevard de Belleville** connects the two arrondissements and has some of the best (and cheapest) African and Asian restaurants in the city. But as soon as the sun sets, this place turns into a Parisian mini-Marseille, and that's not where you want to be.

SUGGESTED ITINERARIES

Dîner et un Film

There are a million options for cute dates in Paris; after all, it didn't earn the nickname City of Love for nothing. Here's how to take the classic dinner and a movie and make it more authentically French.

1. MUSÉE DU VIN: What's more romantic than starting your date in a wine museum? Plus, the price of admission gets you a glass of wine (p. 88).

2. CHEZ MAURICE: The wooden interior and traditional French cuisine of this 10ème restaurant will surely bring romance to your date (p. 110).

3. CINÉMATHÈQUE FRANÇAISE: Head to this theater to snuggle during a classic French film, or peruse the exhibits of costumes and props from the history of cinema (p. 144).

4. PONT DES ARTS: End your date at this famously romantic bridge—for the past few years, couples have been attaching *cadenas d'amour* (love padlocks) to it to express their burning passions. Although the government is barring visitors from continuing this practice, you can still head here to express your newfound love (p. 123).

Walk of Fame

If you truly wanted to walk in the footsteps of every famous person who's been to Paris, you'd never finish. So here is a shortened route through the 6ème that lets you experience the lives of some great thinkers of the past.

1. SHAKESPEARE AND CO. BOOKSTORE: Start at this historic shop that attracted such literary artists as Ernest Hemingway, Ezra Pound, and James Joyce (p. 72).

2. BOULEVARD SAINT-GERMAIN: This street was the popular stomping ground for Existentialists and Surrealists. Today, it's lined with something a little less subversive: boutiques from famous designers like Louis Vuitton and Armani.

3. ÉGLISE SAINT-GERMAIN DES PRÉS: The church itself is famous—it's the oldest one in Paris—but it also holds the tomb of philosopher René Descartes (p. 72).

4. LES DEUX MAGOTS: The first in a pair of historic cafes, Les Deux Magots was the popular hangout of Simone de Beauvoir and Picasso (p. 75).

5. CAFÉ DE FLORE: Although Café de Flore was less popular with the intellectuals, it still saw the likes of André Breton and Picasso (when he wasn't at the rival cafe down the block) (p. 75).

Three-Day Weekend

Let's start by saying that three days is nowhere near enough time to see everything in Paris; the city is far too expansive for that. However, if you just want a best-of-the-best itinerary, you're in luck. Here's how to have the ultimate experience in Paris in just three days, including the best sights, food, and nightlife to be found.

Day One

1. ARC DE TRIOMPHE: Start your day off in the Champs-Élysées to get a 360-degree view of Paris from the top of this famous monument (p. 80). When you're done taking in the panorama, explore the av. des Champs-Élysées and its side streets to get a taste for how the French elite lives.

2. CHEZ LUCIE: Hope you brought your appetite—this Creole restaurant features a three-course lunch special, and the portions are enormous (p. 106).

3. MUSÉE D'ORSAY AND MUSÉE RODIN: When you're ready to move after that large meal, explore this pair of museums, for which you can buy a combined ticket for €12. The Musée d'Orsay (p. 78) is a large collection of Impressionist and Post-Impressionist works, while the Musée Rodin (p. 77) features a couple of must-sees: *The Thinker* and *The Gates of Hell*.

4. EIFFEL TOWER: Once the sun has begun to set, head to your second iconic sight of the day (p. 76). Not only will the lines be much shorter at night, but you'll see the City of Light in its twinkling nighttime glory. Plus, every hour after dark, the tower itself sparkles, and that's a sight not to be missed.

5. LA METHODE: By now you (might) feel hungry again after your filling lunch, so take your final Metro ride of the day to the Latin Quarter for an appetizing dose of southern French cuisine (p. 102).

6. LE VIOLIN DINGUE: Spend part (or all) of your night at this bar and club that is filled with locals after 1am (p. 128). You're also in close proximity to the happening rue Mouffetard, which has some of the cheapest bars in the city.

Day Two

1. CENTRE POMPIDOU: Head to the Marais to explore this complex whose museum features international modern art, a research laboratory, and a pretty trippy room that chronicles the growth of wars and violence (p. 66).

2. LAO SIAM: The outer arrondissements beckon you this afternoon. This 19ème restaurant has cheap Vietnamese fare, which includes unique flavors like some concoction they've dubbed "hip-hop sauce" (p. 121).

3. CIMETIÈRE DU PÈRE LACHAISE: Over one million people have been laid to rest in this cemetery, and you'll want time to explore and find the most famous residents, Jim Morrison and Oscar Wilde (p. 92).

4. LE REFLET DU MIROIR: For dinner, try this Montmartre creperie that takes international cuisine and slips it into standard French pancakes (p. 119).

5. L'ESCALE: You can end your night here filling up on L'Escale's cheap drinks, but be careful, since their concoctions are rather on the strong side (p. 139). You don't want to be hungover for the Louvre tomorrow.

Day Three

1. MUSÉE DU LOUVRE: Honestly, you could probably devote an entire week to the Louvre (p. 62) and still not make it all the way through—there's just so much to see, and you can easily lose yourself in the miles of galleries. Make sure to see the famous *Venus de Milo* and *The Coronation of Napoleon,* then gasp (and squint) at how surprisingly compact the *Mona Lisa* is.

2. MA SALLE À MANGER: You deserve a meal—and maybe a drink—after your explorations in the Louvre, and this restaurant and cocktail bar on Île de la Cité delivers them both (p. 95).

3. NOTRE DAME: Head to the other side of the island to see this famous cathedral (p. 58) that has been hosting Catholics, revolutionaries, and hunchbacks since 1163. Make sure to check out the stained-glass windows and climb up to the bell tower to get the full Quasimodo experience—just don't start talking to the gargoyles.

4. PANTHÉON: If you didn't get enough dead people yesterday, return to the Latin Quarter to see this historical monument and the crypt that's within it (p. 70).

5. LE JARDIN DU LUXEMBOURG: Stroll through these beautiful and expansive gardens to see statues, fountains, and picnicking locals (p. 71).

6. L'AS DU FALAFEL: You've probably spent enough on all those entrance fees by now, so grab an affordable but delicious falafel dinner in the Marais (p. 98).

7. THE MARAIS: The neighborhood teems with nightlife options every night of the week, whether you're looking for chill bars or exciting GLBT clubs. For the former, try **Stolly's** (p. 126); for the latter, brace yourself for **Raidd Bar** (p. 126), which will end your Paris weekend in some style.

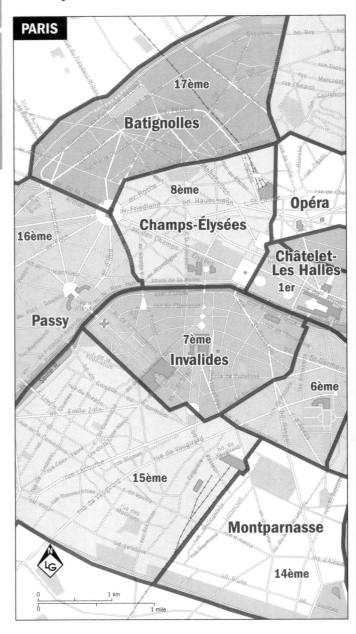

PARIS

17ème

Batignolles

8ème
bd. Haussmann

Opéra

Champs-Élysées

16ème

Châtelet-
Les Halles

1er

Passy

7ème

Invalides

6ème

15ème

Montparnasse

14ème

0   1 km
0   1 mile

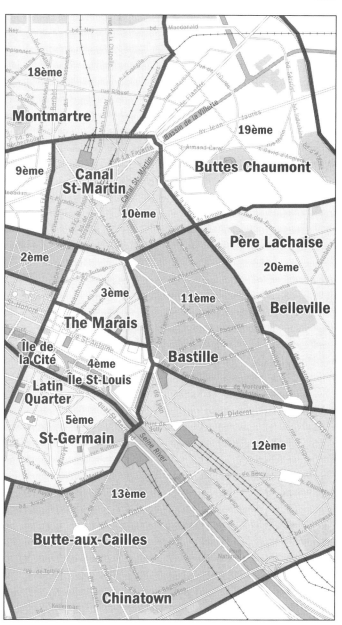

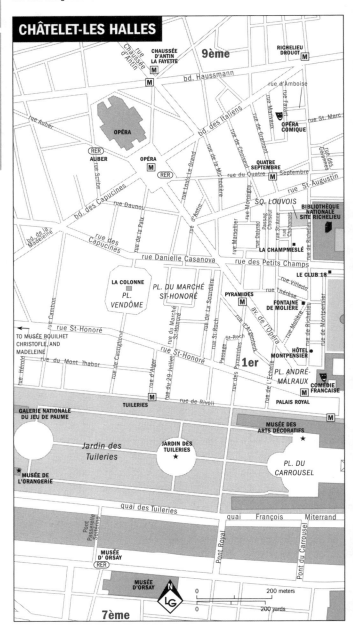

CHÂTELET-LES HALLES

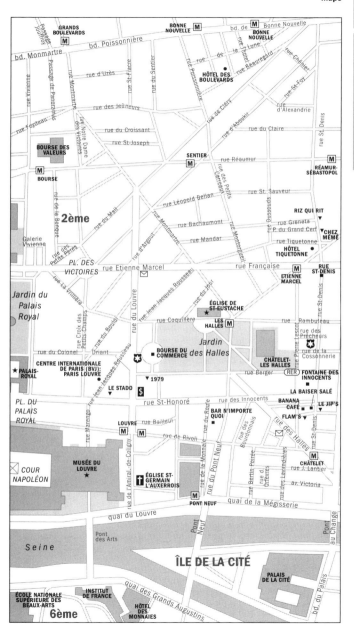

Planning Your Trip

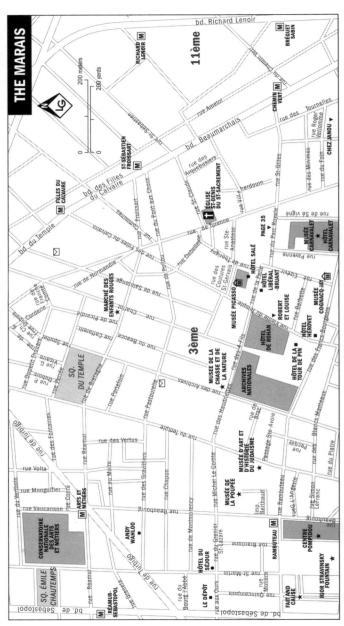

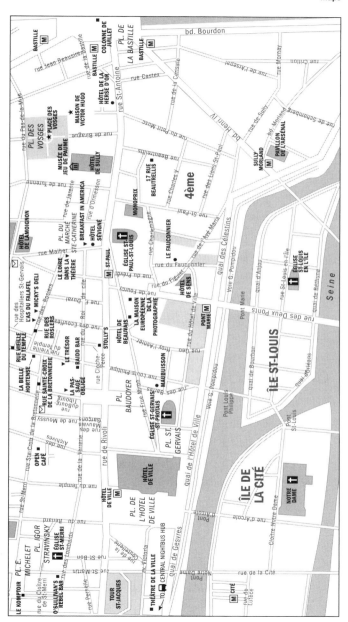

bd. Bourdon

rue Jean Beaustreet

rue Castex

rue St-Antoine

BASTILLE Ⓜ

COLONNE DE JUILLET ★

PL. DE LA BASTILLE

Ⓜ BASTILLE

LA BASTILLE

rue de la Cerisaie

rue de Sully

PAVILLON DE L'ARSENAL

Ⓜ SULLY MORLAND

MAISON DE VICTOR HUGO

HÔTEL DE LA HERSE D'OR

PL. DES VOSGES

★ PLACE DES VOSGES

MUSÉE DE JEU DE PAUME

HÔTEL DE SULLY

17 RUE BEAUTRELLIS

MONOPRIX

4ème

LE FAUCONNIER

rue de Turenne

HÔTEL DE LAMOIGNON

PL. DU MARCHÉ STE-CATHERINE

BREAKFAST IN AMERICA

HÔTEL SÉVIGNÉ

ÉGLISE ST-PAUL ST-LOUIS

Ⓜ ST-PAUL

ÉGLISE ST-LOUIS EN L'ÎLE

rue St-Louis en l'Île

Seine

LE LOIRE DANS LA THÉIÈRE

MICKY'S DELI

L'AS DU FALAFEL

rue des Rosiers

RUE VIEILLE DU TEMPLE

RUE DES ROSIERS

LE TRÉSOR

RAIDD BAR

STOLLY'S

HÔTEL DE BEAUVAIS

LA MAISON EUROPÉENNE DE LA PHOTOGRAPHIE

HÔTEL DE SENS

PONT MARIE Ⓜ

Pont Marie

ÎLE ST-LOUIS

LA BELLE HORTENSE

RUE SAINTE-CROIX DE LA BRETONNERIE

LA PASSAGE OBLIGÉ

MAUBUISSON

quai de Bourbon

quai d'Orléans

Pont St-Louis

OPEN CAFÉ

PL. BAUDOYER

ÉGLISE ST-GERVAIS ST-PROTAIS

PL. ST. GERVAIS

rue de Rivoli

HÔTEL DE VILLE

Ⓜ HÔTEL DE VILLE

PL. DE L'HÔTEL DE VILLE

quai de l'Hôtel de Ville

ÎLE DE LA CITÉ

Pont Louis Philippe

LE KOMPTOIR

PL. E. MICHELET

IGOR STRAVINSKY

ÉGLISE ST-MERRI

O'SULLIVAN'S REBEL BAR

TOUR ST-JACQUES

THÉÂTRE DE LA VILLE

CENTRAL NIGHTBUS HUB

quai de Gesvres

Pont Notre Dame

NOTRE DAME

rue de la Cité

Ⓜ CITÉ

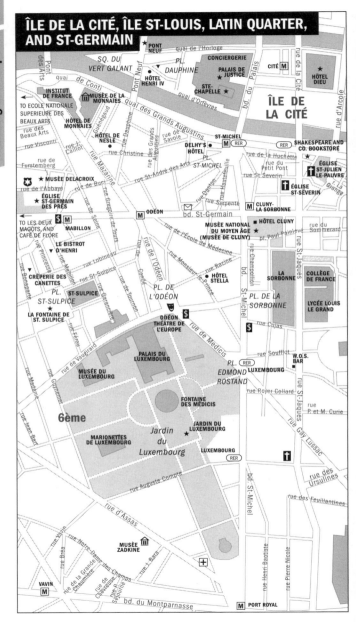

ÎLE DE LA CITÉ, ÎLE ST-LOUIS, LATIN QUARTER, AND ST-GERMAIN

PONT NEUF
quai de l'Horloge
SQ. DU VERT GALANT
CONCIERGERIE
PL. DAUPHINE
CITÉ M
PALAIS DE JUSTICE
Pont des Arts
HÔTEL HENRI IV
HÔTEL DIEU
quai de Conti
STE-CHAPELLE
bd. du Palais
rue de la Cité
rue d'Arcole
INSTITUT DE FRANCE
MUSÉE DE LA MONNAIES
quai des Grands Augustins
ÎLE DE LA CITÉ
TO ECOLE NATIONALE SUPÉRIEURE DES BEAUX-ARTS
HÔTEL DE MONNAIES
quai d'Orfèvres
rue des Beaux-Arts
ST-MICHEL M RER
RER SHAKESPEARE AND CO. BOOKSTORE
rue de Visconti
HÔTEL DE NESLE
DELHY'S HÔTEL
rue de la Huchette
ÉGLISE ST-JULIEN LE-PAUVRE
rue de Furstemberg
rue Christine
PL. ST-MICHEL
rue du Petit Pont
la Grange
rue J. Callot
rue St-André des Arts
rue St Severin
MUSÉE DELACROIX
rue St-Séverin
ÉGLISE ST-SÉVERIN
rue de l'Abbaye
rue de Buci
rue Serpente
ÉGLISE ST-GERMAIN DES PRÉS
rue St-Grégoire de Tours
CLUNY-LA SORBONNE M
TO LES DEUX MAGOTS, AND CAFÉ DE FLORE
ODÉON M
bd. St-Germain
HÔTEL CLUNY
rue du Sommerard
MABILLON M
MUSÉE NATIONAL DU MOYEN ÂGE (MUSÉE DE CLUNY)
pl. Paul Painlevé
rue de l'École de Médecine
rue St-Jacques
LE BISTROT D'HENRI
LA SORBONNE
COLLÈGE DE FRANCE
rue de Princesse
rue Monsieur le Prince
HÔTEL STELLA
CRÊPERIE DES CANETTES
rue St-Sulpice
PL. DE L'ODÉON
PL. DE LA SORBONNE
LYCÉE LOUIS LE GRAND
PL. ST-SULPICE
rue de Tournon
ST-MICHEL
rue Cujas
LA FONTAINE DE ST. SULPICE
ODÉON THÉÂTRE DE L'EUROPE
rue de Vaugirard
rue de Médicis
rue Soufflot
W.O.S. BAR
PALAIS DU LUXEMBOURG
PL. EDMOND ROSTAND
LUXEMBOURG RER
rue Royer Collard
MUSÉE DU LUXEMBOURG
rue Gay Lussac
FONTAINE DES MÉDICIS
rue P. et M. Curie
6ème
rue Jean Bart
Jardin du Luxembourg
JARDIN DU LUXEMBOURG
MARIONETTES DE LUXEMBOURG
LUXEMBOURG
RER
rue Auguste Compte
rue des Ursulines
bd. St-Michel
rue d'Assas
rue des Feuillantines
rue Brea
rue Notre-Dame des Champs
MUSÉE ZADKINE
rue J. Bara
rue Henri-Baptiste
rue Pierre Nicole
VAVIN M
rue de la Grande Chaumière
rue de Chevreuse
bd. du Montparnasse
PORT ROYAL M

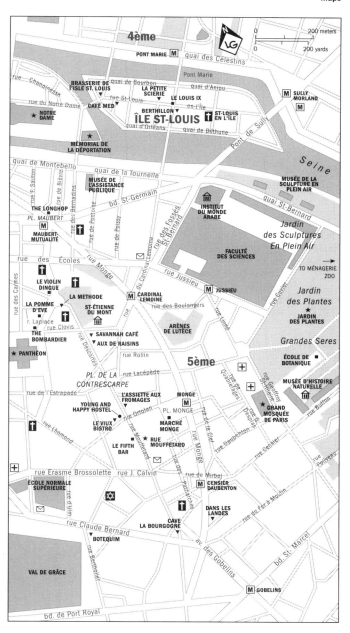

4ème

PONT MARIE Ⓜ quai des Célestins

0   200 meters
0   200 yards

Pont Marie

quai de Bourbon

rue Chanainesse

rue du Notre Dame

BRASSERIE DE
L'ISLE ST. LOUIS

quai d'Anjou

Ⓜ SULLY
MORLAND

LA PETITE
SCIERIE

rue St-Louis

CAFÉ MED ▼

BERTHILLON ▼

LE LOUIS IX
en-l'île

ÎLE ST-LOUIS

★ ST-LOUIS
EN L'ÎLE

★ NOTRE
DAME

quai d'Orléans   quai de Béthune

Pont de Sully

★ MÉMORIAL DE
LA DÉPORTATION

Seine

quai de Montebello

quai de la Tournelle

MUSÉE DE LA
SCULPTURE EN
PLEIN AIR

rue de Bièvre

rue F. Sauton

MUSÉE DE
L'ASSISTANCE
PUBLIQUE

bd. St-Germain

quai St-Bernard

INSTITUT
DU MONDE
ARABE

Jardin
des Sculptures
En Plein Air

THE LONGHOP

PL. MAUBERT

rue des Bernardins

rue de Pontoise

rue de Poissy

MAUBERT-
MUTUALITÉ Ⓜ

rue du Cardinal Lemoine

rue des Fossés
St-Bernard

FACULTÉ
DES SCIENCES

rue des   Écoles

rue Monge

rue Jussieu

Ⓜ JUSSIEU

TO MÉNAGERIE
ZOO →

rue des Carmes

LE VIOLIN
DINGUE

LA METHODE

Ⓜ CARDINAL
LEMOINE

rue des Boulangers

rue Linné

rue Cuvier

Jardin
des Plantes

LA POMME
D'EVE

ST-ÉTIENNE
DU MONT

rue Descartes

★ JARDIN
DES PLANTES

r. Laplace

rue Clovis

THE
BOMBARDIER

SAVANNAH CAFÉ ▼

AUX DE RAISINS ▼

ARÈNES
DE LUTÈCE

Grandes Seres

★ PANTHÉON

rue Rollin

5ème

ÉCOLE DE
BOTANIQUE ■

PL. DE LA
CONTRESCARPE

rue Lacépède

rue Quatrefages

rue Geoffroy St-Hilaire

MUSÉE D'HISTOIRE
NATURELLE

rue de l'Estrapade

L'ASSIETTE AUX
FROMAGES

MONGE

Ⓜ

rue Buffon

YOUNG AND
HAPPY HOSTEL

rue Ortolan

PL. MONGE

rue du B. Despres

★ GRAND
MOSQUÉE
DE PARIS

LE VIUX
BISTRO

MARCHÉ
MONGE

rue Lhomond

rue Daubenton

rue Gracieuse

rue Censier

LE FIFTH
BAR

★ RUE
MOUFFETARD

rue Monge

rue de la Clef

rue du Fer à Moulin

rue Erasme Brossolette   rue J. Calvin

rue de Mirbel

Ⓜ CENSIER
DAUBENTON

rue Polyveau

ÉCOLE NORMALE
SUPÉRIEURE

rue d'Ulm

rue des Patriarches

DANS LES
LANDES ▼

rue Claude Bernard

CAVE
LA BOURGOGNE ▼

rue Berthollet

BOTEQUIM

av. des Gobelins

bd. St-Marcel

VAL DE GRÂCE

bd. de Port Royal

Ⓜ GOBELINS

Planning Your Trip

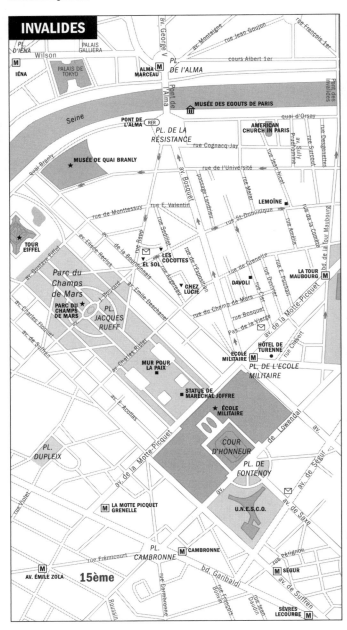

INVALIDES

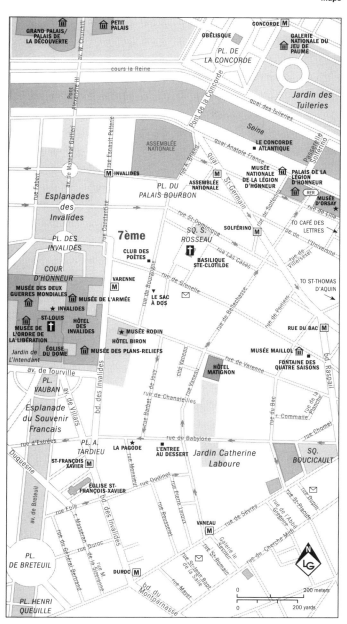

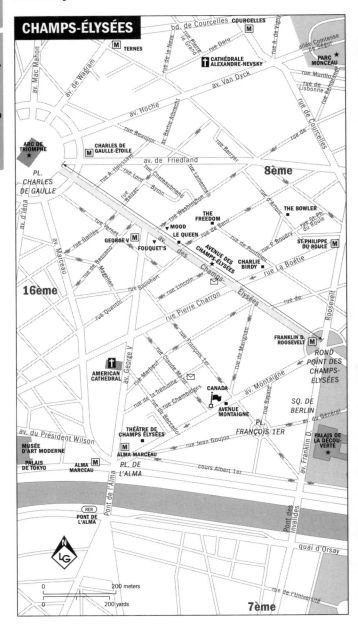

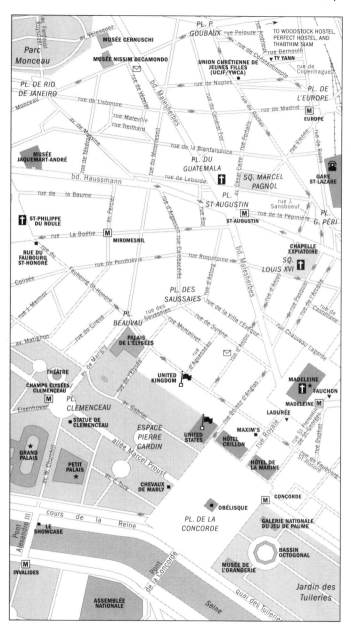

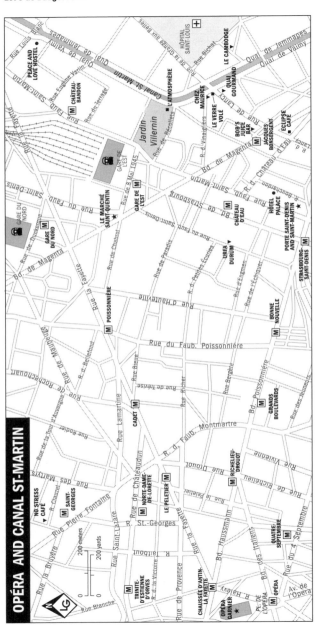

OPÉRA AND CANAL ST-MARTIN

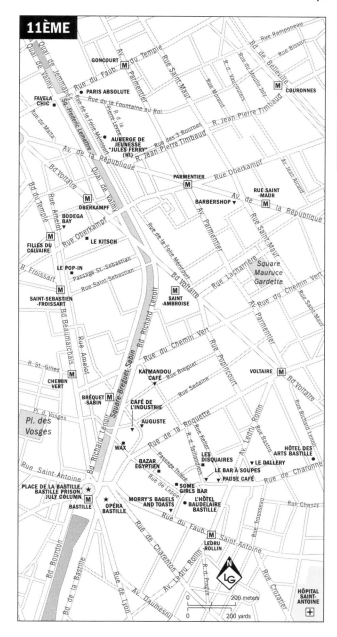

11ÈME

GONCOURT Ⓜ

COURONNES Ⓜ

FAVELA CHIC ■

● PARIS ABSOLUTE

Rue de la Fountaine au Roi

Bd de Belleville

R. Jean-Pierre Timbaud

● AUBERGE DE
JEUNESSE
"JULES FERRY"
(HI)

Rue Jean-Pierre Timbaud

Av. de la République

PARMENTIER Ⓜ   Rue Oberkampf

RUE SAINT-
MAUR Ⓜ

Av. de la République

BARBERSHOP ▼

OBERKAMPF Ⓜ

BODEGA
BAY ▼

FILLES DU
CALVAIRE Ⓜ

■ LE KITSCH

Rue Oberkampf

LE POP-IN ●

Passage St.-Sebastian

Rue Saint-Sebastian

Square
Maurice
Gardette

SAINT-SEBASTIEN
-FROISSART Ⓜ

R. Froissart

SAINT-
AMBROISE Ⓜ

Bd Voltaire

Rue du Chemin Vert

CHEMIN
VERT Ⓜ

R. St.-Gilles

VOLTAIRE Ⓜ

Bd Voltaire

KATMANDOU
CAFÉ ■   Rue Bréguet

BRÉQUET-
SABIN Ⓜ

Pl. d. Vosges

*Pl. des
Vosges*

Rue Sedaine

CAFÉ DE
L'INDUSTRIE
▼

● AUGUSTE

Rue de la Roquette

HÔTEL DES
ARTS BASTILLE ■

WAX ■

BAZAR
EGYPTIEN ■

LES
DISQUAIRES ■

▼ LE DALLERY

Passage Thiéré

LE BAR À SOUPES ▼

Rue de Lappe

▼ PAUSE CAFÉ

Rue de Charonne

Rue Saint-Antoine

● SOME
GIRLS BAR

PLACE DE LA BASTILLE,
BASTILLE PRISON,
JULY COLUMN ★

MORRY'S BAGELS
AND TOASTS ★

L'HÔTEL
BAUDELAIRE
● BASTILLE

Rue Chanzy

BASTILLE Ⓜ

OPÉRA
BASTILLE ★

Rue du Faub. Saint-Antoine

LEDRU-
ROLLIN Ⓜ

Bd Bourdon

Rue de Charenton

Av. Ledru-Rollin

N
LG

HÔPITAL
SAINT-
ANTOINE ✚

0   200 meters
0   200 yards

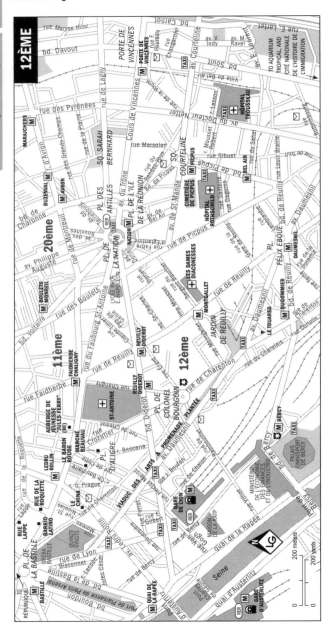

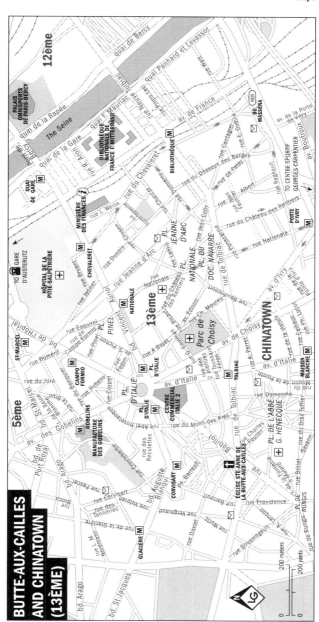

BUTTE-AUX-CAILLES
AND CHINATOWN
(13ÈME)

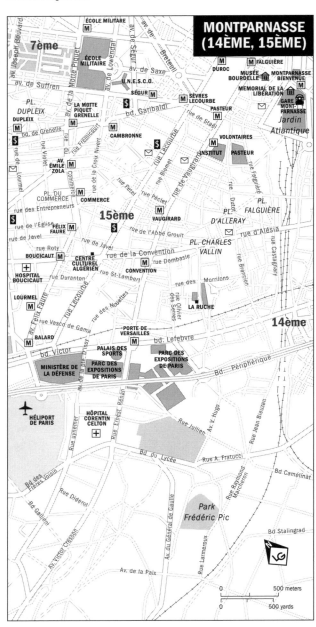

MONTPARNASSE (14ÈME, 15ÈME)

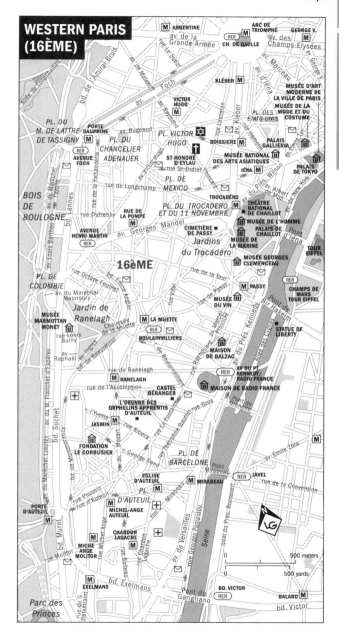

WESTERN PARIS (16ÈME)

M ARGENTINE

ARC DE TRIOMPHE

GEORGE V. **M**

av. de la Grande Armée

RER CH. DE GAULLE

av. des Champs-Elysées

bd. de l'Amiral Bruix

rue de Longchamp

av. de Malakoff

Foch

av. de la Grande Armée

rue de la Faisanderie

av. Raymond Poincaré

KLÉBER **M**

av. Marceau

av. d'Iéna

MUSÉE D'ART MODERNE DE LA VILLE DE PARIS

VICTOR HUGO **M**

av. Bugeaud

av. Victor Hugo

av. Kléber

MUSÉE DE LA MODE ET DU COSTUME

PL. DU M. DE LATTRE DE TASSIGNY

PORTE DAUPHINE **M**

av. Bugeaud

PL. VICTOR HUGO ✡

PL. DES ÉTATS-UNIS

PL. DU CHANCELIER ADENAUER

RER

AVENUE FOCH

ST-HONORÉ D'EYLAU ✝

rue St-Didier

BOISSIÈRE **M**

PALAIS GALLIERA 🏛

av. du Prés. Wilson

MUSÉE NATIONAL DES ARTS ASIATIQUES

IÉNA **M**

PALAIS DE TOKYO

BOIS DE BOULOGNE

av. du Maréchal Fayolle

bd. Lannes

bd. Lannes

av. Louis Barthou

rue de la Faisanderie

rue de Longchamp

PL. DE MEXICO

av. Victor Hugo

av. Georges Mandel

TROCADÉRO

PL. DU TROCADÉRO ET DU 11 NOVEMBRE

M **THÉÂTRE NATIONAL DE CHAILLOT**

av. du Prés. Albert de Mun

av. de New York

rue Dufrenoy

RUE DE LA POMPE **M**

av. Georges Mandel

CIMETIÈRE DE PASSY

MUSÉE DE L'HOMME 🏛

AVENUE HENRI MARTIN

RER

Jardins du Trocadéro

PALAIS DE CHAILLOT

🏛 **MUSÉE DE LA MARINE**

TOUR EIFFEL

16ÈME

rue Octave Feuillet

bd. Émile Augier

rue de la Tour

MUSÉE GEORGES CLEMENCEAU 🏛

PL. DE COLOMBIE

av. du Maréchal Maunoury

rue de la Pompe

rue de Passy

rue Vital

M **PASSY**

RER

CHAMPS DE MARS TOUR EIFFEL

Pont de Bir-Hakeim

Jardin de Ranelagh

MUSÉE MARMOTTAN MONET 🏛

Chaussée de la Muette

M **LA MUETTE**

MUSÉE DU VIN 🏛

rue Raynouard

av. Marcel Proust

rue Louis Boilly

RER

BOULAINVILLIERS

av. du Prés. Kennedy

STATUE OF LIBERTY

av. Raphaël

av. du Ranelagh

bd. de Beauséjour

rue du Ranelagh

M **RANELAGH**

rue de Boulainvilliers

MAISON DE BALZAC 🏛

av. du Prés. Kennedy

AV DU PT KENNEDY RADIO FRANCE

av. du M. Franchet d'Esperey

rue de l'Assomption

RER

🏛 **MAISON DE RADIO FRANCE**

bd. de Montmorency

bd. Suchet

CASTEL BÉRANGER

rue Mozart

L'OEUVRE DES ORPHELINS APPRENTIS D'AUTEUIL

rue La Fontaine

Pont de Grenelle

av. du Maréchal Lyautey

l'Yvette

rue Ribera

rue Gros

JASMIN **M**

rue La Fontaine

rue Théophile Gautier

FONDATION LE CORBUSIER

f. George Sand

PL. DE BARCELONE

Pont Mirabeau

av. Émile Zola

ÉGLISE D'AUTEUIL

M **MIRABEAU**

RER **JAVEL**

rue de la Convention

PORTE D'AUTEUIL **M**

rue Poussin

rue d'Auteuil

PL. D'AUTEUIL

MICHEL-ANGE AUTEUIL

rue Mirabeau

av. de Versailles

CHARDON LAGACHE

rue Chanez

rue Chardon Lagache

Seine

quai du Prés. Kennedy

MICHEL ANGE MOLITOR **M**

rue Molitor

rue Michel Ange

av. Georges Pompidou

VG

0 _____ 500 meters

0 _____ 500 yards

EXELMANS **M**

rue du G. Delestraint

bd. Exelmans

bd. Exelmans

Pont du Garigliano

BD. VICTOR **RER**

BALARD **M**

Parc des Princes

rue du Cdt. Guilbaud

bd. Victor

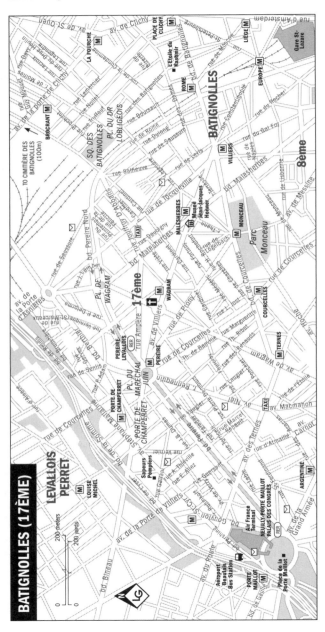

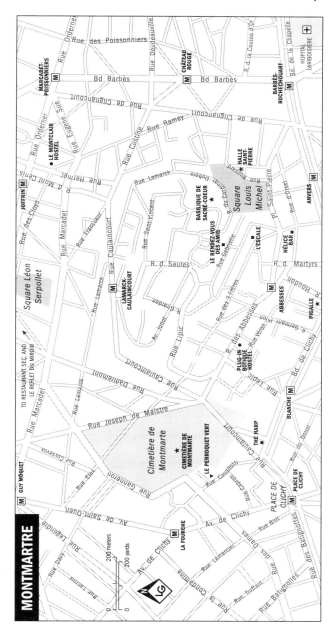

MONTMARTRE

Rue des Poissonniers

Rue Ordener

Rue Doudeauville

R. d. la Goutte d'Or

R. d. la Chapelle

HÔPITAL LARIBOISIÈRE

MARCADET-POISSONNIERS

CHÂTEAU ROUGE

Bd Barbès

BARBÈS-ROCHECHOUART

Rue de Clignancourt

Rue de Clignancourt

Rue Ramey

Rue Custine

Rue Ordener

Rue Eugène Sue

R. d. Mont Cenis

Rue Hermel

LE MONTCLAIR HOSTEL

JOFFRIN

Rue des Clovis

Rue Marcadet

Rue Francœur

Rue Caulaincourt

Rue Lamarck

Rue Saint-Vincent

HALLE SAINT-PIERRE

Cardinal Dubois

Rue Lamarck

BASILIQUE DE SACRÉ-COEUR ★

Square Louis Michel ★

Rue du Chevalier de la Barre

Pl. Saint-Pierre

ANVERS

Rue d'Orsel

LE RENDEZ-VOUS DES AMIS ★

L'ESCALE

R. d. Saules

Rue Gabrielle

HÉLICE BAR ●

R. d. Martyrs

Square Léon Serpollet

LAMARCK-CAULAINCOURT

Rue Lamarck

R. Girardon

Av. Junot

Rue des 3-Frères

ABBESSES

R. Houdon

PIGALLE ★

Rue Germain Pilon

Rue Véron

Rue Lepic

R. des Abbesses

TO RESTAURANT SEC, AND LE REFLET DU MIROIR

Rue Caulaincourt

Rue Damrémont

Rue Lamarck

PLUG-IN BOUTIQUE HOSTEL ●

Bd de Clichy

BLANCHE

Rue Joseph de Maistre

Cimetière de Montmarte

CIMETIÈRE DE MONTMARTRE ★

LE PERROQUET VERT ▼

Rue Cavallotti

Rue Caulaincourt

THE HARP ■

Rue Ganneron

Rue Coysevox

Rue Cardinet

PLACE DE CLICHY

PLACE DE CLICHY

Rue Biot

Rue Forest

Rue de Douai

GUY MÔQUET

Av. de Saint-Ouen

Av. de Clichy

LA FOURCHE

Av. de Clichy

Rue Lamandé

Rue Dames

Rue des Batignolles

Rue Legendre

Rue Davy

Rue Lacroix

Rue la Condamine

Rue Truffaut

Rue des Batignolles

200 meters

200 yards

N

Planning Your Trip

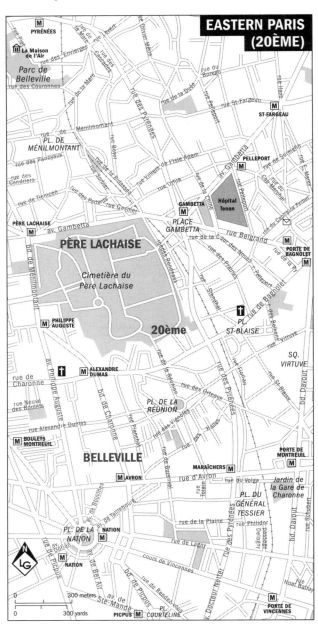

EASTERN PARIS (20ÈME)

Accommodations

Budget accommodations (or budget anything, for that matter) can be difficult to find in Paris. Hostels and hotels generally get cheaper as you journey out of the center into the less trafficked arrondissements. Once you get to the 17ème, though, you're looking at a pretty long Metro ride, and an inconvenient location doesn't always translate into a decent price. But there are still deals for savvy travelers who know where to look. Both Châtelet-Les Halles and Bastille are home to youth hostels with rock-bottom prices that are ridiculously close to Paris's main attractions. When it comes to hotels, be on the lookout for exceptionally good two-stars, especially in the 5ème and 6ème. Expect to pay about €40-60 for the best budget hotels, which can be very quirky or forgettable but are always clean and more peaceful than the alternatives. Free Wi-Fi and cheap breakfasts are almost always provided, and it's not uncommon for hotels and hostels to have adjoining bars. But if you're doing Paris on the cheap, be warned that you can't always count on having your own bathroom or shower, even if you shell out for a single. What better way is there to get to know your neighbors?

Budget Accommodations

If you're looking for cheap accommodations, it might be a good idea to make like the arrondissements and spiral away from Paris's center. The closer you are to the Seine and the big sights, the harder it will be to pinch your pennies. Consider staying in Opéra and Canal St-Martin or in Montparnasse and Southern Paris. Luckily, the partiers who plan to spend late nights raging in Bastille or Montmartre will also be able to find convenient places to stumble home.

CHÂTELET-LES HALLES

While affordable hotels in this trendy neighborhood are usually hard to come by, there are a few high-quality budget locations that are worth checking out. Be sure to make reservations far in advance; cheap spots in such a central location fill up quickly year-round. Also, be vigilant around Châtelet, where passersby won't stick up for you (or even tell you) when a pickpocket or mugger is about to strike.

🏛 Centre Internationale de Paris (BVJ): Paris Louvre   HOSTEL $$

20 rue Jean-Jacques Rousseau
☎01 53 00 90 90; www.bvjhotel.com

This monstrous 200-bed hostel has clean rooms. (Even the lofts are clean—they must have high-reaching dusters.) In the summer, it's packed with international youths and backpackers. Despite the hostel's location next to the old Parisian stock market, you won't pay much for a huge entry, glass ceiling foyer, and the free language lessons you get when conversing with your bunkmates.

▶ ✠ ⓂLouvre-Rivoli. Walk north on rue du Louvre and turn left onto rue St-Honoré. Turn right onto rue Jean-Jacques Rousseau. *i* Breakfast included. Lockers €2. Wi-Fi in dining hall €2 per hr., €3 per 2hr. Reservations can be made no more than 2 months in advance Jul-Aug, no more than 15 days in advance Sept-June. Ⓢ Dorms €29; doubles €70. Cash only. ⌚ Reception 24hr. 3-night max. stay; extensions can be arranged on arrival.

Hotel Tiquetonne   HOTEL $$

6 rue Tiquetonne
☎01 42 36 94 58; www.hoteltiquetonne.fr

Extremely close to the center of the 1er, Hotel Tiquetonne is a very confused one-star budget hotel: it serves breakfast in your room, but charges €6 for shower tokens if you are in a single *sans-douche.*

▶ ✇ ⓂÉtienne Marcel. Walk against the traffic on rue de Turbigo and turn left onto rue Tiquetonne. *i* Breakfast €6. Hall showers €6. Must reserve in advance. Parking available. Ⓢ Singles €40, with bath €50; doubles with bath €60. Ⓩ Reception 24hr.

Hôtel Montpensier   HOTEL $$$
12 rue de Richelieu
☎01 42 96 28 50; www.hotelmontpensierparis.com

One of few affordable hotels in the area, Hôtel Montpensier doesn't skimp on amenities, offering marble bathrooms and large beds. It has a convenient location up the street from the Place du Palais Royal, and the rooms will remind you of the Belle Époque.

▶ ✇ ⓂPalais Royal-Musée du Louvre. Facing la Comédie Française, turn left and walk up rue de Richelieu. The hotel is 1½ blocks up on the right. *i* Breakfast €9. Free Wi-Fi. Ⓢ Singles €60, with bath €70; doubles with shower €99; with full bath €100; triples €149; quads €159. Ⓩ Reception 24hr.

Hôtel des Boulevards   HOTEL $$$
10 rue de la ville Neuve
☎01 42 36 02 29; www.hoteldesboulevards.com

Hôtel des Boulevards is a simple hotel that clearly couldn't afford a decorator. If you aren't looking for more than clean, cheap rooms and complimentary breakfast, then you won't be disappointed. Rooms cost the same if you're solo or traveling with someone else, so find a friend and split the cost.

▶ ✇ ⓂBonne Nouvelle. Walk 2½ blocks down rue de la ville Neuve. The hotel

Bike It Out

You may notice a number of gray bikes scattered around the city. These are part of a city-wide bike-sharing program called **Vélib.** If you're going to be in Paris for a while and have a credit card with an EMV-chip (few US cards currently have them; most European ones do), it may be worth getting a subscription. Bikes are €1 per day and you can take unlimited 30min. trips. Longer rides face extra charges, but, as long as you're staying in the central part of Paris, you'll rarely need it for more than half an hour.

Accommodations

is on the right. *i* Breakfast included. Free Wi-Fi. **⑤** Singles and doubles €55, with toilet €63, with full bath €68.

THE MARAIS

The Marais provides budget accommodations with a bit of flair in the center of Paris's action. The trendy, down-to-earth 4ème is home to some of the best deals and most worthwhile splurges in the city.

🖾 Le Fauconnier   HOSTEL $$

11 rue du Fauconnier

☎01 42 74 23 45; www.mije.com

Le Fauconnier is an ivy-covered, sun-drenched building just steps from the Seine and Île St-Louis. Clean rooms have beds arranged in every possible way: lofts, bunks, and even Tetris-inspired arrangements. But don't worry, you'll get to know your neighbors after soaking in the sun on the terrace.

▶ ⚉ Ⓜ Pont Marie. Walk east on quai des Célestins and turn left onto rue du Fauconnier. *i* Breakfast included. Lockers €1 deposit. MIJE membership required. Reserve 45 days before arrival online or 1 week ahead if by phone. Ages 18-30 only. Internet €0.50 initial connection fee, €0.10 per min. thereafter. **⑤** Dorms €30; singles €49; doubles €72; triples €96. MIJE membership €2.50. 🕐 Curfew 1am; notify in advance if returning later. Lockout noon-3pm. 1-week max. stay.

🖾 Maubuisson   HOSTEL $$

12 rue des Barres

☎01 42 74 23 45; www.mije.com

Run by the same company as Le Fauconnier, Maubuisson is in a former 17th-century convent on a quiet street by the St-Gervais monastery. In a move that would make Mother Superior nervous, the hostel only accommodates individual travelers between the ages of 18 and 30, but the quality of the hostel benefits from the lack of foot traffic.

▶ ⚉ Ⓜ St-Paul. Walk against traffic on rue François Miron for several blocks and turn right onto rue des Barres. *i* Breakfast included. Lockers €1 deposit. Internet €0.50 initial connection fee, €0.10 per min. thereafter. MIJE membership required. Reserve 45 days before arrival online or 1 week ahead if by phone. Ages 18-30 only. **⑤** Dorms €30; singles €49; doubles €72; triples €96. MIJE membership €2.50. 🕐 Lockout noon-3pm. Curfew 1am; notify in advance if returning later. 1 week max. stay.

Accommodations

Hotel de la Herse d'Or   HOTEL $$$

20 rue St-Antoine

☎01 48 87 84 09; www.parishotelherseor.com

Quiet, peaceful rooms can be difficult to find in the Marais. The Hotel de la Herse d'Or, though, provides a tranquil place to crash just a block from the pl. des Vosges. Though not the best budget option for a couple nights' stay, the lavish doubles and apartment-sized triples create a bohemian escape that can be affordable for stays over one week.

▶ ✈ ⓂBastille. Walk toward the Marais on rue St-Antoine for 1½ blocks. *i* Discounts up to 20% for stays of 1 week or longer. ⓈSingles €69; doubles €79, with bath €109; triples with bath €139.

Hôtel Sévigné   HOTEL $$$$

2 rue Malher

☎01 42 72 76 17; www.le-sevigne.com

Everyone knows that the French are skinny, but even Twiggy would have a hard time squeezing around this hotel. The air-conditioned rooms are more spacious than the cramped stair-case and come with full baths. The rooms have small balconies that overlook rue de Rivoli, and with such a central location, you probably won't come back except for a quick nap after a meal in the Marais.

▶ ✈ ⓂSt-Paul. Walk against traffic on rue de Rivoli for 1 block and turn left onto rue Malher. *i* Breakfast €8. ⓈSingles €71-81; doubles €88-98; quads €140.

Hôtel du Séjour   HOTEL $$$$

36 rue du Grenier St-Lazare

☎01 48 87 40 36; www.hoteldusejour.com

Bringing the spirit of minimalism to the hotel industry (read: no TV or air-conditioning), Hôtel du Séjour features 20 basic rooms decorated with Pop Art of Parisian landmarks and colorful stripes. It's a little loud, but worth the price for the ideal location one block away from Les Halles and the Centre Pompidou.

▶ ✈ ⓂÉtienne Marcel. Walk 3 blocks down rue aux Ours, turn left onto rue St-Martin, and right onto rue du Grenier St-Lazare. *i* Reserve 2-3 weeks in advance. ⓈSingles €82; doubles €87, with shower and toilet €97. 🕐 Reception 7:30am-10:30pm.

LATIN QUARTER AND ST-GERMAIN

Hotels in these neighborhoods are generally a bit overpriced due to their central locations. Even with this handicap, secret gems that are accessible to budget travelers are usually located down quiet alleys right around the corner from some of the most popular nightlife spots.

◪ Young and Happy Hostel   HOSTEL $$

80 rue Mouffetard

☎01 47 07 47 07; www.youngandhappy.fr

A funky, lively hostel with 21 clean (if basic) rooms, some with showers and toilets, Young and Happy Hostel is where you want to stay in the 5ème. It's a great option if you're young, fun, and on a budget, as it's on the rue Mouffetard and in the center of the cheapest student watering holes in Paris. While impromptu, their reception doubles as a bar and serves drinks if you ask for them.

▶ ✠ ⓜPlace Monge. From rue Monge, walk behind the pl. Monge on rue Ortolan and turn left onto rue Mouffetard. The hostel is on the right. *i* Breakfast included. Internet €2 per 30min. Ⓢ High-season dorms €28-45.

◪ Hôtel de Nesle   HOTEL $$$

7 rue de Nesle

☎01 43 54 62 41; www.hoteldenesleparis.com

Hôtel de Nesle is a phenomenal place to stay. Each room is unique and represents a particular time period or locale. The Molière room is ideal for the comically minded, and a Colonial room is available for undying proponents of the good ol' days of the Scramble for Africa (don't let that be you). Reserve in advance, because space fills up quickly, especially in the summer.

▶ ✠ ⓜOdéon. Walk toward the church on bd St-Germain and turn right onto rue Mazarine. Turn right onto rue Dauphine and head toward the river. Rue de Nesle is the 1st street on the left. *i* Laundry facilities on-site as well as a Turkish bath (Le Hammam). Ⓢ Singles €55-65; doubles €75-100. Extra bed €12.

Hôtel Stella   HOTEL $$

41 rue Monsieur-le-Prince

☎01 40 51 00 25; http://site.voila.fr/hotel-stella

Designed in the style of Old World Paris, Hôtel Stella has no place for TVs or even an elevator. The rooms are huge and boast high ceilings, exposed beams, the occasional piano, and oriental rugs. With a location down the street from the Jardin de Luxembourg, Hôtel Stella could charge twice as much for their rooms, so thank God they don't.

▶ ⚕ ⓜOdéon. Walk up rue Danton in the direction of traffic past Université René Descartes Paris V and turn left onto rue Monsieur-le-Prince. The hotel is just past the intersection with rue Racine. Ⓢ Singles €30-50; doubles €60; triples €80; quads €100.

Delhy's Hôtel   HOTEL $$$
22 rue de l'Hirondelle
☎01 43 26 58 25; www.delhyshotel.com

This might be the easiest hotel to find in the Latin Quarter. It's close to pl. St-Michel and the Seine, yet tucked away from the hustle and bustle down a quiet cobblestone alleyway. Cheaper rooms have just a sink, but we would advise against bathing in the St-Michel fountain.

▶ ⚕ ⓜSt-Michel. Facing the St-Michel fountain, turn to your right and walk through the passage to the left of La Rive Gauche cafe. The hotel is on the right. *i* Breakfast included. Check website for promotions. Ⓢ Singles €58, with shower €73; doubles €76/83; triples €119. Extra bed €15.

INVALIDES

Budget travel isn't exactly synonymous with the elegant 7ème. Outside the touristy areas, you will find many expensive apartments. If you absolutely must stay here, there are a couple of options that are easy to get to and affordable, by local standards. You have been warned.

Hôtel de Turenne   HOTEL $$$
20 av. de Tourville
☎01 47 05 99 92; www.france-hotel-guide.com/h75007turenne.htm

Centrally located Hôtel du Turenne offers little more than what you would expect from every forgettable hotel you've ever stayed at. What you do get is the much sought-after air-conditioning, full bath, and satellite TV in every room.

▶ ⚕ ⓜÉcole Militaire. Exit the metro facing away from the Tour Eiffel and walk down av. de Tourville. Hotel is at the intersection of av. de Tourville and rue Chevert. *i* Breakfast €9. Ⓢ Singles €69; doubles €85-100; twins €105; triples €140.

CHAMPS-ÉLYSÉES

If you are staying for more than a month, you can stay in the 8ème. If not, there are very few places that are affordable, especially for solo travelers.

Woodstock Hostel   HOSTEL $
48 rue Rodier
☎01 48 78 87 76; www.woodstock.fr

Woodstock's reception instills an intimate vibe, with a back wall covered in stickers (the backpacker's version of a guestbook) and a Beatles-decorated VW bug that pays homage to the hippies of old. Rooms are basic but clean, and the quiet inner courtyard terrace comes complete with odd vagabonds reading or chilling with a cigarette.

▶ ✢ ⓜAnvers. Facing away from the metro, walk down the right side of pl. d'Anvers and turn right onto rue Rodier. The hostel is 1½ blocks down on the left. *i* Wi-Fi included. Computers €2 per 30min. Towels €1. Ⓢ High-season dorms M-F €25, Sa-Su €28; doubles M-F €56, Sa-Su €62. Low-season dorms M-F €22, Sa-Su €25; doubles M-F €50, Sa-Su €56. ⏰ Lock-out 11am-3pm. Curfew 2am.

Perfect Hostel   HOSTEL $$$
39 rue Rodier
☎01 42 81 18 86

Perfect Hostel actually claims to be a "Hotel-Hostel," which probably just gives it an excuse to have lockout hours, a shared kitchen, and private rooms with maid service. While the decor is not the most original, the real deal here is that the apartments

---

Money-Making Decision

When Disney proposed the construction of its multi-million dollar theme park in Paris, many locals scoffed at the idea. They called it "cowboy colonialism" saying that the park would threaten French culture. But when the French government realized how much revenue the park could rake in, it gave Disney the green light. Thus began the era of **Disneyland Paris,** whose 15 million annual visitors make it the most popular tourist attraction in France. Sorry to disappoint you, Walt, but money has a lot more pull than Mickey Mouse.

Accommodations

have full kitchens (oven, microwave, coffee maker, and fridge) and cost the same as a simple room. You can't get more perfect than that.

▶ ✇ Ⓜ Anvers. With your back to the Metro, walk down the right side of the pl. d'Anvers and make a right onto rue Rodier. The hotel is 1½ blocks down on the right. *i* Breakfast included. Reserve 2 months ahead—there are only 10 rooms, and with these prices, the hotel fills up weeks in advance during the summer. Ⓢ Singles €52; doubles €52-72, double apartments €72; triples and triple apartments €87.

OPÉRA AND CANAL ST-MARTIN

You should know better than to stay in a hotel close to the **Gare du Nord.** Whether its because you're coming in late and don't want to go far or you're only in Paris for a night (shame on you), resist the urge to park yourself there. Instead, hop on the Metro to the canal, which is more central, cheaper, and infinitely more scenic (not to mention less sketchy).

🛏 Hôtel Palace   HOTEL $$
9 rue Bouchardon
☎01 40 40 09 45

Try as we might, we cannot figure out why this newly renovated (as of November 2011) hotel has such low prices. Its quiet location and brand new breakfast terrace in the inner courtyard make this a hard place to leave, even with the Metro stop less than two blocks from this wannabe-Art Deco hotel. People are catching on to this deal, so book well in advance.

▶ ✇ Ⓜ Strasbourg-St-Denis. Exit Metro and walk east on bd St-Martin for 1 block. Walk through the roundabout and turn left onto rue René Boulanger. Rue Bouchardon is the 1st left. The hotel is on the left. *i* Breakfast €4. Free Wi-Fi. Ⓢ Singles €23-35; doubles €28-45; triples €60; quads €70. Prices increase with each additional bathroom accoutrement (sink, sink and toilet, full bath).

Peace and Love Hostel   HOSTEL $
245 rue la Fayette
☎01 46 07 65 11; www.paris-hostels.com

This is one of the only hostels in this neighborhood, but the low prices come with some drawbacks. The reception doubles as a bar and stays open until 2am serving the cheapest pints (€3.80) around for mostly Anglo-backpackers. But the limited hours for Wi-Fi, cash-only policy, and strict adherence to check-in times (read: they will give away your bed if you are more than 3hr. late) make this a hostel for those who can stick to a schedule. That's what backpacking, peace, and love are all about, right?

▶ ☏ ⓂJuarès. Like, right there. Or from Gare du Nord, it's a 10min. walk up rue la Fayette, and the hostel is on the left. *i* Wi-Fi 8am-6pm only. Ages 18-35 only. Cash only. Ⓢ High-season dorms €23; private rooms €30. Low-season dorms €18; private rooms €26.

BASTILLE

The 11ème is littered with hotels (among other things) and offers something for everybody, including many quality budget hotels. The neighboring 12ème offers relatively inexpensive and simple accommodations, which work hard to make up for being more remote. The best options cluster around the **Gare de Lyon.**

Auberge de Jeunesse "Jules Ferry" (HI)   HOSTEL $$
8 bd Jules Ferry
☏01 43 57 55 60; www.fuaj.org/Paris-Jules-Ferry

Located on the Seine in the 11ème, Jules Ferry provides the perfect location for Bastille bar hopping. The hostel's colorful rooms with sinks, mirrors, and tiled floors match the carefree atmosphere.

▶ ☏ ⓂRépublique. Walk down av. de la République, cross over Canal St-Martin, and turn left onto bd Jules Ferry. *i* Breakfast included. Wi-Fi €5 per 2hr. Kitchen available for guest use. Ⓢ Dorms from €25. ⌚ Reception 2pm-10:30am. Lockout 10:30am-2pm.

Paris Absolute   HOSTEL $$
1 rue de la Fontaine au Roi
☏01 47 00 47 00; www.absolute-paris.com

Paris Absolute is made popular by its location a few blocks from the party center of Oberkampf. Clean, lime green dorms will welcome you after a long night out, when you'll be grateful there's no curfew.

▶ ☏ ⓂRépublique. Walk toward Canal St-Martin on rue du Temple and cross the canal. The hostel is on the right. *i* Breakfast included. Ⓢ Dorms €29; doubles €75-85.

Hôtel des Arts Bastille   HOTEL $$$
2 rue Godefroy Cavaignac
☏01 43 79 72 57; www.paris-hotel-desarts.com

If you're traveling in a small group, this hotel can be cheaper

Accommodations

(sidebar) Accommodations

than a hostel. Bright rooms with large windows light up the already arresting orange color scheme. Reserve online for almost 60% off listed prices; take an additional €10 off if you book a three-night stay.

▶ ⚑ Ⓜ Charonne. Walk down bd Voltaire away from the Ⓜ Voltaire and turn right onto rue de Charonne. Walk for 200m and turn right onto rue Godefroy Cavaignac. Ⓢ If booking online, singles €55; doubles €55; twins €60; quads €89. By phone or in person, singles €90; doubles €99; twins €109; quads €130.

Auberge Internationale des Jeunes (AIJ)   HOSTEL $
10 rue Trousseau
☎01 47 00 62 00; www.aijparis.com

The AIJ attracts a steady stream of 20-somethings with what it claims are the cheapest dorms in Paris (we believe them). Clean bathrooms are located in the hallways, and vending machines provide late-night snacks for those sober enough to sort through their coins. Guests really just get the basic amenities, but AIJ does throw in a free map of Paris, which has to be worth something.

▶ ⚑ Ⓜ Ledru-Rollin. Walk 3 blocks away from Bastille down rue du Faubourg St-Antoine and turn left onto rue Trousseau. AIJ is on the right. *i* Breakfast included. Under 30 only. Ⓢ Dorms €18; doubles €40. ⌚ Lockout 11am-4pm.

MONTPARNASSE AND SOUTHERN PARIS

This area is calmer than others in Paris, so you won't pay as much for more comfort. Stay close to public transport, as this area is large and hard to navigate at night.

🖾 Oops!   HOSTEL $$
50 av. des Gobelins
☎01 47 07 47 00; www.oops-paris.com

Why it's named Oops!, we have no idea. Maybe it's the creative use of bright colors and patterns that vary by room (and sometimes by wall). Both private rooms and dorms are remarkably clean and have balconies that overlook av. d'Italie. Book well in advance for the summer months, as Oops! is very popular among young backpackers.

▶ ⚑ Ⓜ Les Gobelins. Walk south on av. des Gobelins toward pl. d'Italie. The hostel is 3 blocks from the Metro, on the right. *i* Breakfast included.

Reserve online. **$** High-season dorms €30; private rooms €70. Low-season dorms €23; private rooms €60.

FIAP Jean-Monnet   HOTEL $$$
30 rue Cabanis
☎01 43 13 17 00; www.fiap.asso.fr

With a bar, two restaurants, an outdoor terrace, and regular parties on Wednesdays and Fridays, this student-friendly hotel definitely has a vibrant social scene. The rooms match the '60s-meets-modern-art-museum feel. This is one of the only hotels we've ever heard of that allows six people in one room, although they don't have air-conditioning and have to check out at the ungodly hour of 9am.

▶ 🚇 Ⓜ Glacière. Walk down bd Auguste Blancqui and turn left onto rue Dareau. Walk 2 blocks, turn left onto rue Broussais, and then left onto rue Cabanis. *i* Lockers €3 per day. Reserve at least 1 month in advance. **$** Singles €59; doubles €79; triples €105; quads €140; 5- and 6-person rooms €136-162. ⏰ Reception 24hr.

Three Ducks Hostel   HOSTEL $
6 pl. Étienne Pernet
☎01 48 42 04 05; www.3ducks.fr

It's always happy hour at the Three Ducks Hostel: the concierge desk doubles as a bar. They're so laid-back that they haven't gotten around to painting the walls or trimming the plants in the garden recently. If the frequency of people coming and going makes you feel more uneasy than social, you can ask to store your belongings in the safe at reception.

▶ 🚇 Ⓜ Félix Faure. Exit the Metro across from St-Jean-Baptiste de Grenelle Church and follow the street to the left. *i* Reserve at least 1-2 months in advance. Free Wi-Fi and computer. **$** High-season dorms €23; doubles €52. Low-season dorms €18; doubles €46. Beer €2.20-7. ⏰ Reception 24hr.

Hôtel de Blois   HOTEL $$$
5 rue des Plantes
☎01 45 40 99 48; www.hoteldeblois.com

Those who get a thrill from finding a bargain should try their hand at the website for this 25-room boutique hotel. Prices vary between €65 and €200—it takes a bargain hunter's will and determination to nab one of the cheaper rooms. The pastel-colored rooms are in good shape and the neighborhood is peaceful.

▶ 🚇 Ⓜ Alésia. Walk 2 blocks toward the Tour Montparnasse on rue du Maine and turn left onto rue de la Sablière. Turn right onto rue des Plantes. *i* Breakfast

€12. Reserve at least 1 month in advance. **$** Prices vary depending on availability; check the website for current prices. 🕐 Reception 7am-10:30pm.

Aloha Hostel   HOSTEL $$
1 rue Borromée
☎01 42 73 03 03; www.aloha.fr

Although Aloha serves cheap cocktails, the lockout and 2am curfew might put a damper on your wild side. Then again, it does ensure that you don't have to take a taxi back, since the Metro will still be open, and the bar stays open late enough for you to get your nightcap on. There's free computer access, and the dorms and bathrooms are nothing to quibble with.

▶ ⚐ Ⓜ Volontaires. Walk with traffic on rue des Volontaires. Turn left onto rue Blomet and walk 2 blocks to the corner of rue Blomet and rue Borromée. *i* Breakfast included. Reserve a few weeks in advance. **$** Dorms €28; doubles €64. Reserve with a credit card; pay in cash. 🕐 Curfew 2am. Lockout 11am-5pm.

WESTERN PARIS

Don't say we didn't warn you about this posh area. In the 16ème you'll find some "budget" areas by parental standards, whereas the 17ème has slightly more affordable options. But really, if you're staying in the 17ème, cancel your booking and go next door to the 18ème where hostels abound and budget hotels (the kind that don't rent by the hour) line the red light district and surround the Sacré-Cœur.

Hôtel Champerret Héliopolis   HOTEL $$$$
13 rue d'Héliopolis
☎01 47 64 92 56; www.champerret-heliopolis-paris-hotel.com

This brightly lit boutique hotel with a quiet, flowery (as in full of flowers) inner courtyard and private wooden balconies is perfect for grandparents or those who appreciate the "homey" feel. Just make sure you can speak French, since the reception doesn't speak English.

▶ ⚐ Ⓜ Porte de Champarret. **$** Singles €77; doubles €90, with bath €96; twin €96; triples with bath €120.

Hôtel de l'Europe   HOTEL $$$
67 rue de Moins
☎01 53 31 01 20; hotel.europe75@gmail.com

Close to the 18ème, this Art Deco hotel explodes with

random colors and patterns and has a room to suit just about anyone, from a long backpacker's single with just a sink to a large room with a kitchenette and bathroom for families or friends. Not to worry if you prefer to rough it: there are shared toilets on every floor and a shared kitchen on the ground floor.

▶ ♯ ⓂBrochant. With your back to the post office, walk 1 small block and turn left onto rue de Moins. The hotel is ½ a block down on the left. Ⓢ Singles €55, with shower €65, with full bath €75; doubles €65/75/88. Email reservations for triples and quads with kitchenette and bathroom; prices vary with availability and season but hover around €20-30 per person.

Don't Get Stuck

If you need a break from hectic city life, visit rue du Chat-qui-Pêche, the narrowest street in Paris. Built in 1540, the road contains only a few windows and no doors. The street's name, "Street of the Fishing Cat," comes from an ancient tale about a cat who fished in the flooded cellars of houses during monsoon season before the harbor was built on the Seine. A word of caution to prospective visitors: walking through the 1.8m wide street is not for the claustrophobic or faint of heart—it wasn't named for the stealthiest and most flexible of mammals for nothing.

MONTMARTRE

🕅 Plug-Inn Boutique Hostel   HOSTEL $
7 rue Aristide Bruant
☎01 42 58 42 58; www.plug-inn.fr

Recently opened, this hostel is named for the unlimited free Wi-Fi and computer use. The brand new rooms and untouched bathrooms make you feel slightly cleaner after being in the cabaret- and sex-shop-infused neighborhood, and the views of Paris from the roof are stunning. Check out their blog for details on *soirées* and various discounts.

▶ ♯ ⓂBlanche Sarl. Face the Moulin Rouge and walk 5 blocks up rue Lepic. Turn right onto rue des Abbesses. Rue Aristide Bruant is the 1st right. *i* Breakfast included. Free Wi-Fi and computer use. Ⓢ Dorms €25; doubles €60; triples €90. ⏰ Lockout 10am-3pm.

Le Montclair Hostel   HOSTEL $$

62 rue Ramey

☎01 46 06 46 07; www.montclair-hostel.com

Complete with funky striped walls, a foosball table, and vending machines, Le Montclair is a standard young and hip hostel. Clean dormitories have shared bathrooms, but Montclair offers doubles with either a shower or full bath for those looking for more privacy.

▶ ✄ Ⓜ Jules Joffrin. Follow rue Ordener and turn right onto rue Hermel and rue Ramney is the 1st left. *i* Breakfast included. Computer €1.50 per 30min., €2.50 per hr. Ⓢ Dorms €29, with full bath €35; doubles €76, with toilet €80, with full bath €88. ⌚ Lockout 10am-3pm.

EASTERN PARIS

This area is devoid of tourist accommodations, and its not a place you want to be stumbling home to after bar hopping. The places below are decent, but be sure to call a cab if you indulge too much on your night out. You shouldn't stay this far out unless you want to be near the **Gare Routière International.**

Auberge de Jeunesse "Le D'Artagnan"   HOSTEL $

80 rue Vitruve

☎01 40 32 34 56; www.fuaj.org

A healthy walk from the Metro and a stone's throw from the Cimetière du Père Lachaise, this is everything you'd expect from FUAJ: clean rooms (around 440 beds), a bar, a majority of French or non-anglophone clients, and a totally relaxed atmosphere. Mingle with French transients and pregame at the bar before heading out.

▶ ✄ Ⓜ Porte de Bagnolet. Exit onto bd Davout and take the first right onto rue Vitruve. The hostel is on the left. *i* Breakfast included. Lockers €2-4 per day. Wi-Fi €2 per hr. Reserve online. Ⓢ Beds from €27. Discounts for International Youth Hostels Association members. ⌚ Lockout noon-3pm. Max. stay 4 nights.

Sights

For those who aren't *Let's Go* researchers, seeing everything in Paris is exhausting if not impossible (even we struggled a bit). For a short trip, visiting the main attractions can mean waiting in lines, feeling the urge to add the annoying couple in front of you to the body count at the Catacombs, and becoming completely desensitized to some of mankind's greatest feats of engineering and art. Give yourself a break. Before heading off to see something because you saw it on a postcard, check this section for what's really worth it. Some of Paris's most interesting sights are devoid of tourists. To save money and give yourself a more authentic Parisian experience, picnic in a park that once housed a palace; go to a less famous museum when the line for the Louvre is more than the flight time to CDG; and realize that some of the best (and cheapest) history lessons are found in the city's churches, squares, and public landmarks. When you can appreciate the small things, the Louvre and the Eiffel Tower will be even more awe-inspiring.

Budget Sights

Paris has sights for everyone: the whimsical will head to d'Orsay, the ones captivated by fairy tales and unicorns will inevitably end up at Musée de Cluny, and those interested in the macabre will find themselves attracted to Cimetière du Père Lachaise. However, these sights can rack up quite the bill. To save some euro, consider checking out Paris's many free 🎨**galleries.** The Marais, a haven for starving artists, certainly has plenty of works to display. Hit up Galerie Emmanuel Perrotin (76 rue de Turenne and 10 Impasse St-Claude) or Galerie Thuillier (13 rue de Thorigny). For some more eye candy, head over to the Left Bank to Galerie Claude Bernard (7/9 rue des Beaux Arts), Galerie Loevenbruck (6 rue Jacques Callot), and Galerie Kamel Mennour (47 rue St-André). You never know—this art could be hanging on a wall in the Louvre someday.

ÎLE DE LA CITÉ AND ÎLE ST-LOUIS

Île de la Cité is a pressure cooker of tourists and sights. It's home to two of Paris's oldest and most famous churches and its oldest-running hospital, where you can stroll the gardens for free. On the smaller Île St-Louis, the sights and tourists thin out, but it's still worth a stroll to check out the art galleries, ice cream parlors, and some eateries where you can find locals who have been there since before WWII.

🎨 Notre Dame   CATHEDRAL
Île de la Cité
☎01 53 10 07 00

Centuries before it witnessed Quasimodo's attempts to rescue Esmeralda, Notre Dame was the site of a Roman temple to Jupiter. Having decided that a pagan temple would be a good place for some Catholic infusion, Rome began building churches, the last of which was Notre Dame in 1163. Taking a liking to the high Gothic ceilings and explosion of color from the large stained-glass windows, the French nobility claimed it for most of their weddings (we can only assume Maui was booked at the time.) Among those who took their vows were François II to Mary Queen of Scots and Henri of Navarre to Marguerite de Valois. On the other side of the happiness spectrum, this is also where **Joan of Arc** was tried for heresy. She was only 19 at the time of her trial and subsequent barbecue. To make up for that tiny injustice, she was made a patron saint of France (after almost 500 years) and has her own shrine next to the Treasury.

The revolution had the same effect on Paris, and especially Notre Dame, as a drunken weekend in Vegas has on the individual. Everyone woke up five years later to discover that Notre Dame had been renamed the Temple of Reason and covered with a Neoclassical facade. It was later reconsecrated and served as the site of **Napoleon's** famed coronation in 1804. However, the building fell into disrepair, and for two decades it was used to shelter livestock. **Victor Hugo** cleared away the donkeys and pigs when he wrote his famed novel *The Hunchback of Notre Dame* in 1831, which revived the cathedral's popularity and inspired Disney to introduce the French idea of "gypsycide" to children all over the world. Restorations (read: major changes) by **Eugène Viollet-le-Duc** included a third tower, gargoyles, and a statue of himself admiring his work. Most of the 20th century included more praying against German invasion (we know how that ended up) and famous masses for the funerals of both Charles de Gaulle and François Mitterrand.

If you've read this far, stay with us for a little longer. Here is what you need to see and do when visiting Notre Dame. First, as you enter, notice the headless figures above the doors. Revolutionaries thought that the King of Judah was somehow related to the French monarch (he's not) and decapitated him. From the entrance, you'll see massive crowds. Keep to the right and follow the arrows past Joan of Arc to the Treasury, where you can see Napoleon's sweet emperor cloak as well as relics like St. Louis's tunic. Jesus's thorny crown rests here too, but it's only revealed on the first Friday of the month at 3pm. Round the church and get a good look of the stained-glass window in the back and the altar from the priest's point of view. For the towers, you'll have to brave a line that only lets in 20 people at a time and a 422-step climb to the bell towers to take in the views of the Latin Quarter and the Marais. The *crème de la crème* is the 13-ton bell in the South Tower that requires eight men—or one hunchback—to ring.

▶ ✠ Ⓜ Cité. Ⓢ Free. Audio tour €5, includes treasury visit. Treasury €3, ages 12-25 €2, 5-11 €1. 🕐 Cathedral open daily 7:45am-6:45pm. Towers open daily 10am-5:30pm, last entry 4:45pm. Free tours in French M-F 2 and 3pm; English W-Th 2pm, Sa 2:30pm. Treasury open M-Sa 9:30am-6pm, Su 1:30-5:30pm; last entry 15min. before close. Su mass 8:30am (French), 10am (Gregorian Chants), 11:45am (international i.e. easy French with some English thrown in), 12:45pm, and 6:30pm.

🏛 Sainte-Chapelle   CHURCH
6 bd du Palais
☎01 53 40 60 97; www.monuments-nationaux.fr

Everybody needs the occasional diversion to get through a service. Take the 13th-century equivalent of TVs in church: the stunning floor-to-ceiling stained-glass windows in the **Upper Chapel** of Sainte-Chapelle, illuminating dreamscapes of no fewer than 1113 individual Biblical stories. They really tried, but you just can't squeeze that many depictions onto stained glass and make it understandable without a priest (or tour guide) explaining each one. The easiest to make out is the Passion of the Christ, located at the apex of the Chapel. Originally designed to house the Crown of Thorns and an actual piece of the crucifix, Sainte-Chapelle has a good reason for its smaller size: most of the budget was blown on the crown itself, purchased for the ungodly sum of UKE135,000 (adjust that puppy for about 800 years of inflation). They lost out anyway, since the crown now resides in Notre Dame. The **Lower Chapel** has a blue vaulted ceiling dotted with the golden symbol of the French monarchy, the *fleurs-de-lis,* and contains a few "treasures"—platter-sized portraits of saints. This was where mortals served God, while royalty got to get a little closer in the Upper Chapel.

▶ 🚹 Ⓜ Cité. Within Palais de la Cité. Ⓢ €8, ages 18-25 €5, under 18 free. Twin ticket with Conciergerie €11, ages 18-25 €7.50, under 18 free. 🕐 Open daily Mar-Oct 9:30am-6pm; Nov-Feb 9am-5pm. Last entry 30min. before close. Guided tours in French 11am, 3, and 4:40pm; in English 3:30pm.

Hôtel-Dieu   BUILDING, HOSPITAL
1 pl. Parvis Notre-Dame
☎01 42 34 82 34

Upon realizing that it might be helpful to save actual people in addition to their Christian souls (this was the Dark Ages, it was a pretty revolutionary idea), Bishop St. Landry built this hospital in 651 CE. If you're wondering why you want to visit a hospital, we would probably share your skepticism. However, the open-air colonnade and impeccably kept gardens are open to the public and are worth a look for multiple examples of irony, including memorial plaques to Louis Pasteur (in a country that doesn't pasteurize most of its milk and cheese) or doctors and nurses using the garden as a smoking lounge.

▶ 🚹 Ⓜ Cité. Ⓢ Free. 🕐 Open M-F 8am-8pm, Sa-Su 10am-5pm.

Mémorial des Martyrs de la Déportation HOLOCAUST MEMORIAL

Hidden away at the east end of the Île de la Cité, this small, concrete, incredibly depressing monument pays tribute to the French citizens deported to concentration camps during WWII. A flight of narrow concrete stairs leads you to a sunken platform, from which the high, spiked gates resemble those of the concentration camps. Inside the memorial, you see a long tunnel of 200,000 lit quartz pebbles, that represent each of the French citizens killed. Famous quotes are carved into the walls of the memorial, the most arresting of which is at the exit: *"Pardonne. N'oublie Pas"* ("Forgive. Do Not Forget").

▶ ⚓ Ⓜ Cité. At the eastern tip of the Île de la Cité, on quai de l'Archevêché. A 5min. walk from the back of Notre Dame cathedral and down a narrow flight of steps. Ⓢ Free. 🕓 Open Tu-Su 10am-noon and 2-7pm. Last entry 11:45am and 6:30pm.

Palais de Justice   COURTHOUSE

4 bd du Palais

☎ 01 44 32 51 51

The Palais has witnessed the German spy Mata Hari's death sentence, Sarah Bernhardt's divorce from the Comédie Française, and Alfred Dreyfus's guilty verdict and subsequent declaration of innocence. Learning from the Joan of Arc mistake of the past, the court managed to declare Dreyfus innocent while he was still alive, but only after 12 years of solitary confinement on the hard-labor penal colony Devil's Island. While the courtrooms and legal consultants are open to the public, "public" does not mean foreigners. For those without an EU passport, you'll have to settle for the massive 1760 sq. m colonnade **Conciergerie,** through which every prisoner with a death sentence was marched (when they still did that). You can gain entry through a joint ticket with Sainte-Chapelle.

▶ ⚓ Ⓜ Cité. Within Palais de la Cité. Ⓢ Conciergerie and Sainte-Chapelle €11, ages 18-25 €7.50, under 18 free. 🕓 Open daily Mar-Oct 9:30am-6pm; Nov-Feb 9am-5pm. Last entry 30min. before close.

Pont Neuf   BRIDGE

Though its name might suggest otherwise, the bridge cutting through the western tip of Île de la Cité is the oldest in Paris. Completed in 1607, it would have been the busiest street in Paris for tourists in the 17th century. Today the bridge is lined with lip-locked lovers, seated in the many romantic enclaves overlooking the Seine. That's about it, though: youthful romance and the occasional gargoyle (which you can find at just about every Gothic building in Paris) are all that Point Neuf has to offer nowadays.

▶ ✠ Ⓜ Pont Neuf.

CHÂTELET-LES HALLES

Châtelet-Les Halles is perhaps Paris's densest tourist area, and that's saying something. From the commercial indulgence of the pl. Vendôme to the mind-numbing grandeur of the Louvre to the bizarre trends on display at the Musée des Arts Décoratifs, the 1er and 2ème have it all.

🖼 Musée du Louvre 　　　　　　　　　　　　MUSEUM
rue de Rivoli
☎ 01 40 20 53 17; www.louvre.fr

Try as you might, it's impossible to see everything in the Louvre. The museum's miles (yes, miles) of galleries stretch seemingly without end, and their collections span thousands of years, six continents, countless artistic styles, and a vast range of media. It's no wonder that the Louvre sees an average 8.5 million visitors per year. Like most of Paris's spectacular sights, the Louvre was initially commissioned by kings and intended as a tribute to... themselves. Thinking that those tributes should be shared with everyone, revolutionaries made the museum permanent after kindly asking the monarchy to leave. Napoleon filled the Louvre with plundered goods from just about everywhere he went, and its massive bankroll has allowed the museum to continue acquiring pieces that make Jean Paul Getty look like a stamp collector. Successful trips to the Louvre require two things: a good sense of direction and a great plan of attack. If you're looking for detailed tours, the Louvre's website describes several thematic trails you can follow.

The museum sprawls four floors and three main wings: **Sully, Richelieu,** and **Denon.** To make this easier for you, we'll give you the breakdown of the floors, as the wings really have nothing in common other than to tell you where you are. The basement is where you'll be shuffled to buy tickets and make the daunting selection of which wing to enter first. Here you'll see the medieval foundations of the Louvre as well as its history, which reads like a European History 101 textbook. Appropriately, this is where some of the Louvre's oldest pieces are stored, which include sculptures from the 10th and 11th centuries and the first items from the Egyptian collection.

The **ground floor** houses some of the works that people flock to Paris to see. The *Venus de Milo* is in room 16 in the Sully wing, while the *Law Code of Hammurabi* is stored with the Near Eastern Antiquities in Room 3 of Richelieu. You can find the full extent of the Egyptian collection as well as Greek and Roman sculpture sprawled out on this level.

The biggest crowds are located on the **first floor,** and rightfully so. The most impressive halls of the museum are rooms 77 and 75 in the Denon wing, which house Théodore Géricault's *Raft of the Medusa,* Eugène Delacroix's *Liberty Leading the People,* Jacques-Louis David's *Coronation of Napoleon,* and Paolo Veronese's *The Wedding at Cana.* These paintings are all gigantic, which makes the crowds seem less of a hassle, as everyone can get a good view. We wish we could say the same for Leonardo's **Mona Lisa** (*La Jaconde* for those of you who like to sound lofty and enlightened). The tiny painting has an entire wall to itself, and there is almost always a crowd surrounding it. In the Richelieu wing, the museum has more Jesus-inspired paintings from the Renaissance as well as Napoleon III's fully furnished apartments.

On the **second floor,** only Sully and Richelieu are accessible. In Sully, all of the rooms are filled with French paintings that typically require some background study in art history to fully appreciate. Richelieu is filled with student groups and more obscure tours checking out the remaining Belgian, Dutch, German, Russian, and Scandinavian paintings. These are pretty to look at, but you may be better off spending a little more time getting friendly with your favorites from earlier. At the Louvre, unless you're planning on bunking up next to the *Venus de Milo,* seeing everything is impossible. Just getting a glimpse of what's in front of you, though, is a pretty good start.

▶ ⚑ Ⓜ Palais Royal-Musée du Louvre. *i* The Carte Louvre Jeunes entitles the owner to 1 year unlimited access without waiting in line and free access for the owner and a guest W and F after 6pm. Ⓢ €10, under 18 and EU citizens ages 18-25 free. Special exhibits €11. Combined ticket €14. Carte Louvre Jeunes ages 18-25 €15, 26-29 €30. 1st Su of every month (does not include special exhibits) free. F after 6pm free for under 26 of all nationalities. Audio tour €6, under 18 €2. ⓩ Open M 9am-6pm, W 9am-10pm, Th 9am-6pm, F 9am-10pm, Sa-Su 9am-6pm. Last entry 45min. before close; rooms begin to close 30min. before museum. "Discovery trails" tours in English, French, or Spanish daily 11am, 2, and 3:45pm; sign up at the info desk.

Poor Francis

Francis I wasn't the most successful king. He failed to become the Holy Roman Emperor, lost a series of wars in Italy, and was captured by the actual Holy Roman Emperor. He was held in Madrid until he agreed to sign over all claims to Milan and Naples and hand over his two sons as payment for the ransom. Having done this, he returned to his comfy Palais du Louvre, only to invade Italy again and again until he ran out of money. Perhaps his only success was picking up a portrait for the palace during his conquests: The *Mona Lisa.* You win some, you (mostly) lose some.

◪ Jardin des Tuileries   GARDEN
pl. de la Concorde, rue de Rivoli

Covering the distance from the Louvre to the pl. de la Concorde, the Tuileries are a favorite of tourists during the summer and Parisians when there aren't too many tourists to scare them off (read: annoy them). In the tradition of matching garden size to house size, the Tuileries are a massive complex of hedges, trees, and a very large fountain. Originally built for Catherine de' Medici, the garden was modeled after her native Florence to make her feel more at home—or to take her mind off the fact that her husband, Henry II, was much more infatuated with his mistress. The gardens grew as each successive king added something to call his own. Today, the Tuileries are filled with food stands, merry-go-rounds, and a huge ferris wheel near the rue de Rivoli entrance, quite different from the Tuscan sanctuary Henry imagined.

▶ ⚲ Ⓜ Tuileries. Ⓢ Free. ⏲ Open daily June-Aug 7am-11pm; Sept 7am-9pm; Oct-Mar 7:30am-7:30pm; Apr-May 7am-9pm. Amusement park open June to mid-Aug.

◪ Église Saint-Eustache   CHURCH
2 rue du Jour

☎01 42 36 31 05; www.saint-eustache.org

What do Cardinal Richelieu, Molière, Louis XIV, and Mme. de Pompadour have in common? Église St-Eustache is where each of them was baptised. As a result of some poor fundraising (surprising, since their marketing plan was to tax baskets of fish from the market at Les Halles), the church took over a century to build. You can still see the impact of this dearth of funds on its two towers, one of which is complete while the other is nothing more than a stump. The interior houses a pipe organ larger than that of Notre Dame, paintings by Peter Paul Rubens, and a silver sculpture dedicated to the victims of the AIDS epidemic. Église St-Eustache sees few tourists, allowing the intrepid few to enjoy the silence and grandeur of the 34m vaulted Gothic ceilings.

▶ ✦ Ⓜ Les Halles. *i* Audio tours available in English, ID required. Ⓢ Free. Audio tour suggested donation €3. ⌚ Open M-F 9:30am-7pm, Sa 10am-7pm, Su 9am-7pm. Mass Sa 6pm; Su 9:30, 11am, 6pm.

Musée de l'Orangerie   MUSEUM
Jardin des Tuileries
☎01 44 77 80 07; www.musee-orangerie.fr

Once the greenhouse of the Jardin des Tuileries, l'Orangerie opened as a museum in 1927. Today, it displays works by Impressionist and post-Impressionist painters including Monet, Matisse, Picasso, and Renoir. Since its conversion into a museum, L'Orangerie has become home to Monet's *Water Lilies* and received the collection of renowned art collector Paul Guillaume in the 1960s. This impressive list probably explains why it's impossible to enter the museum without waiting in line, even on weekdays. On weekends the wait can last up to 2hr. Show up at 9am or on Free Sunday (the first Sunday of every month) if you don't want to roast in the sun for most of the day. If you're okay with a quick visit, the admission fee is reduced for the last hour it's open.

▶ ✦ Ⓜ Concorde. Ⓢ €7.50, students and after 5pm €5. Combined ticket with Musée d'Orsay €13. Free 1st Su every month. ⌚ Open M 9am-6pm, W-Su 9am-6pm.

Musée des Arts Décoratifs   MUSEUM
107 rue de Rivoli
☎01 44 55 57 50; www.lesartsdecoratifs.fr

Fashion-conscious Francophiles could easily spend a full day perusing the Musée des Arts Decoratifs. The complex is comprised of three different museums in addition to many smaller exhibits. **Arts Décoratifs** (Interior Design), **Mode et Textile** (Fashion and Fabric), and **Publicité** (Advertisement) are all dedicated to *haute couture* designs that the average tourist has probably never experienced. In the Arts Décoratifs, you'll find sheep-shaped chairs, elephant-shaped fountains, and chairs whittled into birds. The Mode et Textile has exhibits on the evolution of fashion from the '70s to the '90s and features small exhibits on prominent fashion designers, including Yves Saint Laurent. The jewelry collection, **Galerie des Bijoux,** will make anyone's engagement ring look embarrassing.

▶ ⚥ Ⓜ Palais Royal-Musée du Louvre. Ⓢ All 3 museums €9, ages 18-25 €7.50, under 18 and EU citizens 18-25 free. ⏰ Open Tu-W 11am-6pm, Th 11am-9pm, F-Su 11am-6pm. Last entry 30min. before close.

Palais-Royal   PALACE
25 rue de Valois
☎01 49 27 09 09

This palace has a history plagued with death, bad luck, and low funding. Cardinal Richelieu, who commissioned it, died the same year it was completed. Queen of England Henrietta Maria called the palace home after being kicked out of her own country for being Catholic. (The French reaction to her showing up was apparently "You're Catholic? Move into this palace!") Finally, in 1781, the broke Duke of Orléans had to rent out the space to raise money. It's a place to wander and window-shop, while the interior is occupied by government offices.

▶ ⚥ Ⓜ Palais Royal-Musée du Louvre. Ⓢ Free. ⏰ Fountain, galleries, and garden open daily June-Aug 7am-11pm; Sept 7am-9:30pm; Oct-Mar 7:30am-8:30pm; Apr-May 7am-10:15pm.

THE MARAIS

You'll see more here than just strolling rabbis and strutting fashionistas. The eastern section of the arrondissement is a labyrinth of old, quaint streets dotted with churches and some of Paris's most beautiful mansions (particularly around the **place des Vosges**). The **Centre Pompidou,** the Marais's main attraction, breaks up the beige monotony in the western half (or maybe it's just a tourist eyesore—ask any Frenchman). Though the Pompidou, quite like a spoiled child, steals the show, there are a number of other museums that are just as entertaining. If you aren't the museum-going type, **rue Vieille du Temple** and **rue des Rosiers** are great streets to explore.

🖼 Centre Pompidou   MUSEUM, LIBRARY
pl. Georges Pompidou, rue Beaubourg
☎01 44 78 12 33; www.centrepompidou.fr

Though describing the exterior of the Pompidou in words is almost impossible, we'll give it a shot: the exterior of the Pompidou features a network of yellow electrical tubes, green water pipes, and blue ventilation ducts. You have to see it to really get it. The center's functions are as varied as its colors: it serves as a sort of cultural theme park of ultra-modern exhibition, performance, and research space. It is home to the famous **Musée National d'Art Moderne,** whose collection spans the 20th century. TVs display what can be characterized as Andy Warhol's drug-induced visions alongside amorphous tie-dye colored statues, a giant mushroom, and a wall of globes with layered tape to represent the cancerous growth of wars and violence. The second floor features pre-1960s art with less provocative pieces but just as famous names: Duchamp, Picasso, and Miró. Temporary exhibits on international modern art fill the top floors. Other parts of the complex to explore include **Salle Garance,** which runs an adventurous film series; **Bibliothèque Publique d'Information,** a free, noncirculating library; **Institut de la Recherche de la Coordination Acoustique/ Musique (IRCAM),** an institute and laboratory for the development of new technology; and the rooftop restaurant, **Georges.**

▶ ✝ Ⓜ Rambuteau or Hôtel de Ville. Ⓢ Museum €12, under 26 €9, under 18 and EU citizens ages 18-25 free. Library and forum free. 🕐 Center open M 11am-9pm, W-Su 11am-9pm. Museum open M 11am-8:50pm, W 11am-8:50pm, Th 11am-11pm, F-Su 11am-8:50pm. Last entry 1hr. before close. Library open M noon-10pm, W-F noon-10pm, Sa-Su 11am-10pm.

🖾 Musée Carnavalet   MUSEUM
23 rue de Sévigné
☎ 01 44 59 58 58; www.carnavalet.paris.fr

Located in Mme. de Sévigné's beautiful 16th-century *hôtel particulier* and the neighboring Hôtel Le Peletier de St-Fargeau, this meticulously arranged and engaging museum traces Paris's history from its origins to Napoleon III. The city's urban development is conveyed through paintings, furniture, and sculptural fragments. Highlights include Marcel Proust's fully reconstructed bedroom and a piece of the Bastille prison wall. (We tried, but shouting *"Vive la Revolution!"* doesn't entitle you to touch it.)

▶ ✝ Ⓜ Chemin Vert. Take rue St-Gilles, which becomes rue du Parc Royal, and turn left onto rue de Sévigné. Ⓢ Free. 🕐 Open Tu-Su 10am-6pm. Last entry 5:15pm.

🖾 Musée de la Chasse et de la Nature   MUSEUM
62 rue des Archives
☎ 01 48 87 40 36; www.chassenature.org

The collection may be quirky, but it's sure to elicit some sort

Sights

of response—whether it's fascination or disgust. The museum displays hunting-themed art, weaponry, and stuffed animals from several continents in lavish, elegantly arranged rooms that would bring a tear to Allan Quatermain's eye. While the Trophy Room is the most impressive section of the museum, it's basically a what's what of endangered species, the most arresting of which are a polar bear on its hind legs and a pair of cheetahs in a glass case.

▶ ✠ Ⓜ Rambuteau. Walk against traffic on rue Beaubourg, turn right onto rue Michel le Comte, and left onto rue des Archives. Ⓢ €6, ages 18-25 and seniors €4.50, under 18 free. 1st Su of each month free. Ⓧ Open Tu-Su 11am-6pm.

🏛 Place des Vosges   PARK

Paris's oldest and perhaps snootiest public square has served many generations of residents, from the knights who clashed swords in medieval tournaments to the hipsters who swap bottles during picnics today. All 36 buildings that line the square were constructed by Baptiste du Cerceau in the same architectural style; look for pink brick, slate roofs, and street-level arcades. The quaint atmosphere attracted **Cardinal Richelieu** (who lived at no. 21 when he wasn't busy mad-dogging musketeers), writer **Alphonse Daudet** (who lived at no. 8), and **Victor Hugo** (no. 6). It was also the venue for one of seven-year-old prodigy **Mozart's** concerts, inspiring every "My Child is an Honor Student" bumper sticker. Come here to people-watch, nap in the grass, and wish you were friends with Molière or Voltaire.

▶ ✠ Ⓜ St-Paul or Bastille. Follow rue St-Antoine and turn onto rue de Birague.

Maison de Victor Hugo   MUSEUM

6 pl. des Vosges

☎ 01 42 72 10 16; www.musee-hugo.paris.fr

Dedicated to the father of French Romanticism and housed in the building where he lived from 1832 to 1848, the museum displays memorabilia from his pre-exile, exile, and post-exile days, including his family's little-known paintings and the desk where he wrote standing up. On the first floor, the collection reveals paintings of scenes from *Les Misérables* and other works. Upstairs, you'll find Hugo's apartments; a recreation of the bedroom where he died; and the *chambre chinoise,* which reveals his flamboyant interior decorating skills and just how romantic he really was.

▶ ✠ Ⓜ St-Paul or Bastille. Follow rue St-Antoine and turn onto rue de Birague.

Ⓢ Free. Special exhibits €7-8, seniors €5, under 26 €3.50-4. Audio tour €5.
🕐 Open Tu-Su 10am-6pm. Last entry 5:40pm.

Musée d'Art et d'Histoire du Judaïsme   MUSEUM
71 rue Vieille du Temple
☎01 53 01 86 53; www.mahj.org

Displaying a very select portion of Jewish history in Europe and North Africa, with a focus on community traditions throughout the Diaspora, the Musée d'Art et d'Histoire du Judaïsme begins with the cut-and-dry aspect of circumcision (apparently Abraham did it to himself at the age of 99—that's commitment). Modern testimonials on Jewish identity are interspersed with exquisite ancient relics. While they have extensive collections of art and relics looted by the Nazis from Jewish homes, don't expect to learn anything about the horror of the Vélodrome d'hiver. History buffs, prepare to be appalled.

▶ ♿ Ⓜ Rambuteau. From the Metro, turn right onto rue Rambuteau, and then left onto rue Vieille du Temple. Ⓢ €6.80, ages 18-26 €4.50, under 18 and art students free. Special exhibits €5.50, ages 18-26 €4. Combined ticket

You Say You Want a Revolution?

Paris was the center of one of the most violent and bloody revolutions in history. Here are some key revolutionary sites that can still (sort of) be seen today:

- **CAFE DE FOY:** Appropriately located in front of the Palais-Royal in the center of the city, this was where Camille Desmoulins supposedly sparked the first revolt, ending a speech against Louis XVI with the call "Aux armes!" If only your valedictorian speech stirred up that much commotion.

- **BASTILLE:** Thanks to its storming and subsequent destruction, the infamous fortress isn't there anymore. If you're lucky, there might be a carnival in the open *place* where the mighty armory once stood, where rioting Parisians freed a grand total of seven innocent civilians from tyrannical and unjust imprisonment in 1789.

- **TUILERIES:** This palace was also destroyed, but not by angry peasants. It was purposefully burned down in 1871 during the suppression of the Paris Commune. In its place is a huge garden where you can try to picture Marie Antoinette crying after she was forced here from the Palais du Versailles.

€8.50/6. Guided tours €9/6.50. ⏰ Open M-F 11am-6pm, Su 10am-6pm. Last entry 5:30pm.

LATIN QUARTER AND ST-GERMAIN

Sights, sights, and more sights. There's more to see in the 5ème and 6ème than there is time to do it in. If you're only in Paris for a short while, there are a few things you can't miss. The **Jardin du Luxembourg** is magnificent and, alongside the Tuileries, one of the best relaxation spots in Paris. If you want museums with more than just paintings and sculptures, the **Musée National du Moyen Âge** and the massive **Museum of Natural History** are two of Paris's most important collections. If you're the artsy type, don't miss the slew of galleries in the **Odéon/Mabillon** area. And if you're in the mood to walk in the footsteps of Jean-Paul Sartre, Simone de Beauvoir, and Ernest Hemingway, make sure to visit **Saint-Germain-des-Prés** and **Shakespeare and Co. Bookstore**.

🏛 Panthéon   HISTORIC MONUMENT, CRYPT
pl. du Panthéon

☎01 44 32 18 04; http://pantheon.monuments-nationaux.fr

If there's one building that doesn't know the meaning of antidisestablishmentarianism, it's the Panthéon. Because the Neoclassical building went back and forth between a church and a "secular mausoleum" over the years, it contains some surprising gravemates. Within the crypt, tombs alternate between Christian heroes such as St. Louis and Enlightenment thinkers like Voltaire, who would probably object to being placed so close to icons of church dogma. What's worse, both Foucault's pendulum and revolutionary statues lie above the remains of Joan of Arc and St. Geneviève. The trip up the dome has three stops with 360-degree views of the Marais and Latin Quarter, and you can meander the colonnade at the top for the allotted 10min. before being herded back down.

▶ ✝ Ⓜ Cardinal Lemoine. Head away from the river on rue du Cardinal Lemoine and turn right onto rue Clovis. Walk until you reach pl. du Panthéon. *i* Dome visits Apr-Oct in Dutch, English, French, German, Russian, and Spanish. Ⓢ €8, ages 18-25 €5, under 18 free. Oct-Mar 1st Su of each month free. ⏰ Open daily Apr-Sept 10am-6:30pm; Oct-Mar 10am-6pm. Last entry 45min. before close.

🖼 Le Jardin du Luxembourg   GARDEN
Main entrance on bd St-Michel

As with most ornate things in Paris, these gardens used to be exclusively for royalty. When the great expropriation occurred around 1789, the fountains, statues, rose gardens, and well-kept hedges were opened to the public, ensuring a quick picnic spot for every student in the Latin Quarter and St-Germain. The Palais is still off-limits, but the best and most sought-after spot in the garden is the **Fontaine des Médicis,** a vine-covered grotto east of the Palais complete with a murky fish pond and Baroque fountain sculptures.

▶ ✝ ⓂOdéon or RER B: Luxembourg. *i* Guided tours in French Apr-Oct 1st W of each month 9:30am. Tours start at pl. André Honnorat behind the observatory. Ⓢ Free. ⓉOpen daily in summer from 7am to 1hr. before sunset; in winter from 8am to 1hr. before sunset.

Musée National du Moyen Âge (Musée de Cluny)   MUSEUM
6 pl. Paul Painlevé
☎01 53 73 78 00; www.musee-moyenage.fr

Originally occupied by Gallo-Roman baths and then by the 15th-century Hotel of the Abbots of Cluny, the Musée National du Moyen Âge sits on one of the prime pieces of historic real estate in Paris. The main attraction, *La Dame à la Licorne,* is a collection of tapestries featuring every little girl's dream pet: the unicorn. The horned animal paradoxically represented both a Christ figure and a profane abomination, depending on how it was depicted through the ages. In addition to making you nostalgic for My Little Pony, the museum hosts many exhibitions, including one on medieval sword fighting.

▶ ✝ ⓂCluny-La Sorbonne. Walk up bd St-Michel and turn left onto rue du Cluny. *i* Audio tour included. Ⓢ €8, ages 18-25 €6, EU citizens under 26 free. 1st Su of the month free. ⓉOpen M 9:15am-5:45pm, W-Su 9:15am-5:45pm. Last entry 5:15pm.

Jardin des Plantes   GARDEN, MUSEUM, ZOO
57 rue Cuvier
☎01 40 79 30 00; www.mnhn.fr

This one is a doozy. Within the Jardin des Plantes, you can find a whopping five museums, a garden, and a zoo. The **Museum of Natural History,** divided into three separate institutions, is housed here. Of its constituent parts, the four-floor **Grande Galerie d'Évolution** is the best; while not striking in and of itself, it looks better alongside its positively horrible comrades. The exhibit illustrates evolution with a series of stuffed animals (Curious George not included) and numerous multimedia tools. Next door, the **Musée de Minéralogie** displays rubies, sapphires, and other minerals. The **Galeries d'Anatomie Comparée et de Paléontologie** are at the other end of the garden. Inside is a ghastly cavalcade of femurs, ribcages, and vertebrae from prehistoric animals (all the ingredients to create your own Frankenstein). Despite some snazzy new placards, the place doesn't seem to have changed much since it opened in 1898; it's almost more notable as a museum of 19th-century grotesquerie than as a catalogue of anatomy. The largest part of the garden is taken up by the **menagerie,** which houses an impressive reptile terrarium as well as a huge ape house with orangutans.

▶ ✚ Ⓜ Jussieu. Ⓢ Musée de Minéralogie €8, students under 26 €6. Galeries d'Anatomie Comparée et de Paléontologie €7, under 26 free. Grande Galerie de l'Évolution €7, students under 26 free. 2-day passes for the 3 museums and the menagerie €25. Ⓩ Museums open W-Su 10am-5pm. Last entry for all museums 4:15pm.

Shakespeare and Co. Bookstore   BOOKSTORE

37 rue de la Bûcherie

☎ 01 43 25 40 93; www.shakespeareandcompany.com

Sylvia Beach's original Shakespeare and Co. at 8 rue Dupuytren (later at 12 rue de l'Odéon) is legendary among Parisian Anglophones and American literature nerds alike. An alcoholic expat crew of writers gathered here in the '20s; Hemingway described the bookstore in *A Moveable Feast.* After closing during WWII, George Whitman—no relation to Walt—opened the current ragtag bookstore on the shores of the Seine in 1951, dubbing it "a socialist utopia masquerading as a bookstore." You're free to grab a book off the shelves, camp out, and start reading. This isn't your run-of-the-mill, money-machine bookstore; they're in it for the love of the game.

▶ ✚ Ⓜ St-Michel. Take quai de Montebello toward Notre Dame and turn right onto rue St-Jacques. Rue de la Bûcherie is on the left. Ⓩ Open daily 10am-11pm.

Église Saint-Germain-des-Prés   CHURCH

3 pl. St-Germain-des-Prés

☎ 01 55 42 81 33; www.eglise-sgp.org

The Église St-Germain-des-Prés is the oldest church in Paris, and it shows. A popular place to store loot from the Holy Land, this church was sacked by the Normans and was the trial run for revolutionaries looking to hone their storming abilities before the Bastille. Apparently this didn't send a strong enough message the first time, so the revolutionaries returned in 1792 to kill 186 priests (it probably wasn't fairest fight). The abuse continued after, with someone missing the "No Smoking" sign next to 15 tons of gunpowder in 1794, and the church suffered complete devastation when urban planner Georges-Eugène Haussmann extended rue des Rennes in the 1850s, tearing down what was left of the abbey. It has since been refurbished with frescoes, mosaics, and, oddly enough, the interred heart of René Descartes.

▶ ✠ ⓂSt-Germain-des-Prés. Ⓢ Free. ⏰ Open daily 8am-7:45pm. Information office open M 2:30-6:45pm, Tu-F 10:30am-noon and 2:30-6:45pm, Sa 3-6:45pm.

Rue Mouffetard   HISTORICAL NEIGHBORHOOD

The 5ème's rue Mouffetard hosts one of Paris's oldest and liveliest street markets in addition to stretches of food vendors. Local English-speaking students lovingly refer to a night on rue Mouffetard as "getting Mouffe-tarded"—it's good to see that the *bon vivant* lifestyle of Hemingway (who used to live nearby) continues today. With endless alternating kebab stands and cheap bars, you can keep drinking until you wake up where you never had plans to sleep.

▶ ✠ ⓂCardinal Lemoine, Place Monge, or Censier-Daubenton. *i* Market open Tu-Su in the morning.

La Fontaine de Saint-Sulpice   HISTORIC MONUMENT

pl. St-Sulpice

Situated adjacent to the church in the middle of the pl. St-Sulpice, this fountain by sculptor Louis Visconti is often known as *La Fontaine des Quatre Points Cardinaux.* The rather bitter nickname is to deride the four ambitious bishops—Bossuet, Fénelon, Massillon, and Fléchier—who grace its four sides. None of these men ever became cardinals. How hard you choose to mock them should be based on whether you think becoming a cardinal or being enshrined on a monumental fountain is a bigger achievement.

▶ ✠ ⓂSt-Sulpice.

Musée Delacroix   MUSEUM

6 rue de Furstemberg

☎01 44 41 86 50; www.musee-delacroix.fr

If you really like the Romantic era, you'll have a blast here.

Sights

Found Underground

Paris is a city of appearances, and this extends to the aesthetic effort that the city has put into decorating its Metro stations. With artful posters and complimentary graffiti, certain stops are tourist destinations themselves.

- **ABBESSES.** This Montmartre station has a winding staircase that lets the athletically inclined trek seven stories to the exit. Although there's an elevator, take the stairs to appreciate the mural depicting abstract scenes of Paris.

- **SAINT-GERMAIN-DES-PRÉS.** This station holds a collection of famous poetry books in glass cases. Not only that, projectors blow up quotes from French poets onto the walls, making for some higher quality reading during the morning commute than the usual tabloids.

- **CONCORDE.** This one's for people who love both history and Scrabble. The station has what looks like a gigantic word search, and the letters spell out the Declaration of the Rights of Man penned during the French Revolution.

- **ARTS ET MÉTIERS.** Redesigned in 1994 with inspiration from the Conservatory of Arts and Crafts Museum above, this stop looks like a submarine, complete with metallic walls and portholes. Don't forget your oxygen tank.

Painter Eugène Delacroix, the artistic master behind the famous *Liberty Leading the People* (which is actually housed in the Louvre), lived in this three-room apartment. It has since been turned into a museum filled with his watercolors, engravings, letters to Théophile Gautier and George Sand, sketches for his work in the Église St-Sulpice, and souvenirs from his journey to Morocco.

▶ ⚐ Ⓜ St-Germain-des-Prés. Walk toward Odéon and turn left onto rue Cardinale. The museum is straight ahead as the street bends left. *i* Free same-day entry with a Louvre ticket. Ⓢ €5, students and under 18 free. ⏲ Open June-Aug M 9:30am-5pm, W-Su 9:30am-5:30pm; Sept-May M 9:30am-5pm, W-Su 9:30am-5pm. Last entry 30min. before close.

Grande Mosquée de Paris   MUSEUM, MOSQUE

39 rue Geoffroy-St-Hilaire

☎01 43 31 38 20; www.mosquees-de-paris.net

The Grande Mosquée de Paris was built in 1920 to honor

the contributions of North African countries during WWI. Given the nature of the times, the North Africans had to build it themselves, but the French did at least finance the construction. While prayer and worship spaces are closed to the public, all visitors are welcome to wonder at the 33m minaret, sweat it out in the hammam's marble steam baths, and sip mint tea in the cafe.

▶ ♯ Ⓜ️Censier-Daubenton. Ⓢ Guided tour €3, students €2. Hammam (steam bath), 10min. massage, and black tea €38. 🕗 Cafe open daily 9am-11:30pm. Restaurant open daily noon-evening. Hammam open for women M 10am-9pm, W-Th 10am-9pm, F 2pm-9am, Sa 10am-9pm; open for men Tu 2-9pm, Su 10am-9pm.

Cafe de Flore   HISTORIC CAFE

172 bd St-Germain

☎01 45 48 55 26

Legend has it that when Jean-Paul Sartre dined here, he and his friends (with benefits, if we're talking Simone de Beauvoir) sat opposite from communist Marguerite Duras and company. If the coffee at Fouquet's on the Champs-Élysées was too rich for your taste, you can get the Left Bank's version for almost half the cost and feel just as spiffy and a little bit more intellectual.

▶ ♯ Ⓜ️St-Germain-des-Prés. Ⓢ Coffee €4.10. Cocktail "Le Flore" €15. 🕗 Open daily 7:30am-1:30am.

Les Deux Magots   HISTORIC CAFE

6 pl. St-Germain-des-Prés

☎01 45 48 55 25

Attracting intellectuals and those who just like to be seen, Les Deux Magots was a lot cheaper back when Hemingway, Camus, and Picasso visited, which may have been why it almost went bankrupt in 1913. Today it's far from broke, although the coffee is 10 cents cheaper than at neighboring Le Café de Flore.

▶ ♯ Ⓜ️St-Germain-des-Prés. Ⓢ Coffee €4. Cocktails €13. 🕗 Open daily 7:30am-1am.

INVALIDES

Visit this arrondissement more than once if you can. Unsurprisingly, the Tour Eiffel towers over all of the 7ème attractions, but the posh neighborhood also hosts the French national government, a number of embassies, and an astonishing concentration of famous museums. Be sure to stop by the Musée Rodin and Musée d'Orsay.

🏛 Eiffel Tower   TOWER

Champs de Mars, closest to the Seine

☎01 44 11 23 23; www.tour-eiffel.fr

In 1937, Gustave Eiffel said, "I ought to be jealous of that tower; she is more famous than I am." The city of Paris as a whole could share the same lament, especially since the Eiffel Tower has come to stand for Paris itself. Gustave Eiffel designed it to be the tallest structure in the world, intended to surpass the ancient Egyptian pyramids in size and notoriety. Apparently hard to impress, Parisian society continues to shrug in disappointment; the response they'll give is usually, "*c'est honteux*" (it's shameful). Despite the national love-hate relationship, over 150 million Parisians and (mostly) tourists have made it the most visited paid monument in the world, proving once again the French ability to make a fuss and do nothing about it.

Still, at 324m—just a tad shorter than New York City's Chrysler Building—the tower is a tremendous feat of design and engineering, though wind does cause it to occasionally sway 6 to 7cm (nobody's perfect). The unparalleled view from the top floor deserves a visit. The cheapest way to ascend the tower is by burning off those *pain au chocolat* calories on the world's tallest stairmaster, although the third floor is only accessible by elevator. Waiting until nightfall to make your ascent cuts down the line and ups the glamour. At the top, captioned aerial photographs help you locate other famous landmarks; on a clear day it is possible to see Chartres, 88km away. From dusk until 2am (Sept-May 1am) the tower sparkles with light for 10min. on the hour.

▶ ♿ Ⓜ Bir-Hakeim or Trocadéro. Ⓢ Elevator to 2nd fl. €8.20, ages 12-24 €6.60, 4-11 and handicapped €4.10, under 4 free; elevator to top €13.40/11.80/9.30/free; stair entrance to 2nd fl. €4.70/3.70/3.20/free. Buy your ticket online and pick your time to climb and cut down the wait. Champagne bar on top, €10 per glass (don't say we didn't warn you). 🕐 Elevator open daily June 17-Aug 28 9am-12:45pm; Aug 29-June 16 9:30am-11:45pm; last entry 45min. before close. Stairs open daily June 17-Aug 28 9am-12:45pm, last entry at midnight; Aug 29-June 16 9:30am-6:30pm, last entry 6pm.

🏛 Champs de Mars   PARK

Lined with more lovers than trees, the expansive lawn that stretches from the École Militaire to the Eiffel Tower is called Champs de Mars (Field of Mars). Close to the neighborhood's military monuments and museums, it has historically lived up to the Roman god of war for whom it was named. The open

Top 5 Views in Paris

- **EIFFEL TOWER:** You can see many of the city's famous landmarks from its deck. Buy a postcard and send it to your jealous friends from the post office on the first level of the Tower.

- **ARC DE TRIOMPHE:** See the perfect symmetry of av. des Champs-Élysées, the chaotic Paris traffic, and the majestic Eiffel Tower from the viewing platform on the top of the arch. This ancient monument has no elevator, so be prepared to climb more than 280 steps.

- **MONTMARTRE:** Walk or ride the funicular to the top of Montmartre for a panoramic view of Paris, the highest hill in the city. Try to visit at night to catch a view of Paris glowing in light.

- **TOUR MONTPARNASSE:** Take Europe's fastest elevator to the 56th floor of this modern skyscraper, where you will get an amazing view of the city through floor-to-ceiling windows. You can also walk three more floors for outdoor viewing on the roof.

- **NOTRE DAME DE PARIS:** Walking up nearly 400 steps to the top may be a challenge for the unfit, but the breathtaking view of the Seine and the Latin Quarter, as well as a closer look at the gargoyles, is sure to relieve the pain in your calves. No pain, no gain, right?

field has been used for military boot camp and as a convenient place for violent demonstrations, including but not limited to civilian massacres during the Revolution. At the end toward the Military School is the "Wall of Peace," a glass structure that has 32 languages worth of the word "peace" in an attempt to make up for the field's bloody past.

▶ ⚘ Ⓜ La Motte-Picquet-Grenelle or École Militaire.

Sights

🖼 Musée Rodin   MUSEUM

79 rue de Varenne

☎ 01 44 18 61 10; www.musee-rodin.fr

According to Parisians in the know, this is one of the city's museums. During his lifetime, Auguste Rodin (1840-1917) was among the country's most controversial artists and was considered to be the sculptor of Impressionism. Today, the art world considers him the father of modern sculpture and applauds him for imbuing stone with a downright groovy level of "psychological complexity." While most of his lesser known sculptures are inside the former Hôtel Biron, the 18th-century building where he lived and worked, the two museum must-sees are *Le Penseur (The Thinker)*, and *La Porte de L'Enfer (The Gates of Hell)*. These two are rightfully displayed side by side: *The Thinker* is Dante contemplating the *Divine Comedy*, which is portrayed in the *Gates of Hell*, a bronze mess of lustful pairs swirling in the violent turbulence of the second ring of Hell.

▶ ✝ Ⓜ Varenne. *i* Temporary exhibits housed in the chapel, to the right as you enter. Touch tours for the blind and educational tours available (☎01 44 18 61 24). Ⓢ Museum €6, ages 18-25 €5, under 18 and EU citizens under 26 free. Joint ticket with Musée d'Orsay €12. Garden €1/1/free/free. 1st Su of the month free. Audio tours in 7 languages €4 each for permanent and temporary exhibits, combined ticket €6. ⏰ Open Tu-Su 10am-5:45pm; last entry 5:15pm.

🖼 Musée d'Orsay   MUSEUM
62 rue de Lille
☎01 40 49 48 14; www.musee-orsay.com

Aesthetic taste is fickle. When a handful of artists were rejected from the Louvre salon in the 19th century, they opened an exhibition across the way, prompting both the scorn of stick-up-their-arses *académiciens* and the rise of Impressionism. Today, people line up at the Musée d'Orsay to see this collection of groundbreaking rejects. Originally built as a train station, the Musée d'Orsay opened as President Mitterrand's gift to France. It gathered works from the Louvre, Jeu de Paume, Palais de Tokyo, Musée de Luxembourg, provincial museums, and private collections to add to the original collection the Louvre had refused. On the ground floor, you can see the pre-Impressionist paintings, and it only gets weirder as you go up. In the back sits a model of the Parisian Opera cut in two to reveal the inside. Despite our best efforts, we were unable to find the elusive Phantom. The top floor includes all the big names in Impressionist and Post-Impressionist art: Degas, Manet, Monet, Seurat, and Van Gogh. Degas's famed "dancers" are a particular highlight.

▶ ✝ Ⓜ Solférino. Access to visitors at entrance A off the square at 1 rue de la Légion d'Honneur. Ⓢ €8, ages 18-25 €5.50, under 18 and EU citizens 18-26 free. ⏰ Open Tu-W 9:30am-6pm, Th 9:30am-9:45pm, F-Su 9:30am-6pm. Visitors asked to leave starting at 5:30pm (Th 9:15pm).

Invalides   MUSEUM
Esplanade des Invalides
☎08 10 11 33 99; www.invalides.org

For the history buff, this is a must see. A comprehensive

collection of all things war-like and French (yes, including the defeats), this building is more than just a pretty gold dome. Although you have to pay to enter the various military museums, as well as **Napoleon's tomb,** the majority of the complex is accessible for ✂**free,** including the inner courtyard (tip: it's about 15 degrees cooler in the shade), upper walkway, and the St-Louis des Invalides Chapel, all of which have samples of what's inside the museums, including a battery of 60 cannons. Also check out the Charles de Gaulle *Historial* (film), which outlines the famed president/general's efforts during the Nazi resistance. There are also a number of rotating exhibitions that highlight particular times in French military history, from Louis XI, "The Spider King," to the wars in Indochina.

▶ ♯ Ⓜ Invalides. Ⓢ €9, under 18 and EU citizens 18-25 free. ⏰ Open Apr-Sept M 10am-6pm, Tu 10am-9pm, W-Su 10am-6pm; Oct-Mar daily 10am-5pm. Closed 1st M each month. Charles de Gaulle *Historial* closed M. Films show every 30min. Dome open Jul-Aug until 7pm.

Musée du Quai Branly   MUSEUM

37 quai Branly

☎01 56 61 71 72; www.quaibranly.fr

A gift to the French people from Jacques Chirac, this adventure/time machine/museum sucks you in with its overgrown gardens of exotic plants under the shade of the raised modern building. Don't let the architecture fool you: this museum houses a huge collection of ancient artifacts from tribal cultures around the world. Organized into four areas (Africa, Asia, Americas, and Oceania), the museum has anticipated your impending boredom and made the museum as visually and auditorily stimulating as possible. Timothy Leary would be so proud. In case you can't tell the difference between a Nepalese tunic and an African one, look at the floor: the color under your feet corresponds to what section of the world you are in. Be sure to sit in one of the many hidden sound caves to take in some tribal noises in solitude, but beware of local high school students using the dark spaces as personal make-out rooms.

▶ ♯ Ⓜ Alma-Marceau. Cross Pont de l'Alma and follow quai Branly toward the Eiffel Tower. Ⓢ €8.50, under 18 and EU citizens 18-25 free. ⏰ Open Tu-W 11am-7pm, Th-Sa 11am-9pm, Su 11am-7pm.

CHAMPS-ÉLYSÉES

There's a reason that the 8ème has remained popular with tourists long after the Champs-Élysées ceased to be posh. The neighborhood harbors more architectural beauty, historical significance, and shopping opportunities than almost any other in the city and remains an exhilarating—if hectic—place to spend a day. Champs-Élysées is also home to a variety of art museums in its northern corners; they are often located in *hôtels particuliers,* where they were once part of private collections.

🖼 Arc de Triomphe   HISTORIC MONUMENT

pl. Charles de Gaulle-Étoile

www.arc-de-triomphe.monuments-nationaux.fr

Probably the second most iconic image in the whole city, the Arc de Triomphe dominates the Champs-Élysées and remains strikingly powerful even when viewed from a distance. The original architect imagined an unparalleled tribute to France's military prowess in the form of a giant, bejeweled elephant. Fortunately, Napoleon had the more restrained idea of building an arch. You could probably pull together an exhibition of French history since the arch's 1836 completion based purely on photos of the Arc's use in ceremonial celebrations. It stands both as a tribute to French military triumphs and as a memorial to those who have fallen in battle. The Tomb of the Unknown Soldier, added in 1920, lies under the arch. The Arc is spectacular to look at, and it returns the favor by being spectacular to look from. The observation deck offers a brilliant view of the Historic Axis, which stretches from the Louvre to the Grande Arche de la Défense.

▶ ✠ Ⓜ Charles de Gaulle-Étoile. You will die (and face a hefty fine) if you try to dodge the 10-lane merry-go-round of cars around the arch, so use the pedestrian underpass on the right side of the Champs-Élysées facing the arch. *i* Expect long waits, although you can escape the crowds if you go before noon. Buy tickets in the pedestrian underpass. Ⓢ €9.50, ages 18-25 €6, under 18 and EU citizens 18-25 free. ⏰ Open daily Apr-Sept 10am-11pm; Oct-Mar 10am-10:30pm. Last entry 30min. before close.

Avenue des Champs-Élysées   SHOPPING DISTRICT

From pl. Charles de Gaulle-Étoile to pl. de la Concorde

There's a reason we included it here and not in **Shopping:** you can't afford it. The Champs-Élysées seems to be a magnificent celebration of the elite's pomp and fortuitous circumstance, but it's mostly filled with flashy cars, expensive cafes filled with rich foreigners, and kitschy shops. On the plus side, it does have some of the best people-watching in Europe. The avenue also hosts most major French events: on **Bastille Day,** the largest parade in Europe takes place here, as does the final stretch of the **Tour de France.** While the Champs itself may be deteriorating in class (with the invasion of chain stores), many of its side streets, like **avenue Montaigne,** have picked up the slack and ooze sophistication.

▶ ✟ Ⓜ Charles de Gaulle-Étoile.

Grand Palais   PALACE

3 av. du Général Eisenhower
☎01 44 13 17 17; www.grandpalais.fr

Designed for the 1900 World's Fair, the Grand Palais and the accompanying Petit Palais across the street were lauded as exemplary works of Art Nouveau architecture. Since the novelty of a then-modern building has worn off in the past century, most of the Grand Palais houses a 20th-century fine art exhibit and a children's science museum, **Palais de la Découverte** (see below). Most of the building's beauty can be admired outside for free, especially at night when its 6000 metric ton glass ceiling glows, lighting up the French flag that flies above it.

▶ ✟ Ⓜ Champs-Élysées-Clemenceau. Ⓢ €11.50, students €8. For special exhibits, admission varies; expect €8-16, students €6-9, art students free. Ⓣ Open M-Tu 10am-8pm, W 10am-10pm, Th-Su 10am-8pm. Last entry 45min. before close.

Petit Palais   MUSEUM

av. Winston Churchill
☎01 53 43 40 00; www.petitpalais.paris.fr

The Petit Palais showcases a hodgepodge of European art from Christian orthodoxy to 20th-century Parisian artists. If you are really into obscure works by famous artists, go for it. Otherwise you might be burnt out after d'Orsay and the Louvre. But hey, the Petit Palais is free for the permanent collection, so it's got that going for it.

▶ ✟ Ⓜ Champs-Élysées-Clemenceau or Franklin D. Roosevelt. Follow av. Winston Churchill toward the river. The museum is on the left. Ⓢ Permanent collection free. Special exhibits €5-11, ages 14-27 half price, under 13 free. Audio tour €4. Credit card min. €15. Ⓣ Open Tu-Su 10am-6pm. Special exhibits open Tu-W 10am-6pm, Th 10am-8pm, F-Su 10am-6pm. Last entry 1hr. before close.

Madeleine
CHURCH

pl. de la Madeleine

☎01 44 51 69 00; www.eglise-lamadeleine.com

While this famous church is worth a visit to admire its immensity and large sculpture of Mary Magdalene, there isn't much else to see, though there are frequent chamber and music concerts. Today, pricey clothing and food shops line the square surrounding Madeleine, including the famous macaroon boutique, Ladurée (see **Food**).

▶ ✱ Ⓜ️Madeleine. 🕐 Open daily 9am-7pm. Regular organ and chamber concerts; contact church for schedule and tickets. Mass M-F 12:30 and 6:30pm at the nearby chapel; Sa 6pm; Su 9:30, 11am, and 7pm with organ and choir.

Palais de la Découverte
MUSEUM

av. Franklin D. Roosevelt, in the Grand Palais

☎01 56 43 20 20; www.palais-decouverte.fr

Children tear around the interactive science exhibits in the Palais de la Découverte, and it may be hard not to join them—nothing brings out your inner child like buttons that start model comets on their celestial trajectories, spinning seats that demonstrate angular motion, and displays of creepy-crawlies. What's more, both adults and children are likely to learn a surprising amount about physics, chemistry, astronomy, geology, and biology. The temporary exhibits (four per year) are usually crowd-pleasers; the most recent, entitled "Dinosaur Diet," featured real-sized animated dinosaurs. The planetarium has four shows per day; arrive early during school vacation periods.

▶ ✱ Ⓜ️Franklin D. Roosevelt or Champs-Élysées-Clemenceau. Ⓢ €7; students, seniors, and ages 5-17 €4.50; under 5 free. Planetarium €3.50. 🕐 Open Tu-Sa 9:30am-6pm, Su 10am-7pm. Last entry 30min. before close. Planetarium shows 11:30am, 2, 3:15, 4:30pm.

OPÉRA AND CANAL ST-MARTIN

While the 9ème and 10ème don't offer much in the way of landmarks or museums, there are a few sights that you might want to quickly check out. **Le Marché Saint-Quentin** could be worth a longer perusal.

Opéra Garnier
THEATER

pl. de l'Opéra

☎08 92 89 90 90; www.operadeparis.fr

Formerly known as the Opéra National de Paris before the

creation of the Opéra Bastille in 1989, the Opéra Garnier became world famous when its main six-ton chandelier crashed to the ground in 1896, killing one person. This incident inspired the longest running musical on Broadway and a weird sex idol for drama kids everywhere. Yes, we're talking about the *Phantom of the Opera,* and its songs may run through your head throughout your visit. Today, visit the Opéra (when it's not sporadically closed due to preformances) and see the grand staircase, grand foyer, and stage—all decorated with frescoes and ornate stone and marble designs that often leave visitors speechless.

▶ ♿ Ⓜ Opéra. *i* Tickets usually available 2 weeks before the show. Rush tickets go on sale 1hr. before show. Ⓢ Tickets generally €7-160. Tours €9, under 25 €5. Guided tour €12, over 60 €10, students €9, under 13 €6. ⏲ Open daily 10am-4:30pm. Box office open M-Sa 10:30am-6:30pm.

Le Marché Saint-Quentin   MARKET
Corner of rue de Chabrol and bd de Magenta

The largest covered market in Paris, Le Marché St-Quentin is an overwhelming combination of the finest cheeses, fish, and meats. Even if you're not shopping, come just to experience the mix of aromas and mingle with veteran foodies who spend their days browsing for the perfect Camembert. There's a bistro in the middle of the market for those who can't wait until they get home to chow down on their produce.

▶ ♿ Ⓜ Gare de l'Est. ⏲ Open M-Sa 8:30am-1pm and 4-7:30pm, Su 8:30am-1pm.

BASTILLE

Aside from the **place de la Bastille,** there are few monumental sights left in this neighborhood. Still, the symbolic historical value remains, and this lively area provides many contemporary diversions. The 12ème boasts monoliths of modern architecture like the **Opéra Bastille.** The formerly working-class neighborhood is now mostly commercialized, but a bit of idiosyncratic charm can be seen in the funky **rue de la Roquette,** where clubs and bars sit alongside boutiques and cafes.

Place de la Bastille   SQUARE

Though the revolutionary spirit has faded, a similar fervor still manifests itself nightly in fits of drunken revelry, most marked on **Bastille Day**. At the center of the square, a monument of winged Mercury holding a torch of freedom symbolizes France's movement (albeit a slow one) from monarchy to democracy.

▶ ✝ Ⓜ Bastille.

Bastille Prison   HISTORIC LANDMARK

Visitors to the prison subsist on symbolic value alone—it's one of the most popular sights in Paris that doesn't actually exist. On July 14, 1789, an angry Parisian mob stormed this bastion of royal tyranny, sparking the French Revolution. They only liberated seven prisoners, but who's counting? Two days later, the Assemblée Nationale ordered the prison demolished. Today all that remains is the fortress's ground plan, still visible as a line of paving stones in the pl. de la Bastille. But it was hardly the hell hole that the Revolutionaries who tore it down imagined it to be. The Bastille's elite inmates were allowed to furnish their suites, use fresh linens, bring their own servants, and receive guests; the Cardinal de Rohan famously held a dinner party for 20 in his cell. Notable prisoners included the ★**Man in the Iron Mask** (made famous by writer Alexandre Dumas), the Comte de Mirabeau, Voltaire (twice), and the Marquis de Sade. The anniversary of the storming is July 14th, which (much like a certain celebration 10 days earlier across the Atlantic) is a time of glorious fireworks and copious amounts of alcohol, with festivities concentrated around pl. de la Bastille.

▶ ✝ Ⓜ Bastille.

Opéra Bastille   PERFORMANCE HALL
130 rue de Lyon
☎ 08 92 89 90 90; www.operadeparis.fr

The "People's Opera" has been not-so-fondly referred to as ugly, an airport, and a huge toilet, due to its uncanny resemblance to the coin-operated *pissoirs* on the streets of Paris. Yet the opera has not struck a completely sour note, as it helped renew local interest in the arts. The guided tours offer a behind-the-scenes view of the colossal theater. The modern granite and glass auditorium, which seats 2723, comprises only 5% of the building's surface area. The rest of the structure houses exact replicas of the stage (for rehearsal purposes) and workshops for both the Bastille and Garnier operas.

▶ ✝ Ⓜ Bastille. Look for the box office *(billetterie)*. *i* Tickets can be purchased online, by mail, by phone, or in person. Rush tickets 15min. before show for students under 25 and seniors. Call in advance to arrange English tour. Ⓢ Tickets €5-180. Tours €11, students and over 60 €9, under 18 €6. ⏰ Box office open M-Sa 10:30am-6:30pm. 1hr. guided tours in French fall-spring daily at 1 and 5pm.

July Column

MONUMENT

Towering above the constantly busy pl. de la Bastille, this light-catching column commemorates many groups of French freedom fighters—though, somewhat illogically, not the ones who stormed the Bastille. It celebrates the *Trois Glorieuses,* the "three glorious" days that toppled Charles X's monarchy in favor of a free republic... just kidding, it was another monarch, Louis-Philippe, who took over. When Louis-Philippe was in turn deposed in 1848, the column was rededicated to those fighters as well, and 200 additional bodies were buried under it. Apparently thinking it was a revolutionary good luck trinket, the Communards used the tower as a rallying point for their 1871 uprising, but, after three successful months, the French army came in and deported nearly 7500 and executed 20,000. Sheer numbers prevented any additional burials under the column.

▶ Ⓜ Bastille. In the center of pl. de la Bastille.

Cité Nationale de l'Histoire de l'Immigration

MUSEUM

293 av. Daumesnil

☎01 53 59 58 60; www.histoire-immigration.fr

It's both appropriate and ironic that this recently opened museum on immigration is housed in the Palais de la Porte Dorée, which was built during France's colonial expansion and thus features not-so-politically-correct friezes of "native culture" on its walls. Presented chronologically, the permanent collection traces the arrival and subsequent attempts at integration of immigrants from all over the world. The message is driven home with stories of Algerians seperated from families and a model of a six-person bunk bed. After seeing this, you'll definitely have to stop complaining about how cramped your hostel room is.

▶ Ⓜ Porte Dorée. In the Palais de la Porte Dorée, on the western edge of the Bois de Vincennes. Ⓢ €5, ages 18-26 €3.50, under 18 and EU citizens ages 18-26 free. 1st Su of every month free. ⏰ Open Tu-F 10am-5:30pm, Sa-Su 10am-7pm. Last entry 45min. before close.

MONTPARNASSE AND SOUTHERN PARIS

There are few monuments in Montparnasse and Southern Paris. Diverse, residential, and pleasantly odd, these neighborhoods remain uninterrupted by the troops of pear-shaped tourists in matching fanny packs that plague the more pristine arrondissements. Though short on medieval cathedrals, hidden gems from Paris's recent waves of immigration and perturbed Bo-Bos (Bohemian Bourgeoisie) are scattered throughout the area.

🏛 Catacombs   HISTORIC LANDMARK

1 av. du Colonel Henri Roi-Tanguy

☎01 43 22 47 63; www.catacombes-de-paris.fr

The Catacombs were the original site of Paris's quarries, but were converted into an ossuary in 1785 to help alleviate the stench rising from overcrowded cemeteries (perfume only goes so far). Not for the claustrophobic or faint of heart, this 45min. excursion leads visitors down a winding spiral staircase to a welcoming sign: "Stop! Here is the Empire of Death." Stacks of skulls and femurs line the walls, and the remains of six million people make you feel quite insignificant in the grand scheme of things. Try to arrive before the opening at 10am; hordes of tourists form extremely long lines hoping to escape the beating sun. The visitors' passage is well marked, so don't worry about getting lost. Try trailing behind the group a little for the ultimate creepy experience—you won't be disappointed.

▶ ♯ Ⓜ Denfert-Rochereau. Cross av. du Colonel Henri Roi-Tanguy with the lion on your left. Ⓢ €8, over 60 €6, ages 14-26 €4, under 14 free. Ⓩ Open Tu-Su 10am-5pm. Last entry 4pm.

Tour Montparnasse   TOWER

33 av. du Maine

☎01 45 38 52 56

Built in 1969, this modern tower stands 196m tall and makes Paris look like a miniature model. The elevator is allegedly the fastest in Europe (moving at 5.12m per sec.—not a lot of time to clear the pressure in your ears) and spits you out to a mandatory photo line on the 56th floor. After being shoved in front of a fake city skyline and forced to smile for a picture that you probably don't want, you're finally allowed up to the 59th floor to take in the beauty and meticulous planning of Paris's historic streets. Thankfully, the city ruled that similar eyesores could not be constructed in Paris's downtown shortly after this one was built.

▶ ⚲ Ⓜ Montparnasse-Bienvenüe. Entrance on rue de l'Arrivée. Ⓢ €10, students €7. 🕐 Open M-Th 9:30am-10:30pm, F-Sa 9:30am-11pm, Su 9:30am-10:30pm. Last entry 30min. before close.

Cimetière du Montparnasse   CEMETERY

3 bd Edgar Quinet
☎01 44 10 86 50

Paris certainly has a lot of cemeteries. Despite the repetitiveness of buried celebrities, there are some unique features that make Montparnasse worth visiting. Because it's secluded from the main tourist areas, this cemetery is more of a local park during the day, but one where you can stroll past Jean-Paul Sartre and Simone de Beauvoir (the two are buried together—how cute). Watch out for older kids from the *banlieues* bumming cigarettes off tourists and the occasional homeless drunk. Nonetheless, the cemetery showcases some delightful architecture and an impressive list of tenants.

▶ ⚲ Ⓜ Edgar Quinet, opposite Sq. Delambre. Ⓢ Free. 🕐 High season open M-F 8am-6pm, Sa 8:30am-6pm, Su 9am-6pm; low season open M-F 8am-5:30pm, Sa 8:30am-5:30pm, Su 9am-5:30pm.

Quartier de la Butte-aux-Cailles   NEIGHBORHOOD

Intersection of rue de la Butte-aux-Cailles and rue des 5 Diamants

Traces of the district's original counterculture from the 1968 riots are alive and well here: dreadlocks are the hairstyle of choice, the walls are covered in graffiti, and the fashionably unaffected are armed with guitars at all times. Here you can find some of the cheapest cafes and restaurants, which (as expected) only accept cash. Basically, this neighborhood makes Haight-Ashbury look like Silicon Valley, and provides a good chance for you to get cheap eats and free entertainment from carefree hippies.

▶ ⚲ Ⓜ Place d'Italie. Take rue Bobillot south a few blocks and turn right onto rue de la Butte-aux-Cailles.

Quartier Chinois   NEIGHBORHOOD

Just south of rue de Tolbiac

Spread out over four Metro stops just south of rue de Tolbiac, Paris's Chinatown should really be called Paris's Indo-Chinatown. Thanks to years of colonialism, some of the most authentic and talented chefs have flocked to this region from

Sights

Cambodia, Laos, Vietnam, and Thailand to provide super cheap food. A walk here (especially in the sweltering summers) will transport you to Ho Chi Minh City.

▶ ⚡ Ⓜ Tolbiac, Maison Blanche, Porte de Choisy, or Porte d'Ivry.

WESTERN PARIS

Fortunately for tourists, all of these museums are within walking distance of each other. To keep your sanity, please don't go to all of them at once, even though you might be tempted to cross the road and continue knocking them off your to-do list. We suggest you head to the wine museum first, get a buzz going, then hike up the road to **Trocadéro.**

🖼 Musée du Vin   MUSEUM

rue des Eaux
☎01 45 25 70 89; www.museeduvinparis.com

Formerly a 15th-century monastery, the Musée du Vin's underground tunnels and vaults take visitors through the history of wine production, including the tools that till the soil, the harvesting techniques in different regions of France, and how they make champagne. The exhibits integrate history with models of Louis Pasteur, who cured wine disease by heating the wine in a vacuum, and Napoleon, who cut his wine with water (you know, to stay sharp on the battlefield). The tour ends with a tasting of one of three types of wine (rosé, white, or red—we recommend the last one), but only after a thorough explanation of where each came from. Be patient, and for goodness's sake let them pour it for you.

▶ ⚡ Ⓜ Passy. Go down the stairs, turn right onto pl. Albioni, and then right onto rue des Eaux; the museum is tucked away at the end of the street. Ⓢ Self-guided tour and 1 glass of wine €12; students, seniors, and visitors with disabilities €9.70. 🕐 Open Tu-Su 10am-6pm.

Cimetière de Passy   CEMETERY

2 rue du Commandant-Schloesing
☎01 53 70 40 80

Opened in 1820, this cemetery is home to some of Paris's most notable deceased, including the fashionable Givenchy family, composer Claude Debussy, Impressionist Berthe Morisot, and painter Édouard Manet. The idiosyncrasies and enduring rivalries of these figures continue even in death: the graves here look more like miniature mansions than tombstones. The tomb of the Russian artist Marie Bashkirtseff is a recreation of her studio and stands at an impressive 40 ft. tall. Morisot and Manet are buried in a more modest tomb together; we suspect that Morisot's husband would not have approved. Well-groomed and quiet, the graveyard is more like a shadowy garden, with a wonderful view of the Eiffel Tower.

▶ ✇ Ⓜ Trocadéro. Follow av. Paul Doumer right. The cemetery is on the right. Ⓢ Free. ⏰ Open Mar 16-Nov 5 M-F 8am-6pm, Sa 8:30am-6pm, Su and public holidays 9am-6pm; Nov 6-Mar 15 M-F 8am-5:30pm, Sa 8:30am-5:30pm, Su and public holidays 9am-5:30pm. Last entry 30min. before close. Conservation office open M-F 8:30am-12:30pm and 2-5pm.

Jardins du Trocadéro   GARDEN

The ultimate tourist hub, the gardens provide the perfect "I've been to Paris" photo op, with one of the clearest views of the Eiffel Tower. The fountain and sprawling, sloping lawns are great for a picnic or watching the many street performers working for your spare change.

▶ ✇ Ⓜ Trocadéro.

Musée Marmottan Monet   MUSEUM

2 rue Louis Boilly

☎ 01 44 96 50 33; www.marmottan.com

Even for the artistically challenged, this is worth a visit. Less crowded than any other popular museum in Paris, the gold-detailed, ornately decorated museum brings you back to the Belle Époque. Housing Monet's water lilies as well as Berthe Morisot's works of the same Impressionist genre, this museum also throws a bone to the iconography of the Middle Ages.

▶ ✇ Ⓜ La Muette. Walk through the Jardin de Ranelagh on av. Jardin de Ranelagh. The museum is on the right on rue Louis-Boilly. Ⓢ €10, under 25 €5. ⏰ Open Tu-W 11am-6pm, Th 11am-10pm, F-Su 11am-6pm. Last entry 30min. before close.

MONTMARTRE

Just because the sights in Montmartre aren't captured on postcards doesn't mean they don't exist. While most people come to see the **Moulin Rouge** or **Sacré-Cœur,** you can learn just as much about Paris by grabbing a coffee along the Pigalle while watching seedy crowds roam the streets and gullible tourists fall for souvenir tourist traps. It's more important here than anywhere in Paris to blend in—tourists are frequent targets for pickpockets and scammers, so for Lady Marmalade's sake, don't go wandering around these sights at night.

⬛ Basilique du Sacré-Cœur   CHURCH

35 rue du Chevalier-de-la-Barre

☎01 53 41 89 00; www.sacre-coeur-montmartre.fr

Situated 129m above sea level, this splendid basilica was first planned in 1870. Its purpose? To serve as a spiritual bulwark for France and the Catholic Church, which were under the weight of an imminent military defeat and German occupation. The basilica was commissioned by the National Assembly and was initially meant to be an assertion of conservative Catholic power, but the only people that assert themselves on the steps today are the scammers offering "free" bracelets, so beware. The basilica sees over 10 million visitors per year and offers a free, spectacular view of the city. On a spring day, grab some ice cream and marvel at the view.

▶ ♯ ⓂLamarck-Caulaincourt. Take rue Caulaincourt and turn right onto rue Lamrack. Follow rue Lamrack until you reach the basilica. Ⓢ Free. ⓘ Basilica open daily 6am-10:30pm. Dome open daily Mar-Nov 9am-7pm; Dec-Feb 9am-6pm. Mass M-F 11:15am, 6:30, 10pm; Sa 10pm; Su 11am, 6, 10pm.

Halle Saint-Pierre   MUSEUM

2 rue Ronsard

☎01 42 58 72 89; www.hallesaintpierre.org

Halle St-Pierre is a one-of-a-kind (read: weird) abstract art museum located right down the street from the Sacré-Cœur. Exhibits change constantly, so the museum is hard to pin down. In general, the art tends to be a bit far out. The most recent exhibition, on display until March 4, 2012, is on "Modern Art and Pop Culture," and displays paintings such as Mickey Mouse smoking a cigarette and (to the dismay of Chistendom) three pumas being crucified.

▶ ♯ ⓂAnvers. Follow rue de Steinkerque up the hill and turn right onto pl. St-Pierre. Walk 1 block and turn left onto rue Ronsard. Ⓢ €7.50, students €6. ⓘ Open Sept-July daily 10am-6pm; Aug M-F noon-6pm.

Cimetière de Montmartre   CEMETERY

20 av. Rachel

☎01 53 42 36 30

The vast Cimetière de Montmartre, stretching across a signifi-cant proportion of the 18éme, lies below street level on the site of a former quarry. It is the resting place of multiple acclaimed artists: writer Émile Zola, painter Edgar Degas, saxophone inventor Adolphe Sax, and ballet dancer Marie Taglioni are among the long-term residents. If you have an extra pair in your backpack, you can leave pointe shoes on Taglioni's grave. The other dead celebs prefer coins on their gravestones. One of the most infamous killers in French history is also buried here: Charles Henri Sanson, Royal Executioner, who executed nearly 3000 people, including Louis XVI himself.

► Ⓜ Place de Clichy. Head up bd de Clichy, which becomes rue Caulaincourt. The entrance is at the intersection of rue Caulaincourt and av. Rachel. Ⓢ Free. Open May 16-Nov 5 M-F 8am-6pm, Sa 8:30am-6pm, Su 9am-6pm; Nov 6-May 15 M-F 8am-5:30pm, Sa 8:30am-5:30pm, Su 9am-5:30pm.

Pigalle — NEIGHBORHOOD

This famous, seedy neighborhood has a bad reputation for a reason. Home to strip clubs, sex shops, and fake designer clothing and handbags, Pigalle turns a dark corner at night. Travelers report that you shouldn't take the Metro at night around here; instead, opt for a taxi. Now that the disclaimer is out of the way, the **Moulin Rouge** (82 bd de Clichy ☎01 53 09 82 82; www.moulinrouge.fr) cabaret show is definitely worth the €90 you have lying around, as it's the classiest titty show you'll ever see. The neighborhood is improving as young bohemians take advantage of the low rent rates, so there is a growing rock and hip-hop scene, especially at **Elysée Montmartre** (72 bd de Rochechouart ☎01 44 92 45 36; www.elyseemontmartre.com).

► Ⓜ Pigalle.

EASTERN PARIS

Parc des Buttes-Chaumont — PARK

Not your average Parisian park, the Buttes-Chaumont was modeled after Hyde Park in London, but it seems more like Pandora from *Avatar.* Despite the barrier of trees around the park and walkways, there is more than enough sun for a picnic or laying out on the steep grassy slopes that overlook the high cliff. Bridges lead over the surrounding lake to the top, where designer Adolphe Alphand decided (why? we don't know) to build a small Roman Temple. In the 13th century, this area was the site of a gibbet (an iron cage filled with the rotting corpses of criminals), a dumping ground for dead horses, a haven for worms, and a gypsum quarry (the origin of the term "plaster of Paris"). Thankfully, it's come a long way since then.

▶ ✝ Ⓜ Buttes Chaumont. Ⓢ Free. 🕑 Open daily May-Sept 7am-10:15pm; Oct-Apr 7am-8:15pm.

🪦 Cimetière du Père Lachaise   CEMETERY

16 rue du Repos
☎ 01 55 25 82 10

After Pasteur and his germ theory totally messed with the zoning regulations of the Cimetière des Innocents (right next to the Les Halles food market), Père Lachaise was opened as a place to bury the dead. Parisians have buried over one million bodies here, despite there being only 100,000 graves. Highlights include elbowing your way past leather-studded jackets at Jim Morrison's grave, where people have taken to "madly loving" their rock/drug idol; kissing Oscar Wilde's grave (we passed on that one); or just getting utterly lost in the maze of headstones, Tim Burton-esque mausoleums, and cobblestone paths.

▶ ✝ Ⓜ Père Lachaise or Gambetta. 𝒊 Free maps at the Bureau de Conservation near Porte du Repos; ask for directions at guard booths near the main entrances. For more info on "theme" tours, call ☎ 01 49 57 94 37. Ⓢ Free. 🕑 Open from mid-Mar to early Nov M-F 8am-6pm, Sa 8:30am-6pm, Su

The Kiss of Death

The word "romantic" may not be the right adjective to describe a stroll through a cemetery. But Cimetière du Père Lachaise, the world's most visited cemetery, is a favorite spot for couples to smooch in front of graves and tombstones of famous people like Oscar Wilde or Frédéric Chopin. Not ghoulish at all, right?

When the cemetery first opened in 1804, it was unpopular thanks to its distance from the heart of the city. The cemetery's reputation changed when Honoré de Balzac's novels featured characters buried in Père Lachaise. People infatuated with the story quickly began to flock to the city to visit the gravesites of fictional heroes and heroines.

Today, Jim Morrison's grave is the most visited. His grave was unmarked for many years, but that didn't stop crazy fans from having drug-fueled orgies over his dead body, hoping that Jim's spirit would join them in their outlandish hooliganism. The cemetery officials eventually placed a stone block over his resting place to prevent fans from unearthing the body.

9am-6pm; from Nov to mid-Mar M-F 8am-5:30pm, Sa 8:30am-5:30pm, Su 9am-5:30pm. Last entry 15min. before close. Free 2½hr. guided tour from Apr to mid-Nov Sa 2:30pm.

🖼 Cité des Sciences et de l'Industrie   MUSEUM

30 av. Corentin Cariou

☎01 40 05 12 12; www.cite-sciences.fr

If art isn't your cup of tea and you have a passion for the sciences, welcome to your Louvre. This massive complex has anything that would make Bill Nye giggle like a school girl. Permanent exhibits on energy use, optical illusions, and human genetics all have videos and interactive games to make those subjects palatable for those who couldn't stay awake in biology class, and the constantly rotating temporary exhibits keep up with what's interesting in scientific news. Recent exhibits have tackled climate change, the ocean, and new transport technology (complete with a flight simulator). Carl Sagan would cry tears of joy while watching their planetarium show on the history of the universe, projected onto a nearly 11,000 sq. ft. dome. If you're low on cash, the aquarium is free.

▶ ♿ Ⓜ Porte de la Villette. *i* Free access to job placement assistance, health information center (for medical document consult and translating), and multimedia library. Ⓢ €8-20. Admission price depends on what exhibits you want to see. 🕐 Open Tu-Sa 10am-6pm, Su 10am-7pm. Health info center open Tu-Su noon-6pm.

Food

Say goodbye to foot-long subs and that sticky pre-sliced cheese they sell at Costco; you're not in Kansas anymore. Food is an integral part of French life—while world-famous chefs and their three-star prices are valued Parisian institutions, you don't have to break the bank for excellent cuisine, especially if you come at lunch (when prices are nearly half what they are at dinner). Brasseries are even more casual and foster a lively and irreverent atmosphere. The least expensive option is usually a creperie, which specialize in thin Breton pancakes filled with meat, vegetables, cheeses, chocolate, or fruits. Creperies might conjure images of yuppie brunches and awkward first dates for Americans, but here in Paris you can often eat a crepe for less than you'd pay at the great Golden Arches. Specialty food shops, including *boulangeries* (bakeries), patisseries (pastry shops), and *chocolatiers* (chocolate shops), provide delicious and inexpensive picnic supplies. A number of cheap kebab and falafel stands around town also serve quick, cheap fare. *Bon appétit!*

Budget Food

Lucky for you, cheap food can be found in Paris. Those willing to venture to the outer arrondissements will have their stomachs rewarded by the diversity of options available to them. Opéra and Canal St-Martin, Bastille, Montparnasse and Southern Paris, and Eastern Paris all offer various international fare that will appease both your taste buds and your wallet. You may be surprised to hear that some bars and cafes in Paris offer free food with the purchase of a drink. Granted, the food isn't fancy (you'll most likely be served couscous or *moules frites*), but you'll be happy to get anything for free in a city as expensive as this. Many of these gems of cafes are sprinkled throughout Montmartre and Opéra and Canal St-Martin.

ÎLE DE LA CITÉ AND ÎLE ST-LOUIS

The islands are expensive. Forage all you want, but the cheapest meal you can put together is a crepe and maybe some ice cream. If you want an actual meal, head to Île St-Louis where the tourist crowds (and the prices) tend to diminish. Of course, if you do happen to be loaded, there are a lot of dimly lit, intimate (read: expensive) restaurants where you will pay for the privilege of eating in the true center of Paris.

🗺 Ma Salle À Manger   RESTAURANT, COCKTAIL BAR $$
26 Passage Dauphine
☎01 43 29 52 34

This cafe in the quiet pl. Dauphine gains curb appeal from its funky explosion of color. The establishment is a quirky combo of Corsican posters, old movies, and old French adverts. Think of a French hippie's garage sale, but throw in cheap lamb, *moules-frites,* and a selection of (relatively) affordable cocktails for an early start to the night.

▶ ✢ Ⓜ Cité or Pont Neuf. Ⓢ Entrées €6-10. Menu du jour (entrée and *plat,* or *plat* and dessert) from €13. Cocktails €8. ☉ Open M-F 11am-3:30pm and 7-10:30pm, Sa-Su 11am-10:30pm.

Café Med   RESTAURANT, CREPERIE $$
77 rue St-Louis-en-l'Île
☎01 43 29 73 17

Come here for a fix of Moulin Rouge, where the Red Windmill

Food

is the central theme of this usually packed cafe. The most afford-able meal is a traditional Bretagne crepe/cider combo, but for a healthy dose of carbs, go for the lunch or dinner menu, where most of the main dishes are pasta with *herbes de Provence*.

▶ ⚡ Ⓜ Pont Marie. Ⓢ Galette/crepe/cider combo €10.50. Lunch menu €12. Dinner menu €18. ⏰ Open M-F 11am-3:30pm and 7-10:30pm, Sa-Su 11am-10:30pm.

Berthillon   ICE CREAM $

31 rue St-Louis-en-l'Île

☎ 01 43 54 31 61; www.www.berthillon.fr

If you are the ice cream aficionado who has made pilgrimages to the Ben and Jerry's or Blue Bell factories, this should prob-ably be on your bucket list. While it may not offer the tours or free samples of larger factories, one similarity remains: the ice cream is phenomenal. The sweet dessert is served (mixed with fresh fruit on demand) minutes after it's made in the old parlor room.

▶ ⚡ Ⓜ Pont Neuf. Ⓢ 1 scoop €2.50; 2 scoops €3.50; 3 scoops €5. ⏰ Open from Sept to mid-July W-Su 10am-8pm. Closed 2 weeks in Feb and Apr.

CHÂTELET-LES HALLES

Food in Châtelet caters to tourists and is unabashedly overpriced. While you can get a lot of bang for your buck in the many pizza and pasta places in the center of the area, once you go farther up **rue Saint-Honoré** or past Les Halles you'll find quirkier places that aren't crowded with hungry shoppers and tourists.

🔖 Le Jip's   FUSION $$

41 rue St-Denis

☎ 01 42 21 33 93

Le Jip's has some of the cheapest and most authentic Cuban/African/Brazilian food in Paris (wrap your head around those flavor combos). You could spend the whole day chowing on chicken creole in coconut milk, melt-in-your-mouth lamb, and desserts like *crème de citron vert* (lime green custard) and caramelized pineapple. Tapas platters and mojitos with a choice of four kinds of rum can warm you up until the bar explodes with salsa dancing until 2am.

▶ ⚡ Ⓜ Châtelet. *i* Salsa dancing Su 3-5pm; call ahead to reserve. Ⓢ Tapas platters €12. Lunch menu €15. Mojitos €10. Salsa dancing €10; includes 1 drink. ⏰ Open daily 11am-2am.

Flam's
CAFE $

62 rue des Lombards

☎01 42 21 10 30; www.flams.fr

Flam's is a basic cafe chain that has taken the Alsatian recipe for *flammekueche* ("cake baked in flames"; a thin pizza topped with cheese and cream) and made it available for next to nothing. The bright orange exterior makes it easy to find, and the cheap beer and cocktails make it hard to leave. While this isn't the chain's only location in Paris, it's most attractive here thanks to being one of the cheapest places around.

▶ ✱ Ⓜ Châtelet. Ⓢ *Flammekueche* €5.50-8. *Prix-fixe* menu €17. Beer €2.50-3.50. Cocktails €4.50-7. 🕐 Open M-Th 11:45am-midnight, F-Sa 11:45am-11:30pm, Su 11:45am-midnight.

Le Stado
BASQUE $$

150 rue St-Honoré

☎01 42 60 29 75; www.lestado.com

Don't let the rugby jerseys or Olympic photos make you think Le Stado is a sports bar, because it's almost the opposite. The upscale Basque restaurant serves *canard, salade paysanne,* and regional cakes. Come here for a three-course lunch on a weekday, as it's difficult to afford the dinner menu (€28).

▶ ✱ Ⓜ Louvre-Rivoli. Ⓢ Salads €8-11. *Plats* €10-25. Lunch menu €13. Dinner menu €26. 🕐 Open daily 11:30am-2:30pm and 7-11pm.

Riz qui Rit
KOREAN, VEGETARIAN $$

142 rue St-Denis

☎01 40 13 04 56; www.rizquirit.wordpress.com

This hip Korean restaurant will maintain your Zen (or at least try to explain to you what Zen is) with their eco-friendly meat dishes and vegetarian options. Bento Zen lunch boxes combine a whole meal into one partitioned tray and can be taken to go for those in a hurry.

▶ ✱ Ⓜ Étienne Marcel. Walk against traffic on rue de Turbigo and turn left onto rue St-Denis. Ⓢ Bento Zen lunch box €12. Vegetable and meat dishes €8-16. 🕐 Open daily 9am-7pm.

1979
TRADITIONAL $$

49 rue Berger

☎01 40 41 08 78

Appropriately decorated with Pop Art, mardi gras masks, and the odd faux polar bear mounted on the wall, 1979 serves traditional French foods with a twist, like clams, prawns, and smoked salmon combined with *ravettes de foie gras.*

▶ ✢ ⓂLouvre-Rivoli. Take rue du Louvre north and turn right onto rue Berger. Ⓢ *Prix-fixe* menus €9-16. 🕐 Open M-Th noon-2:30pm and 8-10:30pm, F noon-2:30pm and 8-11pm, Sa 8-11pm.

Chez Mémé   TRADITIONAL $$

124 rue St-Denis

☎01 40 28 43 20

Decorated like an aviary, Chez Mémé serves traditional dishes in a funky, jazz-filled environment with tables topped by fake birds in cages. Chalkboards with messages from past patrons advise you what to order.

▶ ✢ ⓂÉtienne Marcel. Walk against traffic down rue de Turbigo and turn left onto rue St-Denis. Ⓢ *Plats* €8-15. Salads €9-11. 🕐 Open M-Sa noon-2:30pm and 7-10pm.

THE MARAIS

Though it sometimes feels like dining in the 4ème is less about food and more about how you look eating it, there are a number of quality restaurants here that specialize in everything from regional French cuisine to New Age fusion. This is not the cheapest area, but if you're ready for a bit of a splurge, your appetite will be more than satiated, especially by affordable lunch menus or the falafel on **rue des Rosiers.** If you decide on dinner, make sure to make a reservation at the more popular restaurants. Dozens of charming bistros line **rue Saint-Martin,** and kosher establishments are common on **rue du Vertbois** and **rue Volta.**

🔳 L'As du Falafel   FALAFEL $

34 rue des Rosiers

☎01 48 87 63 60

L'As du Falafel has become a landmark, and with good reason. Get a view into the kitchen and you'll see giant tubs of freshly cut veggies and the chef frying falafel as fast as it's ordered. Patrons line up outside for the famous "falafel special"—we saw it as more of a magic trick, because we still don't know how they managed to fit everything into that pita. Seriously, it's huge, especially for only €5.

▶ ✢ ⓂSt-Paul. Take rue Pavée and turn left onto rue des Rosiers. Ⓢ Falafel special €5. Shawarma €7.50. 🕐 Open high season M-Th noon-midnight,

F noon-7pm, Su noon-midnight; low season M-Th noon-midnight, F noon-5pm, Su noon-midnight.

🏅 Chez Janou   BISTRO $$

2 rue Roger Verlomme

☎01 42 72 28 41; www.chezjanou.com

Tucked into a quiet corner of the 3ème, this Provençal bistro serves affordable ambrosia to a crowd of enthusiasts. The duck practically melts in your mouth, and the chocolate mousse (€6.60) comes in an enormous self-serve bowl, though Parisians count on self-control. For those without it, the choice of more pastis (over 80 varieties) than food items will have you channeling your inner Fitzgerald—just don't drive home.

▶ ⚚ ⓂChemin-Vert. Follow rue des Tournelles south until the intersection with rue Roger Verlomme. *i* Reservations recommended, as this local favorite is packed every night of the week. Ⓢ *Plats* from €14. *Prix-fixe* menu €14. 🕗 Open daily noon-midnight. Kitchen open M-F noon-3pm and 7:45pm-midnight, Sa-Su noon-4pm and 7:45pm-midnight.

Micky's Deli   KOSHER $$

23 bis rue des Rosiers

☎01 48 04 79 31

Thanks to Rabbi Rottenberg, every slice of meat and beef patty at this deli is pure to the standards of the Torah. One of the last traditional holdouts of the 3ème, Micky's Deli gets a lot of traffic, so head in early or toward closing to get a hold of its monster-sized hot pastrami or burger, or go for the famous Micky's Burger, which blasphemously combines the two.

▶ ⚚ ⓂSt-Paul. Take rue Pavée and turn left onto rue des Rosiers. Ⓢ Burger and fries with drink €7. Deli sandwiches €11-17. 🕗 Open M-Th 11:30am-3pm and 7-11pm, F 11:30am-3pm, Sa 8pm-midnight, Su noon-11pm.

Robert et Louise   FRENCH $$$

64 rue Vieille du Temple

☎01 42 78 55 89; www.robertetlouise.com

Defined by a firm belief that chicken is for pansies (let's not even talk about vegetarians), Robert et Louise offers a menu that's wholeheartedly carnivorous—we're talking veal kidneys, steak, prime rib, and lamb chops. The only concession to white meat is the *confit de canard*. There's a definite homey vibe here; you'll feel like you've been taken in by a generous French family who found you abandoned and shivering on their way home from a hunt.

Food

▶ ⚑ Ⓜ St-Paul. Follow the traffic on rue de Rivoli and turn right onto rue Vieille du Temple. *i* Reservations recommended. Ⓢ *Entrées* €5.60-8. *Plats* €12-63. Lunch menu €12. Desserts €5.60-6. ⏰ Open Tu-Su noon-2:30pm and 7-11pm.

Breakfast in America   DINER $$

4 rue Malher

☎01 42 72 40 21; www.breakfast-in-america.com

BIA promises to be one thing: "an American diner in Paris." It sure delivers—from the shiny red booths to the delicious fries, shakes, bottomless mugs o' joe, and the expected post-meal tips, it doesn't get more American than this.

▶ ⚑ Ⓜ St-Paul. Ⓢ Burgers and sandwiches €9-12. Student menu (burger, fries, and drink) €8. All-you-can-eat-brunch Su €20. Milkshakes €5. ⏰ Open daily 8:30am-11pm.

Page 35   CREPERIE $$

4 rue du Parc Royal

☎01 44 54 35 35; www.restaurant-page35.com

Instead of picking which type of French restaurant to go to, check out this hip, modern-art gallery/restaurant/creperie that serves anything under the red, white, and blue banner. Page 35 sums up the spirit of the Marais with its extensive menu of sirloin, tartare, *confit de canard,* poached egg on foie gras, and pasta with *herbes de Provence.* For those who haven't tried them yet, they also serve traditional buckwheat crepes from Brittany. Come toward the end of lunch to avoid the heavy crowds.

▶ ⚑ Ⓜ St-Paul. Take rue de Sévigné to the intersection with rue du Parc Royal. Ⓢ Flash your *Let's Go* guide for a free Kir. Ⓢ Lunch menu €13. Dinner menu €24. ⏰ Open Tu-F 11:30am-3pm and 7-11pm, Sa-Su 11:30am-11pm.

Le Loire dans la Théière   PATISSERIE, CAFE $$

3 rue des Rosiers

☎01 42 72 90 61

If we were to rename this cafe, we'd call it "Just Desserts"— and not in the bad-karma sense. Almost like a hip cafe in New York's SoHo, Le Loire dans la Théière serves pies, cakes, tartes, and meringue with a tea for under €10. It's so popular that it closes at 7pm. The walls are covered with ads for jazz and rock concerts, and they serve omelettes at Sunday brunch with mint and goat cheese.

▶ ⚑ Ⓜ St-Paul. Take rue Pavée and turn right onto rue des Rosiers. Ⓢ Pot of tea and dessert €9.50. ⏰ Open daily 10am-7pm.

Food

Marché des Enfants Rouges   MARKET $

39 rue de Bretagne

Paris's oldest covered market is a foodie's paradise of hidden restaurants and chaotic stands where you can grab a meal for under €10. Parisians often stop by for lunch at the wooden tables or heated patios. Since you can find French *boulangeries, fromageries,* and patisseries almost anywhere, your best bet is to go for the more exotic (like Moroccan *tagines* or Japanese sushi bento boxes), since they are much cheaper here than in specialty restaurants.

▶ ⚡ Ⓜ Filles du Calvaire. Turn left onto rue Froissart, which becomes rue de Bretagne. 🕐 Open Tu-Th 9am-2pm and 4-8pm, F-Sa 9am-8pm, Su 9am-2pm.

La Pas-Sage Obligé   VEGETARIAN $$

29 rue du Bourg Tibourg

☎ 01 40 41 95 03; www.lepassageoblige.com

Seemingly defying French culture, this restaurant manages to present traditional dishes without meat. The general VG burger (pronounced VEH-jee) and the more authentic *terrine de champignons* are both satisfying, and carnivores are kept happy with *entrecôte* and tartare.

▶ ⚡ Ⓜ Hôtel de Ville. Walk against traffic on rue de Rivoli and turn left onto rue du Bourg Tibourg. Ⓢ *Plats* €11-15. Su brunch buffet €19. 🕐 Open daily noon-2pm and 7-10:30pm.

Le Trésor   TRADITIONAL $$$

5/9 rue du Trésor

☎ 01 42 71 35 17; www.restaurantletresor.com

If you want to experience swanky side of the Marais (without blowing a hole in your wallet), come here and deliberate between the veal and the bread-encrusted salmon. You might miss it altogether, though, as the restaurant's exterior is hidden by plants and flowers.

▶ ⚡ Ⓜ St-Paul. Walk with traffic on rue de Rivoli, turn left onto rue Vieille du Temple, and turn right onto rue du Trésor. Ⓢ Lunch menu €13. Dinner menu €24. 🕐 Open daily noon-2am.

LATIN QUARTER AND ST-GERMAIN

These neighborhoods are deceptive. What look like cute French restaurants can be total tourist traps where the waitstaff will rush you out as fast as you eat. Yet you can also find food from all over France at a reasonable cost. As a general rule, restaurants between the Seine and bd St-Germain are not as authentic as those south of St-Germain. **Rue Mouffetard** has some smaller, cheaper options that are popular with students and budget travelers.

Savannah Café   LEBANESE $$
27 rue Descartes
☎01 43 29 45 77; www.savannahcafe.fr

A contradictory mix of Lebanese cuisine and French flavors makes Savannah all the rage with Parisian restaurateurs. One of the best deals is the mix of six Lebanese appetizers for €17. The bright yellow interior is covered with stuffed toy zebras, photos of the Middle East, and framed recommendations.

▶ ⚡ Ⓜ Cardinal Lemoine. Walk uphill on rue du Cardinal Lemoine and turn right onto rue Clovis. Walk 1 block and turn left onto rue Descartes. The cafe is on the left. Ⓢ *Entrées* €7-14. *Plats* €14-16. Desserts €6-7.50. ⌚ Open M-Sa 7-11pm.

Crêperie des Canettes   CREPERIE $
10 rue des Canettes
☎01 43 26 27 65; www.pancakesquare.com

Creperies are ubiquitous; however, this one uniquely prepares affordable crepes in the traditional way—square and crispy, not round and soft. The goat cheese and walnut crepes (€7) are a good choice, as is the "Typhoon" (salmon, crème fraiche, and lemon; €9), which appropriately goes with the sailing theme.

▶ ⚡ Ⓜ Mabillion. Walk down rue de Four and turn left onto rue des Canettes. Ⓢ Crepes €3.50-9. Lunch and dinner menus €12. ⌚ Open M-Sa noon-11pm.

La Methode   PROVENÇAL $$
2 rue Descartes
☎01 43 54 22 43

This Provençal restaurant takes French dishes and gives them a southern flair, creating an upscale meal that won't leave you broke. One of the best starters is the artichoke salad and foie gras, or, for the less adventurous, the salmon and ratatouille *entrée* is pretty damn good. The most difficult decision will be where to sit: the terrace overlooks the small plaza while the converted wine cave from the 17th century is perfect for a glass of wine.

▶ ✚ Ⓜ Cardinal Lemoine. Walk uphill on rue du Cardinal Lemoine and turn right onto rue Clovis. Walk 1 block and turn right onto rue Descartes. The restaurant is on the left in the square. ⑤ *Plats* €11-14. Lunch menu €14. Dinner menu €15. ⏰ Open Oct-Aug M-Sa noon-2pm and 7-10pm, Su noon-10pm.

Snack Attack

Parisians prefer traditional patisseries, *boulangeries,* and *fromageries* to supermarket chains that sell pre-packaged cheese and baguettes. But Paris's supermarkets still treat taste buds better than their equivalents in most other cities. Hop into any Carrefour, Monoprix, or Franprix to get ahold of these unique snacks:

- **SPECULOOS BISCUITS.** Based with a Nutella-like spread, this alternative to graham crackers was featured on pastry chef David Lebovitz's famous Parisian food blog.

- **PIMM'S COOKIES.** These crunchy treats based on the British drink are filled with orange or raspberry jelly. Though they won't give you a buzz, the sugar high might make up for your sobriety.

- **KINDER BARS.** This Italian candy bar is highly popular in France. Try a Bueno bar for its wafery goodness with a tongue-numbing hazelnut cream filling. The Duplo bar is a classier alternative with nougat cream, whole walnuts, and milk chocolate. A word of caution: avoid the candy aisle after schools let out, or you'll be duking it out with hungry French children for these treats.

- **FLAVORED YOGURT.** The French love being daring with dairy, so take advantage of the interesting yogurt varieties sold in most grocery stores. Among the unique flavors are citrus *(citron)* and hazelnut *(noisette).* Quality (read: expensive) brands come in glass jars.

Cave la Bourgogne   BRASSERIE $$

144 rue Mouffetard

☎01 47 07 82 80

Whether you go for beer or a full meal, this brasserie's terrace is usually packed (even on Sunday), and its location in the middle of a roundabout makes it great for people-watching. If you don't want to wait for outside seating, the interior is decorated with

Food

wine barrels and empty wine bottles that clue you into what
should be paired with your affordable steak tartar (€15).

▶ ✿ ⓂCensier-Daubenton. Walk down rue Monge and turn right onto rue
Censier. Walk until you reach Sq. St-Médard. It's on the other side of the
roundabout. ⓢ Salads €7-10. Meat dishes €14-18. ⏰ Open daily noon-3pm
and 7:30-11pm.

Le Vieux Bistro   BISTRO $$
54 rue Mouffetard

Visit Le Vieux Bistro for one of the cheapest three-course meals
in the 5ème, served by a staff that won't rush you. The bistro
serves traditional Savoy faire with *escargot,* onion soup, and
tenderloin that melts in your mouth. The local youth make Le
Vieux their hangout spot, despite the somewhat cheesy baskets,
pots, and spices that hang from the ceiling.

▶ ✿ ⓂPlace Monge. Walk down rue Monge and turn right onto pl. Monge.
Keep going as it turns into rue Ortolan and turn right onto rue Mouffetard.
The restaurant is on the left. ⓢ 3-cheese fondue €14. Lunch menu €10. Din-
ner menu €16. ⏰ Open daily noon-3pm and 6pm-midnight.

Dans les Landes   TAPAS $$
119 bis rue Monge
☎01 45 87 06 00

This bistro will have you thinking it's Spanish with their tapas
happy hour (cocktail and choice of *tapa;* €8). The terrace is tempting, but the inside draws you in with its curvy stone-finish walls,
Southern European wine that doubles as decoration, and huge
shared tables that encourage chatting with your neighbors.

▶ ✿ ⓂCensier-Daubenton. Walk down rue Monge. The restaurant is on
the left. ⓢ *Plats* €7-21. Happy hour special €8. ⏰ Open daily noon-11pm.
Happy hour 5-7:30pm.

Le Bistrot d'Henri   TRADITIONAL $$
16 rue Princesse
☎01 46 33 51 12

For a really impressive meal—or to impress your date—this Old
World bistro serves some reasonably priced traditional French
food. The chef recommends the lamb, which is expertly mari-
nated in prune juice for 7hr. (this may strike you as over the top,
but he's an artist), or the duck breast covered in honey. Landing
a table at this Art Deco joint can be difficult, so call ahead for
reservations or hop on La Fourchette (www.lafourchette.com)
to nab a table and get discounts on *entrées* or drinks.

▶ ✈ Ⓜ Mabillon. Walk down rue du Four and turn left onto rue Princesse. Ⓢ *Entrées* €7-11. *Plats* €14-23. 🕐 Open M-Sa noon-2:30pm and 7-11:30pm.

Botequim   BRAZILIAN $$
1 rue Berthollet
☎ 01 43 37 98 46

If you're looking for an escape from traditional Parisian cuisine, enter Botequim and be transported to Brazil. Statues of Catholic saints stand alongside tribal boa headdresses on the shelves. Without a knowledge of Portuguese, it will be a little hard to navigate the menu. Never fear: go for anything, from the coconut shrimp to the *salade tropicale* (hearts of palm, shrimp, cashews, and pineapple) or the salmon with mango sauce. Just be prepared for the culture shock when you leave and discover you're back in France.

▶ ✈ Ⓜ Censier-Daubenton. Walk down rue Monge and turn right onto rue Claude Bernard. The restaurant is at the corner with rue Berthollet. Ⓢ *Entrées* €8-9. *Plats* €15-17. 🕐 Open M-Sa noon-3:30pm and 8pm-2am.

L'Assiette aux Fromages   FONDUE $$
25 rue Mouffetard
☎ 01 43 36 91 59; www.lassietteauxfromages.com

This Swiss establishment is the answer to your authentic-fondue prayers. The smiling cow in the window hints at the wide variety of French cheeses you can order to accompany any salad or melon and ham dish. Choose between the two *formules* (one more expensive than the other) that include *confit de canard* or lamb with rosemary.

▶ ✈ Ⓜ Place Monge. Walk down rue Monge and turn right onto pl. Monge. Keep going as it turns into rue Ortolan and turn right onto rue Mouffetard. The restaurant is 1½ blocks down on the right. Ⓢ Fondues €15-17. *Formules* €16 or €26. 🕐 Open daily noon-2:30pm and 6:30-11:30pm.

Aux Doux Raisins   BISTRO $$
29 rue Descartes
☎ 01 43 29 31 13

While most of the items on the menu of this winery-inspired bistro may be as basic as you'd pack for a picnic in the Jardin du Luxembourg, they do serve popular dishes that would be familiar to any French farmer: *bœuf bourguignon,* foie gras, and *confit de canard* (€13-14). For an impressive spread of meats and cheeses for two, split the *planche doux raisins* (€13).

▶ ✈ Ⓜ Cardinal Lemoine. Walk uphill on rue du Cardinal Lemoine and turn

Food

right onto rue Clovis. Walk 1 block and turn left onto rue Descartes. $ Entrées €7-8.50. *Plats* €13-14. Desserts €7-8. ⏰ Open daily 11:30am-1am.

INVALIDES

The chic 7ème is low on budget options, but there are a number of quality restaurants that are worth the extra euro. **Rue Saint-Dominique, rue Cler,** and **rue de Grenelle** feature some of the best gourmet bakeries in Paris. The steaming baguettes and pastries make for an ideal picnic by the nearby Eiffel Tower.

⬛ Chez Lucie   CREOLE, STUFF YOUR FACE $$

15 rue Augereau
☎01 45 55 08 74

Specializing in dishes from Martinique, this Creole hole in the wall will make you abandon your Eurotrip for a sailboat in the French Antilles. The owner prides himself on his conversation skills; he shoots the breeze with customers and will even show you pictures of his wife while you dine on gumbo, spicy catfish, or—for the more adventurous—shark. The portions are enormous for such a low price, and the *ti' ponch* (rum punch) will knock you on your ass.

▶ 🚇 Ⓜ École Militaire. Walk toward the Eiffel Tower on av. de la Bourdonnais, turn right onto rue de Grenelle, and then take an immediate left onto rue Augereau. The restaurant is on the right (with a bright yellow awning). $ Entrées €7. *Plats* €10-30. 3-course lunch special €16. Dinner special €16-25. ⏰ Open daily noon-2pm and 7-11pm.

Les Cocottes   RESTAURANT $$

135 rue St-Dominique
☎01 45 50 10 31; www.maisonconstant.com

Christian Constant, a famed Parisian chef, realized that not everyone wants to pay an arm and a leg for a good meal. He then opened Les Cocottes and began serving quick gourmet salads (poached egg and dried meat on greens with vinaigrette) and dishes cooked in the famed metal kettles (like caramelized potatoes with pork) for up-and-coming, business-casual French as well as intrepid tourists.

▶ 🚇 Ⓜ École Militaire. Walk toward the Eiffel Tower on av. de la Bourdonnais, turn right onto rue de Grenelle, followed by an immediate left onto rue Augereau. Walk to St-Dominique and turn right. The restaurant is on the right. $ *Mousseline d'artichaut* €16. Salads €10-12. *Mousse au chocolat* €7. ⏰ Open M-Sa noon-4pm and 7-11pm.

Le Sac à Dos
TRADITIONAL $$$

47 rue de Bourgogne

☎01 45 55 15 35; www.le-sac-a-dos.fr

This hidden gem makes up for generic French fare with personality that will make you blush. Or was that because the sun-bleached owner's shirt is unbuttoned to his navel? Choose from one of the main dishes written on chalkboards, and make room for the *mousse au chocolat* that is served in a cookie bowl.

▶ 🚲 Ⓜ Varenne. Walk away from Pont d'Alexandre III on bd des Invalides, turning left on rue de Varenne. Walk 1 block, past the Musée-Rodin, to rue de Bourgogne and turn left. The restaurant is on the right. Ⓢ *Plats* €17. Desserts €6. 🕐 Open M-Sa 11am-2:30pm and 6:30-11pm.

CHAMPS-ÉLYSÉES

Once the center of Paris's glamorous dining scene, the 8ème's culinary importance is on the decline, but its prices are not. We don't recommend eating on the Champs-Élysées, but we do suggest visiting the bakeries, *épiceries,* and cafes below for a small (but expensive) treat. Thabthim Siam is a total exception: eat there. There are also cheaper establishments around **rue la Boétie, rue des Colisées,** and **place de Dublin.**

◪ Thabthim Siam
THAI $$

28 rue de Moscou

☎01 43 87 62 56

Thabthim Siam is where locals come to get their curry fix. The changing menu allows patrons to sample a wide range of Thai cuisine. Linguistically challenged customers beware: authentic Thai names only have French translations, so if those aren't in your repertoire, just point to a neighboring table and order what they're eating—it's most likely delicious.

▶ 🚲 Ⓜ Rome. Ⓢ *Entrées* €8. *Plats* €13-17. 2-course lunch menu with drink €15. 🕐 Open M-Sa noon-2pm and 7-10:30pm.

◪ Ladurée
TEA HOUSE $

18 rue Royale

☎01 49 60 21 79; www.laduree.com

Opened in 1862, Ladurée started off as a modest bakery. It has since become so famous that a *Gossip Girl* employee was flown here to buy macaroons so Chuck could offer his heart to Blair properly. On a more typical day the Rococo decor of this tea salon—the original location of a franchise that now extends to

Food

13 countries—attracts a jarring mix of well-groomed shoppers and tourists in sneakers. Along with the infamous mini maca-roons arranged in pyramids in the window (beware: the rose flavor tastes like bathroom freshener), most items will induce a diabetic coma. Dine in the salon or queue up an orgasm to go.

▶ ♯ Ⓜ Concorde. Ⓢ Macaroons €1.70. Ⓩ Open M-Th 8:30am-7:30pm, F-Sa 8:30am-8pm, Su 10am-7pm. Other locations at 75 av. des Champs-Élysées, 21 rue Bonaparte, and 64 bd Haussmann.

White Is the New Yellow

The McDonald's on av. des Champs-Élysées is not your typical grab-and-go fast food. While taking a bite of your *Croque McDo* (grilled ham and cheese sandwich) and sipping a can of Kro-nenbourg 1664 in the spacious restaurant, you'll notice that the famous golden arches in front of the store look unusually pale. Apparently, Parisians considered the traditional Mickey D's yel-low to be too tacky—the city enforces a regulation that requires shops on this posh avenue to flaunt classy white signs only.

Mood   ASIAN, BURGER BAR $$
114 av. des Champs-Élysées and 1 rue Washington
☎01 42 89 98 89; www.mood-paris.fr

Like the Asian woman's nipple that greets you at the door (don't get too excited; it's only a photograph), Mood is a matter of personal taste, and you may or may not think the restaurant warrants all the fuss. The sensuous melange of Western decor and delicate Japanese accents reflects the fusion cuisine that revisits the classic American hamburger. The *prix-fixe* lunch (€17-21) might be the only affordable way to finagle your way into the beige upper dining room.

▶ ♯ Ⓜ George V. Ⓢ Entrées €10-19. *Plats* €17-35. Cocktails €15. Ⓩ Restau-rant open M noon-2:30pm, Tu-F noon-2:30pm and 7pm-1am, Sa 7pm-1am, Su noon-2:30pm and 7pm-1am. Bar open daily 5pm-1am. Happy hour daily 5-8pm.

Fouquet's   CAFE $$$$
99 av. des Champs-Élysées
☎01 47 23 50 00

Restaurants can only dream of this kind of fame. This sumptu-ous, red velvet-covered cafe once welcomed the likes of Chaplin,

Churchill, Roosevelt, and Jackie Onassis. While Fouquet's past its glory days, the people-watching on the Champs-Élysées alone is worth the €8 coffee. Just so you know, you're paying to sit among the rich, not for your beverage. Still, it's an experience of quintessential old-time Parisian glamour, easy on the eyes and devastating for the bank account (*entrées* start at €30).

▶ ⚘ Ⓜ George V. Ⓢ *Plats* €20-55. 🕑 Cafe open daily 8am-2am. Restaurant open daily 7:30-10am, noon-3pm, and 7pm-midnight.

Fauchon
FOOD STORE $$$

26-30 pl. de la Madeleine

☎01 47 42 60 11; www.fauchon.com

If you didn't blow all your euro at Ladurée, then you might be able to afford this pricey and equally upper-class *épicerie*. Splurge on nougat (€8-13) or *pâte de fruit* (fruit paste; €6.50) to add some class to your picnic, or buy teas and chocolates (€10-145) as a gift for your connoisseur friend.

▶ ⚘ Ⓜ Madeleine. 🕑 *Épicerie* and *confiserie* open M-Sa 9am-8pm. Boulangerie open 8am-9pm, eat-in 8am-6pm. *Traiteur* and patisserie open 8am-9pm. Tea room open 9am-7pm.

Ty Yann
CREPERIE $

10 rue de Constantinople

☎01 40 08 00 17

The ever-smiling Breton chef and owner, M. Yann, cheerfully prepares outstanding and relatively inexpensive *galettes* (€7.50-11) and crepes in a tiny, unassuming restaurant—the walls are decorated with his mother's pastoral paintings. Creative concoctions include La Vannetaise (sausage sautéed in cognac, Emmental cheese, and onions; €10). Create your own crepe (€6.40-7.20) for lunch.

▶ ⚘ Ⓜ Europe. Ⓢ Crepes €7.50-11. Credit card min. €12. 🕑 Open M-F noon-2:30pm and 7:30-10:30pm, Sa 7:30-10:30pm.

OPÉRA AND CANAL ST-MARTIN

It's not a challenge for the average tourist to find the famous places in the 9ème, most of which are located around **rue Saint-Georges.** Here, we're throwing out some harder-to-find but equally good restaurants in price and quality. The unknown secret is the 10ème, which easily outshines the 9ème in terms of quaint, cheap establishments, especially around the canal area. Passage Brady, two blocks north of Ⓜ Strasbourg-St-Denis, has a wealth of Indian and Pakistani restaurants serving the best cheap curries in Paris.

☒ Bob's Juice Bar   SMOOTHIES, BAGELS $

15 rue Lucien Sampaix
☎09 50 06 36 18

This small hippie, eco-conscious smoothie and bagel shack is usually filled with backpackers sharing long tables and snacking on homemade baked goods (€1-3) and bottomless coffee brewed all day.

▶ ✠ ⓂJacques Bonsergent. Walk up bd de Magenta toward Gare du Nord, and turn right onto rue Lucien Sampaix. Juice Bar is ½ a block up on the left. Ⓢ Smoothies €5-6. Bagel sandwiches €5.50. ⏰ Open M-F 8am-3pm.

☒ Chez Maurice   BISTRO $$

26 rue des Vinaigriers
☎01 46 07 07 91

Finally, a real French meal for dirt cheap. If the old-fashioned interior doesn't transport you to the turn of the century, a carafe of wine from the tap will help. Hold out for dessert, where it will be hard to choose between crème brûlée or chocolate fondue, even after stuffing yourself with *escargot* or steak tartare.

▶ ✠ ⓂJacques Bonsergent. Walk up bd de Magenta toward Gare du Nord, and turn right onto rue Lucien Sampaix. Walk 1 block to rue des Vinaigriers and turn right. The restaurant is on the right. Ⓢ Menu €11-16. Cash only. ⏰ Open M-F noon-3pm, Sa 6:30-11pm.

No Stress Cafe   TAPAS, CAFE $$

24 rue Clauzel
☎01 48 78 00 27

The huge terrace and quiet plaza give this funky cafe its namesake vibe. While you can skip most of the food, No Stress has a killer happy hour (Tu-Th 6-8pm) with cheap cocktails (€5) and tapas (€3.50) that draw a young crowd that quickly evaporates once the deal ends, only to reappear again before closing.

▶ ✠ ⓂSt-Georges. Walk up rue Notre Dame de Lorette in the direction of traffic until you reach rue H. Monnier. Turn left and the cafe is in the pl. Gustave Toudouze. Ⓢ Lunch menu €13. *Plats* €14-€18. Woks €15-18. Salads €14-€16. Desserts €7.50-€8.50. ⏰ Open Tu-Su 11am-2am.

Quai Gourmand   PASTA, CAFE $

79 quai de Valmy
☎01 40 40 72 84

This super cheap, albeit tacky, cafe serves the type of food that you could probably prepare yourself in a hostel kitchen. But its location right on the canal and tempting selection of Magnum

Bars for dessert will help you withstand the bright pink and green interior and NRJ pop music soundtrack.

▶ 🍴 Ⓜ République. Walk toward the canal on rue de Faubourg (the one that bisects pl. de la République). Turn left once you get to the canal and walk 3 blocks. The cafe is on the left. Ⓢ Sandwiches €4.50. Lunch menu (until 3:30pm) €8. To-go pasta bowls €6. Crepes €3, additional ingredients €1. 🕐 Open daily 10am-8pm.

Urfa Durum   KURDISH $
58 rue Faubourg St-Denis
☎01 48 24 12 84

In a city full of kebabs and faux Middle Eastern fast food, Urfa Durum stays true to its Kurdish roots. Cheap lamb sandwiches are served in bread baked to order. Top off the experience by eating at the traditional (read: miniature) wooden tables and stools outside the shop.

▶ 🍴 Ⓜ Château d'Eau. Exit onto bd Stasbourg. Facing the Gare de l'Est at the intersection of bd Stasbourg and rue du Château d'Eau, walk left and take the 1st left onto rue Faubourg St-Denis. Ⓢ Sandwiches €6. 🕐 Open daily noon-8pm.

Le Cambodge   CAMBODIAN $$
10 av. Richerand
☎01 44 84 37 70; www.lecambodge.fr

If you can't manage to get a seat because of the obscene crowds, this traditional Cambodian restaurant does takeout. Cambodge prides itself on spicy mixes of herbs, curry, and meats. Specialties include caramelized pork and citronella beef, which can be washed down with (slightly off-theme) Chinese Tsing-Tao beer. Yes, the beer is also available to go.

▶ 🍴 Ⓜ République. Walk toward the canal on rue de Faubourg (the one that bisects pl. de la République). Cross the canal, and turn left onto quai de Jemmapes. Walk 2 blocks to av. Richerand; the restaurant is on the right. Ⓢ Entrées €3-11. Plats €8.50-13. Desserts €4.50-5.50. 🕐 Open M-Sa noon-2:30pm and 8-11:30pm.

BASTILLE

Bastille swells with fast-food joints, so you can choose which of the kebab stands grosses you out the least. But the diverse neighborhood also boasts a number of upscale ethnic restaurants, many of which are cheaper than those in the central arrondissements. The most popular haunts line the bustling

rue de Charonne, rue Keller, rue de Lappe, and **rue Oberkampf.** The 12ème is generally affordable, with casual establishments that serve a variety of cuisines, from North African to Middle Eastern to traditional French. The best places are found on the side streets, while **Viaduc des Arts** hosts a few terrace cafes that are popular with designers.

◪ Auguste   SANDWICHES $

10 rue St-Sabin

☎01 47 00 77 84; www.augusteparis.com

A tiny hole in the wall whose clientele look like throwbacks to the days of the Paris Commune, this *sandwicherie* is packed at lunchtime with students and penny-pinchers looking to get at simple—but huge—sandwiches like the salmon and avocado or goat cheese and honey.

▶ ⚲ Ⓜ Bréguet-Sabin. Cross Canal St-Martin on rue Sedaine and turn right onto rue St-Sabin. Ⓢ Sandwiches €2-4. Soups €3-5. Cash only. ⏰ Open M-Sa 11am-4pm.

Katmandou Cafe   INDIAN $$

14 rue de Bréguet

☎01 48 05 36 36; www.katmandou.fr

Specializing in everything spicy, this Indian restaurant has six types of naan and curry for those who want their taste buds slowly singed off. To wash it down, order a lassi with mint, banana, or rose and mango.

▶ ⚲ Ⓜ Bréguet-Sabin. Cross Canal St-Martin on rue Sedaine, turn left onto bd Richard Lenoir, and turn right onto rue de Bréguet. Ⓢ *Plats* €9.50-13. *Prix-fixe* menu €12. 10% discount for takeout. ⏰ Open M-Sa noon-2:30pm and 7-11:30pm, Su 7-11:30pm.

Morry's Bagels and Toasts   BAGELS $

1 rue de Charonne

☎01 48 07 03 03

Those who miss the towering *grattes-ciel* of NYC should stop at Morry's for heated bagels topped with pastrami, cream cheese, avocado, or salmon. While the young clientele probably don't recognize the picture of a young Bob Dylan, they do know budget eats when they see them.

▶ ⚲ Ⓜ Bastille. Walk down rue du Faubourg St-Antoine and turn left onto rue de Charonne. Ⓢ Bagels €3-5.90. Desserts €1.50-3.40. ⏰ Open M-Sa 8:30am-7:30pm.

Barbershop   BISTRO $$
68 av. de la République
☎01 47 00 12 85

For a Parisian restaurant, Barbershop manages the rather impressive task of making French food seem out of place, since everything else here seems to have come straight from Jamaica. Enjoy your beef in Roquefort sauce or roasted Camembert while pictures of Bob Marley watch over you. DJs take the theme further by spinning soul and reggae tunes during dinner.

▶ ✦ Ⓜ Rue St-Maur. Ⓢ *Plats* €10-18. *Prix-fixe* menu €13. 🕐 Open M-Sa noon-3pm and 8-11pm, Su noon-4pm.

Le Dallery   BISTRO $$
6 Passage Charles Dallery
☎01 47 00 11 72

"French" and "hole in the wall" don't always go together, but this bistro combines them perfectly with express menus of grilled beef, lamb, or *salade paysanne* (€11) with dessert and coffee. The smell alone is enough to make you wander in from the main street.

▶ ✦ Ⓜ Ledru-Rollin. Take av. Ledru-Rollin north, turn right onto rue de Charonne, and then left onto Passage Charles Dallery. Ⓢ Express menu €11. Regular menu €12. 🕐 Open M-Sa noon-8pm.

Pause Cafe   CAFE $$
41 rue de Charonne
☎01 48 06 80 33

Hipster glasses are an unofficial pre-req for working here. People climb over themselves to get a seat on the large outdoor terrace and peruse the basic menu of salads, beer, tartare, and honey-glazed duck breast. It's run-down chic, but it was cool enough to be featured in the film *Chacun Cherche Son Chat,* which we suspect is the main reason people come here.

▶ ✦ Ⓜ Ledru-Rollin. Take av. Ledru-Rollin north and turn left onto rue de Charonne. Ⓢ *Plats* €8-11. 🕐 Open M-Sa 8am-2am, Su 9:30am-9pm. Kitchen open M-Sa noon-midnight, Su noon-5pm.

Le Touareg   AFRICAN $$
228 rue de Charenton
☎01 43 07 69 49

Le Touareg will throw you across the Mediterranean before you realize what you ordered—unless you're familiar with Moroccan cuisine, you won't notice. The *couscous méchoui* piles up with *merguez,* vegetables, and lamb, while their bowls of *chakchouka* (a spicy vegetable and egg dish) are big enough to bathe in. But these spicy dishes might make you sweat, so we suggest having pitchers of water handy.

▶ ⚒ Ⓜ Dugommier. Ⓢ Lunch menu €12. *Plats* €12-17. ⏰ Open M-Sa noon-3pm and 7pm-midnight.

Le Bar à Soupes   SOUP BAR $

33 rue de Charonne

☎ 01 43 57 53 79; www.lebarasoupes.com

This soup bar offers a pick-me-up for anyone feeling under the weather or a little homesick. Their lunch menu has basic soups like lentil and, for those whose hearts flutter when they hear "mmm mmm good," tomato soup. Giant paintings of vegetables match the equally large portions of soup. The rotating menu ensures that no two days are exactly the same.

▶ ⚒ Ⓜ Ledru-Rollin. Take av. Ledru-Rollin north and turn left onto rue de Charonne. Ⓢ Soups €5-6. Lunch menu €9.80. ⏰ Open M-Sa noon-3pm and 6:30-11pm.

Bodega Bay   SOUTH AMERICAN $$

116 rue Amelot

☎ 01 47 00 13 53; www.bodega-bay.fr

Bodega Bay might seem like a cheesy throwback to TexMex and gringos, but you can skip over the nachos and fajitas for the more authentic grilled swordfish and bitter chocolate cake. If you're wondering why there's a large mural of a space invasion, we couldn't figure it out either.

▶ ⚒ Ⓜ Oberkampf. Follow the traffic on rue de Crussol and turn left onto rue Amelot. Ⓢ *Plats* €13-14. *Prix-fixe* menu €12. ⏰ Open M-F noon-3pm and 6pm-midnight, Sa 6pm-midnight.

Cafe de l'Industrie   CAFE $$

16 rue St-Sabin

☎ 01 47 00 13 53

Though the coffee is one of the major draws here, the cafe expands its repertoire to include traditional French dishes (*plat du jour;* €10), including a selection of sliced meats and *tartines* if you just want to nibble as you down cheap wine. If the Cubist artwork starts to morph, we suggest slowing down on the wine.

▶ ⚒ Ⓜ Bréguet-Sabin. Ⓢ *Plats* €9-13. Desserts €2.50-6. ⏰ Open daily 10am-2am. Kitchen closes at 12:30am.

MONTPARNASSE AND SOUTHERN PARIS

More relaxed than the areas constantly full of tourists and the pickpockets that follow them, Montparnasse and southern Paris offer restaurants that are refreshingly affordable. Neighborhoods around the lower half of **boulevard Raspail** in the 14ème serve more traditional French cuisine, while the **Quartier de la Butte-aux-Cailles** and **Chinatown** in the 13ème serve obscure foreign dishes for next to nothing.

🔲 Chez Gladines   BASQUE $

30 rue des 5 Diamants
☎01 45 80 70 10

What Chez Gladines lacks in decoration (beyond a prominent Basque flag) it makes up for by sticking to its separatist roots. Customers constantly line up to enjoy *cassoulets* and *piperade* (scrambled eggs with vegetables).

▶ ♯ Ⓜ Place d'Italie. Take bd Auguste Blanqui away from pl. d'Italie and turn left onto rue des 5 Diamants. Ⓢ *Assiettes* €4-7.90. *Plats* €8.90-12. Cash only. 🕐 Open daily noon-3pm and 7-10:30pm.

🔲 Au Bretzel   ALSATIAN $$

1 rue Léopold Robert
☎01 40 47 82 37

This is a more upscale Alsatian restaurant that still serves affordable *flammekeuche* (a kind of thin pizza). Come here to settle down in the carved wood chairs next to murals of German and French towns. The huge *flammekeuche* can be shared and are some of the most traditional in Paris, despite decor that feels like the inside of a cuckoo clock.

▶ ♯ Ⓜ Vavin. Walk down bd du Montparnasse away from the tower and turn right onto rue Léopold Robert. Ⓢ *Flammekeuche* €8.50-10. *Prix-fixe* menu €18. 🕐 Open M 7:30-10:30pm, Tu-Sa noon-2pm and 7:30-10:30pm.

🔲 Pho 14   VIETNAMESE $

129 av. de Choisy
☎01 45 83 61 15

If you only eat in one place in Chinatown, make it Pho 14. A local favorite that draws starving students and penny-pinching barmen, Pho 14 (not to be confused with Pho 13 next door)

Food

Food in the Fast Lane

Even Paris, a city filled with fine dining, isn't immune to the fast-food invasion. If *escargots* are a little too slow for you, get in the fast lane to some of these cheap joints:

- **QUICK BURGER.** Although it's a clear rip-off of McDonald's, Parisians prefer it to the original, even if they can't get a *Royale* with cheese.

- **FLUNCH.** The chain was named after a *portmanteau* between "fast food" and "lunch," which is now French slang meaning "to eat on the go" *(fluncher)*. The food is cooked in minutes at the grill, including the steak, green beans, and potatoes meal. We're not sure if that gives the cook enough time to determine whether the steak is *"rosé"* or *"à point,"* so dine at your own risk.

- **BRIOCHE DORÉE.** This chain patisserie sells all the usual tarts, morning croissants, and lunchtime baguettes. Located in some Metro stations, these identical shops mass manufacture pastries and are only redeemed by their gleaming glass cases and over-the-top gilded signs. After all, presentation is everything.

serves huge bowls of *pho* beef (flank steak in spicy soup with rice) for next to nothing. This restaurant usually has a line out the door at night, so try to arrive on the early or late side of dinner.

▶ ♯ ⓜTolbiac. Walk east on rue de Tolbiac and turn left onto av. de Choisy. ⑤ *Pho* €6-10. ⓩ Open daily 9am-11pm.

Chez Papa 14   TRADITIONAL $$

6 rue Gassendi
☎01 43 22 41 19

Specializing in cuisine from the wine production regions of southwestern France, Chez Papa serves cheap foie gras, salads, and *cassoulets*. Don't let the low-hanging peppers, grapes, and spices hit you in in the head as you're being seated.

▶ ♯ ⓜDenfert-Rouchereau. Walk toward Cimetière Montparnasse on rue Froidevaux. The restaurant is at the intersection of rue Froidevaux and rue Gassendi. ⑤ *Entrées* €5-7. *Plats* €9-12. *Prix-fixe* menu €12. ⓩ Open daily noon-3pm and 6pm-midnight.

Mussuwam
AFRICAN $$

33 bd Arago

☎01 45 35 93 67; http://mussuwam.fr

Mussuwam serves traditional Senegalese food that provides a spicy break from the creamy and cheesy fare of French establishments. Some of the dishes are listed in a strange dialect that makes us wonder if Senegalese is its own language. Dinner is too pricey to bother, but if you keep an open mind, their lunch menu changes daily and costs a fraction of the regular prices.

▶ ♯ Ⓜ Les Gobelins. *i* Lunch menu Tu-F. Ⓢ Lunch menu €16. Dinner and weekend menu €25. 🕐 Open Tu-Th noon-3pm and 7-10:30pm, F-Sa noon-10:30pm

Les Tontons
BISTRO $$

3 rue des Gobelins

☎08 99 69 76 21

Designed after an old-style bistro with mirrors to make it appear larger than it is, Les Tontons specializes in steak and tartare. You can even order bone marrow. If steak isn't your thing, choose from desserts like tiramisu with strawberry tagada or simple Nutella cake.

▶ ♯ Ⓜ Les Gobelins. Ⓢ Lunch menu €13. Dinner menu €16. 🕐 Open M-Sa noon-2:30pm and 7-10:30pm.

Les Temps des Cerises
TRADITIONAL $$

18 rue de la Butte-aux-Cailles

☎01 45 89 69 48

One of several outrageous menu options at Les Temps des Cerises is a *pot-au-feu* with a mix of pig cheek and duck. Waiters joke with each other and clients and are happy to point you in the direction of more obscure French dishes.

▶ ♯ Ⓜ Place d'Italie. Ⓢ *Entrées* €7.50-11. *Plats* €10-17. Lunch menu €9.20. 🕐 Open M-F 11:45am-2:10pm and 7:15-11:45pm, Sa 7:15-11:45pm.

WESTERN PARIS

These two arrondissements are kind of a challenge. On one side, the 16ème has the upscale restaurants that often charge just for the privilege of breathing in their establishment. Then you have the 17ème, where attitudes and prices are much more relaxed, and the locals are more than willing to befriend you or go out of their way to add an extra table to their terrace to accommodate you.

Food

La Villa Passy

CAFE $$

4 Impasse des Carrières

☎01 45 27 68 76

Tucked away from the main roads in the 16ème, this cafe allows you and your date to swoon under the ivy-covered seating on pink-and-white cushioned benches. Or you can get the same theme inside, since the plants and fountains make the interior look like an outdoor courtyard. La Villa Passy is a bit more expensive than most restaurants, but if you're looking for the 16ème at its best, your search is over.

► ✢ Ⓜ La Muette. Walk in the direction of traffic (toward the Seine) down rue de Passy. Impasse des Carrières is the 5th street on the left, and the restaurant is at the end of the alley. Ⓢ *Plats* (like salad and steak tartare) €15-19. Su brunch (salad, omelette, croissants, and coffee) €25. Ⓞ Open Tu-F noon-3pm and 7-11pm; Sa noon-4pm and 7-11pm; Su noon-4pm.

Café des Petits Frères des Pauvres

CAFE $

47 rue des Batignolles

☎01 42 93 25 80

It's not so impressive in the food department, but this cafe is among the most affordable around: the €1.50 breakfast includes croissants, jam, and coffee. If that doesn't do it, some of the **cheapest coffee in Paris** (€0.45) will surely make you fall in love. The older regulars and staff are quick to chat and welcome you into their artsy community. In the afternoon, stop by to see local performances by poets, singers, and bands, plus the occasional movie showing.

► ✢ Ⓜ Place de Clichy. With your back to Montmartre, walk down bd des Batignolles 3 blocks and turn right onto rue des Batignolles. The cafe is 3 blocks down on the left. Ⓞ Open M 9am-12:30pm and 2-6pm, Tu 9am-12:30pm, W-Th 9am-12:30pm and 2-6pm, F 9am-12:30pm and 2-5pm, 1st and 3rd Sa each month 9am-12:30pm.

Les Filaos

AFRICAN $$$

5 rue Guy de Maupassant

☎01 45 04 94 53; www.lesfilaos.com

The first joint in Paris to specialize in Mauritian cuisine, Les Filaos provides an ethnic touch to the 16ème restaurant scene. *Ti' ponches* (rum punches; €5) are made fresh behind the straw hut bar. Curries (€15-16) can be made as spicy as you like, and be sure to save room for the coconut tarts. Saturday night *soirées* feature live Mauritian dancers.

► ✢ Ⓜ Rue de la Pompe. Walk toward the RER station Henri Martin, and turn

left onto bd Emilie Augier. Walk 1 block and turn left onto rue Guy de Maupassant. The restaurant is on the left. Ⓢ *Prix-fixe* lunch €20; dinner €35. 🕐
Open Tu-F noon-2pm and 7-10pm, Sa 7-10:30pm.

Le Manoir
BRASSERIE $$

7 rue des Moines

☎01 46 27 54 51

> A local favorite (if the packed terrace of chattering Parisians
> didn't give it away), this restaurant and cafe attracts laid-back
> 17ème residents. To keep up with high demand in the summer
> months, the owner makes a habit of expanding his outdoor seat-
> ing well into the public sidewalk.

▶ ♣ ⓂBrochant. With your back to the post office, walk down av. de Clichy 1
block and turn right onto rue des Moines. The restaurant is 3 blocks down
and on the left. *i* Wi-Fi. Ⓢ *Plats* €10-20. 2-course lunch €12. Su brunch
€20. 🕐 Open daily 7:30am-2am.

MONTMARTRE

Montmartre has bistros from the turn of the last century, creative
chefs looking for new ways to do the same thing, and a host of
nicer internationally influenced establishments. The upscale op-
tions are in **Clichy** and **Jules Joffrin.**

Le Reflet du Miroir
CREPERIE, INTERNATIONAL $

161 rue Ordener

☎01 42 62 23 97; www.lerefletdumiroir.fr

> If you stare into the mirrors that decorate this "creperie," you'll
> probably have a confused look on your face. These aren't your
> average crepes, and it's not your average creperie. Drawing
> inspiration from around the world, Le Reflet du Miroir uses
> chutney from London or shredded parmesan from Italy and
> puts them in French wrapping. Apparently beside themselves
> with what to do with American cuisine, they gave up and
> served plain ol' burgers (€11).

▶ ♣ ⓂJules Joffrin. With your back to the church, walk to the left of the tri-
angular building and up rue Ordener. Ⓢ Crepes €8-10; deluxe crepes €11.
Plats €4-12. 🕐 Open Tu-F 7-10pm, Sa noon-10pm, Su 7-10pm.

Le Perroquet Vert
BISTRO $$$

7 rue Cavallotti

☎01 45 22 49 16; www.perroquet-vert.com

> This French bistro is named after a book by Marthe Bibesco,

Food

a scandalous writer from the 1920s (don't worry, we had to Wikipedia her too). While we can't promise artistic talent after eating here, we can promise one of the oldest bistros in Montmartre with traditional French fare like veal and market fish with chorizo sauce. Enjoy your food while sitting in red velvet chairs and waiting for an epiphany. Try to dine here during the week, as the weekend selection is pricey.

▶ ✤ ⓂPlace de Clichy. Walk up av. de Clichy for 3 blocks. Turn right onto rue Capron, walk 1 block, and turn left onto rue Cavallotti. ⓈEntrées €8. Plats €16-17. Weekday lunch menu €14; weekend €29. ⏰ Open M-Sa 12:15-2:30pm and 7:30-10:30pm.

Parisian Bistro?

Think that bistros are a French invention? Think again. The word "bistro" originated during the occupation of Paris by the Russian army. In the 1814 Montmartre neighborhood, Cossack Russians set up a cafe that aimed to serve food quickly, or быстро (Russian for "quickly," pronounced "BEE-struh"). French linguists, however, dismiss this claim and say "bistro" is a shortening of the word *bistrouille,* meaning brandy and coffee.

Restaurant Seç   TURKISH $$
165 rue Ordener
☎01 42 51 18 46; http://restaurant-sec.com

This upscale Turkish restaurant serves one hell of a lunch menu, with choices like stuffed peppers, kebabs, and grilled meatballs. But be sure not to miss the the Middle Eastern take on yogurt and honey—after all, it is the region that invented it.

▶ ✤ ⓂJules Joffrin. With your back to the church, walk to the left of the triangular building and walk up rue Ordener. The restaurant is on the left. ⓈEntrées €4-7. Plats €10-14. Lunch menu €15. ⏰ Open M-Sa 11:30am-3:30pm and 6:30pm-midnight.

EASTERN PARIS

This neighborhood has some of the best international food in the city. **Rue de Belleville** has the cheapest options, but be careful walking around this area after dusk.

◢ Massai Mara   AFRICAN $

66 rue Armand Carrel

☎01 42 08 00 65; www.massaimara.fr

For students, €5 at lunch gets you whatever the chef whips up, a drink, and a seat in one of the low leather-backed chairs. Fried plantains, rice, and white fish topped with some spicy sauce are some of the staples.

▶ ❖ ⓂJuarès. $ *Plats* €8-13. Student lunch menu €5. ⏰ Open daily noon-3pm and 7-11pm.

◢ Lao Siam   VIETNAMESE $$

48 rue de Belleville

☎01 40 40 09 68

While most of the dishes here are cheap, Lao Siam sneaks a few more euro from your wallet by charging separately for rice (€2.20). The decor is nothing fancy, and paper napkins leave no room for pretension. But the food speaks louder than the decor, and the place is generally packed. The *filet du poisson* with "hip-hop sauce" (€8.80) is not to be missed. They also feature very tasty and salty duck selections.

▶ ❖ ⓂBelleville. $ *Entrées* €7-11. *Plats* €6.80-22. Beer €3.50. Wine by the bottle €11-55. ⏰ Open daily noon-3pm and 7-11pm.

Nightlife

You may have told your parents, professors, and prospective employers that you've traveled to Paris to compare the works of Monet and Manet (hint: its not just one letter), but after 52 years in the business, we at *Let's Go* know it isn't just art that draws the young and the restless to Europe. If you're traveling to drink and mingle, Paris will not disappoint you. Nightlife here is debaucherous, and there's something for everyone. Bars are either chic cafes bursting with people-watching potential, party joints all about rock and teen angst, or laid-back local spots that double as havens for English-speakers. Clubbing in Paris is less about hip DJs and cutting-edge beats than it is about dressing up and being seen. Drinks are expensive, so Parisians usually stick to the ones included with the cover. Many clubs accept reservations, which means there's no available seating on busy nights. It's best to be confident (but not aggressive) about getting in. Bars in the 5ème and 6ème draw international students, while Châtelet-Les Halles attracts a slightly older set. The Marais is the center of Parisian GLBT nightlife.

Budget Nightlife

Paris nightlife has something for everybody. You can stay out at a brasserie ordering wine, or hit up a neighborhood pub with your new backpacker friends. But if you want to forgo €5 glasses of wine or €10 covers, grab a bottle of white, red, or rosé from any local *supermarché* and head down to the water. During any spring or summer night, you'll find various Parisians picnicking on Pont des Arts or passing bottles of Bordeaux around on Canal St-Martin. So, forget your romantic idea of stylish Parisians sipping wine at a cafe, grab a *bouteille de vin* and a *tire-bouchon,* and head to the river to practice your rusty French and partake in the fun.

ÎLE DE LA CITÉ AND ÎLE ST-LOUIS

Far from a party spot, the islands are a bit of a nightlife wasteland. Still, there are a few overpriced brasseries that are worth a stop. The bars are a lot more fun and a lot less expensive on either side of the bank in the neighboring 4ème and 5ème.

▨ Le Louis IX   CAFE, BRASSERIE

25 rue des Deux-Ponts
☎01 43 54 23 89

> The islands are quiet. And so is the rough-looking bearded man in the corner who's working on his third or fourth *pastis* at this local bar. While the clientele may be the kind that go to bed at 8:30pm, its good place to debate whether to go to the Latin Quarter or Marais over a pint of blond beer.

▶ ♯ ⓜPont Marie. Ⓢ Wine €3.50-4.60. Beer €3.80-5. Apéritifs €3.80-4.50. ⓩ Open daily 7:30am-8:30pm.

CHÂTELET-LES HALLES

The bars in Châtelet are close together and easy to find. This neighborhood has its fair share of GLBT bars (though it's no Marais) and small bars that are packed until dawn. Watch yourself around Les Halles, since the area is a prominent location for pickpockets.

▨ Banana Café   BAR, CLUB, GLBT

13 rue de la Ferronerie
☎01 42 33 35 31; www.bananacafeparis.com

> Situated in the heart of Châtelet, Banana Café proclaims itself

the most popular GLBT bar in the 1er, and rightly so. The club suits a wide range of clientele that range from the somewhat reticent patrons who occupy the terrace, to the erotic dancers/strippers stationed outside. Head downstairs after midnight for a piano bar and more dance space. There are weekly theme nights like "Go-Go Boys," which takes place Thursday through Saturday from midnight to dawn.

▶ ⚏ Ⓜ Châtelet. Walk 3 blocks down rue St-Denis and turn right onto rue de la Ferronerie. Ⓢ Cover F-Sa €10; includes 1 drink. Beer €5.50. Cocktails €11. Happy hour pints €3; cocktails €4. ⏰ Open daily 5:30pm-6am. Happy hour 6-11pm.

Bar N'Importe Quoi   BAR

16 rue du Roule

☎01 40 26 29 71; www.nimportequoi.fr

Almost anything goes at this bar that's normally packed on the weekends. Bras hang above the bar, possibly as a result of the "le boob shot" policy (flash the bartender for a free shot; women only). The downstairs doubles the size of the bar, alleviating some of the crowds. American sports are shown on Sunday nights, and early in the week draft beer is €5 all night—anything to keep people knocking 'em back.

▶ ⚏ Ⓜ Louvre-Rivoli. Walk against traffic on rue de Rivoli and turn left onto rue du Roule. Ⓢ Shots €3. Beer €7-8. Cocktails €8.50. Happy hour cocktails €5.50. ⏰ Open M-W 6pm-4:30am, Th-Sa 6pm-5:30am, Su 6pm-4:30am. Happy hour 6-8pm.

Bare it All

Don't be surprised to find statues or advertisements of topless, bottomless, or completely nude people on the streets of Paris. At Fontaine de l'Observatoire, visitors will find three fully dis-robed statues of women atop the fountain. On Paris billboards, Yves Saint Laurent created a new ad for M7, a cologne for men, that featured a full-frontal naked model. In this city, the human body is seen as art rather than a promiscuous eyesore, so don't snicker, giggle, or react in typical *American Pie* fashion.

Le Club 18   CLUB, GLBT

18 rue Beaujolais

☎01 42 97 52 13; www.club18.fr

Flashing lights and pop, house, and dance beats make for a

wild night in this intimate (read: tiny), almost exclusively gay bar. Couches and mirrors line the walls, which means getting cozy with your neighbor is guaranteed. Younger crowds don't show up until after 1 or 2am.

▶ ⚤ ⓂPalais Royal-Musée du Louvre. Follow rue de Richelieu and turn right onto rue de Montpensier. Follow rue de Montpensier around the Jardin du Palais Royal until rue Beaujolais. Ⓢ Cover €10; includes 1 drink. Cocktails €6-9. 🕐 Open W midnight-6am, F-Sa midnight-6am.

La Champmeslé   CLUB, GLBT
4 rue Chabanais
☎01 42 96 85 20; www.lachampmesle.com

This welcoming lesbian bar is Paris's oldest and most famous. Head under the rainbow for discussions on art, books, and current events. Josy, the owner, still works the bar, knows almost every customer by name, and enthusiastically promotes the bar's late-night spectacles (which, when they happen, are at 2am). The crowd is friendly; straight folk are warmly welcomed. The club hosts weekly cabaret shows and monthly art exhibits.

▶ ⚤ ⓂPyramides. Walk up av. de l'Opéra and turn right onto rue des Petits Champs. After a few blocks, turn left onto rue Chabanais. *i* Cabaret shows Sa 10pm. Ⓢ Beer before 10pm €5, after €7. Cocktails €8-10. 🕐 Open M-Sa 4pm-3am.

Le Baiser Salé   JAZZ BAR
58 rue des Lombards
☎01 42 33 37 71; www.lebaisersale.com

This jazz bar is not the stereotypically hip, pretentious place you imagine. Housing African jazz and local alternative bands, Le Baiser Salé offers a quieter night for the partying type, with people intensely dancing in the packed upstairs lounge. Le Baiser Salé will please hipsters and their mainstream friends alike.

▶ ⚤ ⓂChâtelet. Take rue St-Denis 2 blocks and turn left onto rue des Lombards. *i* Tickets available at FNAC stores and online. Free jam sessions M at 10pm, 1-drink min. Ⓢ Cover €12-22. Beer €6.50. Cocktails €9.70. Happy hour beer €4-5; mojitos €4.50; cocktails €7. After 10pm, €1.30 increase on all drink prices. 🕐 Open daily 5pm-6am. Happy hour 5:30-8pm.

Nightlife

THE MARAIS

There are about as many bars and clubs in the Marais as people. Paris's GLBT nightlife scene and other fashionable bars and clubs crowd **rue Sainte-Croix de la Bretonnerie.** Trendy establishments with outdoor seating are piled on top of one another on **rue Vieille du Temple** and between **rue des Francs Bourgeois** and **rue de Rivoli.** The places on **rue des Lombards** are more rough and convivial, though they're often filled with tourists. The 3ème is more laid-back for the most part, so women (and men) can leave the stilettos at home. There are a number of GLBT bars on and around **rue Saint-Martin,** and casual bars host live music, especially around the Pompidou.

🔳 Raidd Bar   BAR, CLUB, GLBT
23 rue Vieille du Temple
☎01 42 77 04 88

If you want a penis or just want to see one, come here. Sparkling disco balls light up Raidd Bar, as do the muscular, tank-topped torsos of the sexy male bartenders. After 11pm, performers strip down in the glass shower built into the wall (yes, they take it all off). There's a notoriously strict door policy: women aren't allowed unless they are outnumbered by (gorgeous) men.

▶ ♯ ⓜHôtel de Ville. ⑤ Beer €6.50. Cocktails €10. Happy hour beer €4.20; cocktails €4.50. 🕐 Open M-Th 5pm-4am, F-Sa 5pm-5am, Su 5pm-4am. Happy hour 5-11pm.

🔳 Stolly's   BAR
16 rue Cloche Percé
☎01 42 76 06 76; www.cheapblonde.com

This small Anglophone hangout takes the sketchy out of the dive bar, but leaves the attitude. The pitchers of cheap blonde beer (€14) ensure that the bar lives up to its motto: "Hangovers installed and serviced here." Come inside, have a pint, and shout at the TV with the decidedly non-trendy, tattoo-covered crowd.

▶ ♯ ⓜSt-Paul. From the Metro, turn right onto rue Pavée and then left onto rue du Roi de Sicile. Turn left onto rue Cloche Percé. ⑤ Beer pints €5-6; 1.5L €13. Cocktails €6.50-8. Happy hour pints and cocktails €5. 🕐 Open M-F 4:30pm-2am, Sa-Su 3pm-2am. Happy hour 5-8pm. Terrace open until midnight.

Andy Wahloo   BAR
69 rue des Gravilliers
☎01 42 71 20 38; www.andywahloo-bar.com

The walls may be covered with pictures of African women, but the clientele certainly dresses less conservatively. Andy Wahloo, which means, "I have nothing" in a certain Moroccan dialect, serves ambitious mint cocktails with chutney and banana liqueur (€10-14). DJs on Wednesdays start the weekend early with a mix of '90s rap, dance, and some salsa.

▶ ⚲ ⓂArts et Métiers. Follow rue Beaubourg for 2 blocks and turn left onto rue des Gravilliers. Ⓢ Cocktails €9-13. ⏲ Open Tu-Sa 5pm-2am.

O'Sullivan's Rebel Bar   BAR

10 rue des Lombards

☎01 42 71 42 72; http://chatelet.osullivans-pubs.com

A tattooed take on an Irish bar, O'Sullivan's Rebel Bar makes Paris's chain bars look like classy English tea rooms. The bartenders serve drinks so quickly that they sometimes use the water gun to cool off (or to squirt shots directly into their mouths). Come on the weekends when the music is loud and the crowd is rowdy.

▶ ⚲ ⓂHôtel de Ville. Walk up rue du Renard and turn left onto rue de la Verrerie, which becomes rue des Lombards. Ⓢ Pints €4-5.30. Cocktails €7-9; cocktail of the evening €5. ⏲ Open M-Th 5pm-2am, F-Sa 5pm-5am, Su 5pm-1am. Happy hour 5-9pm.

Open Café   BAR, GLBT

17 rue des Archives

☎01 42 72 26 18; www.opencafe.fr

Popular almost to the point of absurdity, this GLBT-friendly bar draws a large crowd of loyal, mostly older male customers. Though women are welcome, they will slowly find themselves outnumbered as the ever-expanding sea of Y-chromosomes grows later in the evening.

▶ ⚲ ⓂHôtel de Ville. 𝒊 ½-price beer 6-10pm. ½-price champagne 10pm-close. Ⓢ Beer €3.80. Cocktails €7.90. ⏲ Open M-Th 11am-2am, F-Sa 11am-4am.

Le Komptoir   BAR

27 rue Quincampoix

☎01 42 77 75 35; www.lekomptoir.fr

Head to this tapas bar for the cheapest happy hour pints and cocktails in the Marais. Le Komptoir's distinctive backward "K" in its name hints at its backward behavior of cheap drinks, free entry to Thursday and Fridays concerts, and catering to the businessmen who come for afternoon shakes.

▶ ⚲ ⓂHôtel de Ville. In the pl. Michelet. Walk up rue du Renard, turn right

Nightlife

onto rue St-Merri and then left onto rue Quincampoix. *i* Jazz concerts Th 9pm. Pop rock concerts F 9pm. ⑤ Beer €6.60. Cocktails €8. Happy hour beer €4, cocktails 2 for 1. Concerts free. 🕐 Open Tu-Su 10am-2am. Happy hour 6-8:30pm.

Le Dépôt
CLUB, GLBT

10 rue aux Ours

☎01 44 54 96 96; www.ledepot.com

Le Dépôt is a gay club that revolves around sex—literally. Winding passages lead to dance floors that shoot off into private rooms. Meanwhile, porn stars get off on mounted TVs. A steady stream of men and boys filter in at all hours, hoping for success in the designated "cruising" area. Women, as a rule, are not allowed.

▶ ♯ Ⓜ Étienne Marcel. Follow the traffic on rue Étienne Marcel, which becomes rue aux Ours. ⑤ Cover M-Sa before 9pm and Su before 4pm €8.50; increases incrementally after that. 🕐 Open daily 2pm-8am.

LATIN QUARTER AND ST-GERMAIN

This neighborhood is awesome. **Rue Mouffetard** has the cheapest bars in Paris. At night they flood with students and backpackers. You should definitely wander down **rue de la Montagne Sainte-Geneviève** for the English-speaking bars.

🏠 Le Violin Dingue
BAR, CLUB

46 rue de la Montagne Ste-Geneviève

☎01 43 25 79 93

Known as "le VD" to locals, this bar has some of the cheapest happy hour drinks, and it's open the latest. Upstairs feels like a pub with a strong American influence (they show American football, after all). After 1am, though, it floods with young French locals who swarm to get into the huge downstairs club, where the latest pop blasts against the vaulted stone ceilings until 5am.

▶ ♯ Ⓜ Cardinal Lemoine. Walk uphill on rue du Cardinal Lemoine and turn right onto rue Clovis. Walk 1 block and turn right onto rue Descartes. When you hit the plaza, the bar is on the left. ⑤ Beer €6. Cocktails €7-10. Happy hour beer €3. Happy hour cocktails €4. Prices increase €1.50 after 1:30am. 🕐 Open daily 8pm-5am. Happy hour 8-10pm.

⚑ Le Fifth Bar   BAR

55 rue Mouffetard

☎01 43 37 09 09

The prized possession of rue Mouffetard, this bar is frequented by students and international travelers—the popularity shows on the scratched-up bar and stools. The drinks are cheap, and there is a sitting area in the back and a small dance floor downstairs that you might confuse with a sweatbox.

▶ ⚑ Ⓜ Place Monge. Walk down rue Monge and turn right onto pl. Monge. Keep going as it turns into rue Ortolan and turn right onto rue Mouffetard. The bar is on the left. Ⓢ Shots €4. Beer €5.50. Cocktails €7-10. Happy hour specials €1-3 cheaper. Ⓧ Open M-Th 4pm-2am, F-Sa 4pm-6am. Happy hour 4-10pm.

La Pomme d'Eve   BAR, CLUB

1 rue Laplace

☎01 43 25 86 18; www.lapommedeve.com

The only South African bar in Paris, La Pomme d'Eve is a night owl's hangout that explodes around 2am when the rest of the bars close. Ask George to make you a "Springbuck" (Amarula and Get 27; €5), then mingle under the zebra skin with local bartenders (French and international) who flock here after work.

▶ ⚑ Ⓜ Cardinal Lemoine. Walk uphill on rue du Cardinal Lemoine and turn right onto rue Clovis. Walk 1 block and turn right onto rue Descartes. Walk until the plaza, turn uphill, walk 1 block, and take the 1st right. The bar is on the left. Ⓢ Beer €6.50. Cocktails €7-12. Happy hour beer and cocktails €5. Ⓧ Open Tu-Su 8pm-5am. Happy Hour 6-9:30pm.

The Bombardier   PUB

2 pl. du Panthéon

☎01 43 54 79 22; www.bombardierpub.fr

This laid-back traditional British pub has one of the best locations in Paris, right behind the Panthéon between rue Mouffetard and rue Ste-Geneviève. Come for the cask ale, hang out with expats, and see where the night takes you. The Bombardier is not recommended for the faint of heart—everyone at this pub goes hard, especially the bartenders after closing.

▶ ⚑ Ⓜ Cardinal Lemoine. Walk uphill on rue du Cardinal Lemoine and turn right onto rue Clovis. Walk 2 blocks and turn right onto pl. du Panthéon. *i* Student happy hour night on M. Trivia Su 9pm. Ⓢ Beer €5.50-6; happy hour €4.50-5. Cocktails €8; happy hour €7. Ⓧ Open daily noon-2am. Happy hour 5-9pm.

INVALIDES

While there aren't a lot of hopping clubs and bars in this area, there are a few gems that are geared toward the thinky-artsy types and the more party-hardy travelers. Most of the brasseries stay open until 8 or 9pm in this area (especially in summer when it stays light past 10pm). Find them around rue St-Dominique. For some free hanging out, head to the **Champs de Mars,** but some travelers report that despite seeing droves of youths drinking in public, it is illegal and police will pick up on any non-French behavior and pick off oblivious tourists.

Le Concorde Atlantique   CLUB

23 quai Anatole France

☎01 40 56 02 82; www.bateauconcordeatlantique.com

Take a three-story club with themed *soirées,* add copious amounts of booze deals, and stick it right on the Seine. You have just imagined Le Concorde Atlantique. This boat/nightclub keeps going until 4 or 5am. *Soirées* are shamelessly promoted, often with cover charges that include free drinks, and the occasional ladies' night. The deals don't end there: the website **www.paris-bouge.com** is an invaluable resource, giving out cheap tickets and drink passes to save travelers as much as 50%.

▶ ⚡ Ⓜ Assemblée Nationale, right on the Seine in between Pont de la Concorde and walking bridge Solférino. Ⓢ Cover from €10-20, includes (sometimes up to 5) free drinks. Some nights men pay extra €5-10 and must pay online before. ⓧ Open Tu-Sa 8pm-4am (unless its a special *soirée,* which occur occasionally on Su).

Club des Poètes   LOUNGE, RESTAURANT

30 rue de Bourgogne

☎01 47 05 06 03; www.poesie.net

If you want to drink and feel cultured, this restaurant-by-day and poetry-club-by-night is exactly what you're looking for. It brings together an intimate community of literati for supper and sonnets as local actors and singers take to the stage for improv poetry readings from around the world. Despite giving off a slightly intimidating hipster vibe, the crowd is well versed in English and welcomes visitors and travelers to cram in next to them on the long L-shaped table.

▶ ⚡ Ⓜ Varenne. Walk towards Pont d'Alexandre III on bd des Invalides, turning right onto rue de Grenelle. Walk 1 block to rue de Bourgogne and turn left. The club is on your right. *i* Poetry readings M-Sa 10pm. Ⓢ *Prix-fixe*

entrée-plat or plat-dessert €10-25. Wine €6 per glass. 🕐 Open for lunch
M-F noon-3pm. In the evening arrive between 8-10pm for dinner or drinks.
Kitchen open until 10pm. No entry after 10pm.

CHAMPS-ÉLYSÉES

Glam is the name of the game at the trendy, expensive bars and
clubs of the 8ème. Dress up, bring some atractive friends, and a
fat wallet.

⬛ Le Queen   CLUB
102 av. des Champs-Élysées
☎01 53 89 08 90; www.queen.fr

A renowned Parisian institution where drag queens, superstars,
tourists, and go-go boys get down and dirty to the mainstream
rhythms of a 10,000-gigawatt sound system. Open all night,
every night, Le Queen has *soirées* for just about every party
demographic you can think of, as long as you can make it past
the bouncer. Be prepared to show ID to gain entrance to this
flashy disco with a light-up dance floor, which features theme
nights that includes the occasional gay *soirée*.

▶ ⚥ Ⓜ Georges V. *i* Disco Night on M. Ladies Night on W; no cover for
women 11:30pm-1am. Live DJ on F. Ⓢ Cover €20; includes 1 drink. Drinks
€10. 🕐 Open daily 11:30pm-6am.

Le Showcase   CLUB
Under Pont Alexandre III, Port des Champs-Élysées
☎01 45 61 25 43; www.showcase.fr

One of the most popular clubs with the bohemian bourgeoisie in
Paris (a.k.a. kids with money), Le Showcase's limited operation
days and even more limited entrance make it nearly impossible
to get in without some good-looking friends. To be sure you'll
make it in, get on the "guest list" by registering your name for
free online, then dance 'til dawn in this dungeon-esque club.

▶ ⚥ Ⓜ Champs-Élysées-Clemenceau. *i* Entrance typically free before
midnight. Register for free on their website or Facebook page to be added
to the guest list. Ⓢ Cover €10-15. Beer €9. Cocktails €15. 🕐 Open F-Sa
11pm-dawn.

The Bowler   BAR, RESTAURANT
13 rue d'Artois
☎01 45 61 16 60; www.thebowler.fr

The Bowler's upscale clientele will make you rethink the

stereotypical British pub. With (relatively) cheap drinks in the heart of the 8ème it's hard to say no, especially to the weekly Quiz Night or live music. The large interior bar plays sports (tennis, cricket, rugby, and, of course, soccer are the popular ones) as patrons debate whether they are going to continue their night elsewhere or camp out and relax here.

▶ ⚡ Ⓜ St-Philippe du Roule. Walk down rue de la Boétie toward the Champs and turn right onto rue d'Artois. The Bowler is on the left. *i* Live music M 7pm. Quiz Night on Su. Ⓢ Beer €6-9. Cocktails €9-12. Happy hour beer and cocktails €5. Brunch €10. 🕐 Open M-F noon-2am, Sa-Su 1pm-2am. Happy hour M-F 5-7pm, Sa-Su 1pm-2am. Brunch Sa-Su 1-3:30pm.

The Freedom   BAR

8 rue de Berri

☎01 53 75 25 50

The Freedom might not have the decor or class of the rest of the neighborhood, but it makes up for it in sheer party spirit (we mean both kinds of "spirit"). Student Night has the cheapest shooters in all of Paris.

▶ ⚡ Ⓜ George V. Walk away from the Arc de Triomphe and turn left down rue de Berri. *i* Student Night on Th. Ladies night F-Sa 11pm-5am. Ⓢ Shots €5. Beer €6. Cocktails €8-9. Student Night shots €2.50; beer €4. Ladies Night cocktail and shot €6. 🕐 Open M-Th 5pm-2am, F-Sa 5pm-5am, and Su 5pm-2am.

OPÉRA AND CANAL ST-MARTIN

Stay on major streets and avoid heading to the Metro on back alleys in the 10ème late at night. Pickpockets, muggers, and general scumbags abound.

Le Pachyderme   BAR, RESTAURANT

2 bis bd St-Martin

☎01 42 06 32 56

More of a lounge bar than a party spot, this African-themed joint has statues of elephants and black leather love seats inside and a huge heated terrace outside. We would make some jokes about low lighting and elephants, but it's mean to pick on the overweight.

▶ ⚡ Ⓜ Strasbourg-St-Denis. 3 blocks toward pl. de la République, on the left. Ⓢ Beer €6.80. Cocktails €9.70; "Cocktail of the moment" €7. Entrées €14-19. *Plats* €17-25. 🕐 Open daily noon-1:30am.

Eclipse Cafe   BAR, CLUB
12 rue du Château d'Eau
☎01 42 00 15 41

The party here depends on the size of the crowd. On a calm night, it's just some local youth drinking on the terrace with the bartenders and listening to music. When it gets packed, tables are moved and dancing gets going, aided by the cheap pints and cocktails.

► ♯ ⓂJacques Bonsergent. Walk down bd de Magenta toward pl. de la République, turn right onto rue de Lancry, and then left onto rue du Château d'Eau. The bar is on the left. ⑤ Pints and cocktails €5. ⚟ Open daily 6pm-2am.

Le Verre Volé   RESTAURANT, BAR
67 rue Lancry
☎01 48 03 17 34

You'll need a reservation to dine here, but not if you just want to drink. While you won't hang out here all night, this great location on the canal is the perfect spot to mingle with young Parisian hipsters over a glass of one of the restaurant's many wines.

► ♯ ⓂJacques Bonsergent. Walk down bd de Magenta and turn left onto rue de Lancry; it's just before the canal. ⑤ Wine from €5. Beer €5.50. Entrées €5-6. *Plats* €10-11. ⚟ Open Tu-Su noon-3:30pm and 6:30-11:30pm.

L'Atmosphère   BAR
49 rue Lucien Sampaix
☎01 40 38 09 25

L'Atmosphère has the cheapest beer in the 10ème—or at least the cheapest you can find at 1:30am. An older, laid-back crowd sits on the raised terrace overlooking the canal. When they thin out around 1am, 20-somethings flood the place for beer and cocktails and take up the everlasting effort to keep the bar open past closing time.

► ♯ ⓂJacques Bonsergent. Walk down bd de Magenta and turn left onto rue Lancry. When you get to the canal, turn left and walk 2-3 blocks; the bar is on the left. *i* Live music some nights. ⑤ Beer €2.50-5. ⚟ Open Tu-F 10am-2am, Sa 2pm-2am, Su 2-9:30pm.

Nightlife

BASTILLE

Nightlife in the 11ème has long consisted of Anglophones who drink too much and the French who hide from them. With a few exceptions, **rue de Lappe** and its neighbors offer a big, raucous night on the town dominated by expats and tourists, while **rue Oberkampf, rue Amelot,** and **rue Thaillandiers** are more eclectic, low-key, and local. All four streets are worth your time, even if you have only one night in the area. **Rue Faubourg St-Antoine** is a world of its own, dominated by enormous clubs who only let in the well dressed.

🔲 Favela Chic   BAR, CLUB
18 rue du Faubourg du Temple
☎01 40 21 38 14; www.favelachic.com
> A Franco-Brazilian joint, Favela Chic is light on the Franco and heavy on the brassy Brazilian. Wildly popular with locals, this restaurant-bar-club is covered in palm trees, Mardi Gras masks, and sweaty gyrating bodies.
> ▶ ♯ ⓂRépublique. Walk down rue du Faubourg du Temple and turn right into the arch at no. 18; the club is on the left. Ⓢ Cover F-Sa €10; includes 1 drink. Beer €5.50-6. Cocktails €9-10. ⓄOpen Tu-Th 8pm-2am, F-Sa 8pm-4am.

🔲 Le Pop-In   BAR, ROCK CLUB
105 rue Amelot
☎01 48 05 56 11; www.popin.fr
> Le Pop-In takes the pretension out of hipster and replaces it with booze. Hosting (almost) nightly concerts and open-mic nights, this mix of punk rock, Swedish metal, and British pop attracts the dreadlocked and skinny-jeaned.
> ▶ ♯ ⓂSt-Sébastien-Froissart. 𝒊 Open-mic night on Su. Check website for concerts. Ⓢ Beer €2.80-5.50. ⓄOpen daily 6:30pm-1:30am. Happy hour 6:30-9pm.

Le Kitsch   BAR
10 rue Oberkampf
☎01 40 21 94 41
> This might be the most random collection of objects that we've ever seen on a single wall—particularly the garden gnome next to the tie-dyed porcelain cow next to the Virgin Mary. It is Le Kitsch, after all. Priding itself on the nonsense factor, this bar named its signature drink, a mojito-cum-slushy, Shrek (€7.50). The bar attracts a more laid-back local crowd—or as laid-back as they can be in this weird establishment.

▶ ✦ Ⓜ Oberkampf. Ⓢ Beer €3. Cocktails €7.50; happy hour cocktails €5. 🕐 Open daily 5:30pm-2am. Happy hour 5:30-9pm.

Barrio Latino   CLUB

46/48 rue du Faubourg St-Antoine
☎01 55 78 84 75; www.buddha-bar.com

Barrio Latino reminds us of a modern remake of *Scarface:* well-dressed clientele, Latin music broken up with house and techno, and tables filled with G-men watching over a raging five-story party. Enthusiastic and aspiring salsa dancers shake it in various corners and on tables (despite security's best efforts to dissuade them). The giant dance floor heats up around 11pm, but you'll pay a lot to get buzzed enough to fit in.

▶ ✦ Ⓜ Bastille. Ⓢ Cover Th-Sa €20. Beer €6.50-9. Cocktails €12-14. Shooters €6.50. 🕐 Open daily noon-2am.

Some Girls Bar   BAR

43 rue de Lappe
☎01 48 06 40 33

No, it's not a strip joint. It's actually a rock-themed bar that proudly plays the Rolling Stones and other bands from the '60s-'90s in a thoroughly confused, kitschy setting of neon lights, leopard skins, and palm trees. Take advantage of the happy hour that lasts until 10pm, then make your way out before another favorite song convinces you to stay.

▶ ✦ Ⓜ Bastille. Walk down rue de la Roquette and turn left onto rue de Lappe. Ⓢ Pints €5. Cocktails €7-9. Happy hour cocktails €5. 🕐 Open M-Sa 9pm-2am. Happy hour 7-10pm.

Wax   CLUB

15 rue Daval
☎01 40 21 16 16

Wax is a rare Parisian miracle—a place that is actually fun to dance in and almost free (you have to buy at least one drink to stay, though). Housed in a concrete bunker, the club is packed on the weekends with young locals and tourists. On Tuesdays they host a "soirée groove," making them some of the only people in the world who use the word "groove" unironically.

▶ ✦ Ⓜ Bastille. Take bd Richard Lenoir and turn right onto rue Daval. 𝒊 Mandatory coat check F-Sa €1.50. "Soirée groove" on Tu. House and techno on Sa-Su. Ⓢ Beer €4-6. Cocktails €10. 🕐 Open W-Th 5pm-2am, F-Sa 5pm-5am.

Les Disquaires   BAR, CONCERT VENUE
6 rue des Taillandiers
☎01 40 21 94 60; www.lesdisquaires.com

Early in the week, Les Disquaires is a laid-back jazz venue.
Come Thursday, it turns into a packed club with DJs mixing
pop rock tunes while patrons carve their initials into the wax-
coated tables—that is, after they spill drinks on them.

▶ ⚑ ⓂBastille. Take rue de la Roquette and turn right onto rue des Taillandiers. *i* Live concerts daily at 8pm. Club W-Sa. Ⓢ Beer €3-4. Wine €3.50.
Shots €4. ⏰ Open daily 6pm-2am.

Le China   JAZZ BAR, RESTAURANT
50 rue Charenton
☎01 43 46 08 09; www.lechina.eu

Le China could be a clone from the lounges in the 16ème: it's
dark, sophisticated, and the prices aim at the well-to-do. Leather
couches line the walls as people chat, sip their drinks, and jam
to piano tunes. Downstairs in Club Chin Chin, things get a
little more energetic (especially on the weekends) but stay classy
with red velvet and dimmed lighting.

▶ ⚑ ⓂBastille. *i* Piano bar M and Su 8pm-midnight. Concerts daily 8:30pm.
Ⓢ Cocktails €9-15. ⏰ Open M-F noon-2am, Sa-Su 5pm-2am.

Frenchism

If you hear a few familiar words while in Paris, even though
you don't speak French, don't be alarmed; the adoption
of English words here is both a common and controversial
phenomenon. *Le hamburger, le jogging,* and *le weekend* are
all words that French-speakers use regularly. As the digital
age introduced words like "podcast," "email," and "Wi-Fi,"
French has struggled to keep up with English in the creation of
new terminology. Most French people find it easiest to simply
say "podcast" or "Wi-Fi" (pronounced *"wee-fee"*), but French
cultural purists feel that this is an outrage. Enlisting French linguists at the Académie Française, nationalists associated with
the stubborn Ministry of Culture have started a movement to
invent new French words for the influx of new terms. Podcast
becomes *"diffusion pour baladeur,"* and Wi-Fi is *"accès sans
fil à l'internet."* It's a valiant crusade, but Wi-Fi is just so much
easier to say.

MONTPARNASSE AND SOUTHERN PARIS

Clubs and Anglophone bars are clustered in Montparnasse near the tower and the train station, while there are some laid-back bars and clubs floating on the Seine near Chinatown. Butte-aux-Cailles has super cheap hippie bars, but they close early due to whiney neighbors. The absolute highlight for anyone between the ages of 18 and 70 is Cafe OZ.

🦘 Cafe Oz   BAR
3 pl. Denfert-Rochereau
☎01 47 38 76 77; www.cafe-oz.com

Opened in May 2011, the newest and largest iteration of this Australian chain is rumored to have the largest terraces in Paris. After midnight, the older crowd vacates and the massive interior becomes packed with young bodies dancing on tables, stairs, or wherever there is room. Things are kept cool by the drafty 30 ft. ceilings. Despite OZ's size, the palm fronds above the bar and walls covered in boomerangs still make you feel like you're in a packed hut on the beach of Queensland.

▶ ⚡ Ⓜ Denfert-Rochereau, behind the RER station. *i* Snacks served until midnight. Ⓢ Shooters €5. Beer €7-8. Cocktails €10. Happy hour cocktails €6. ⏰ Open M-Tu noon-2am, W noon-3am, Th noon-4am, F-Sa noon-5am, Su noon-2am. Happy hour 5-8pm.

La Folie en Tête   BAR
33 rue de la Butte-aux-Cailles
☎01 45 80 65 99; www.lafolieentete.blogspot.com

Decorated with musical instruments, street signs, and newspaper clippings announcing Bob Marley concerts, this reggae bar has one of the cheapest happy hours in the neighborhood. Hipsters, poets, and broke students keep it packed until closing.

▶ ⚡ Ⓜ Place d'Italie. From pl. d'Italie, follow rue Bobillot. Turn right onto rue de la Butte-aux-Cailles and follow it as it turns right. Ⓢ Beer €5-6. Cocktails €7. Happy hour cocktails €5. ⏰ Open M-Sa 5pm-2am, Su 6pm-midnight. Happy hour 5-8pm.

Nightlife

WESTERN PARIS

Usually there is a direct correlation between the spice of the nightlife and the prices of drinks, but in the 16ème, bars are pricey, and people rarely leave their lounge chairs. The 17ème has a few gems and lower-priced lounges and bars, but if you want the lounge scene and don't mind spending the big bucks to feel important, stick around the Arc de Triomphe.

The Honest Lawyer   BAR

176 rue de la Pompe

☎01 45 05 14 23; www.honest-lawyer.com

The happy hour packs this bar, a throwback from the American Prohibition era and the fleet of alcoholic expats it sent to Paris. Cram into the small round tables with your friends if you're not feeling pretentious enough for the rest of the neighborhood.

▶ ⚲ ⓂVictor Hugo. Walk down av. Victor Hugo away from the Arc de Triomphe and turn left at rue de Longchamp. Go 1 block and turn right onto rue de Pompe; the bar is at the corner with av. de Montespan. Ⓢ Beer €5.50. Happy hour cocktails €6. 🕐 Open M-F 7:30am-2am, Sa 10am-2am, Su 7:30am-2am. Happy hour daily 5:30-8:30pm.

La Gare   BAR

19 Chaussée de la Muette

☎01 42 15 15 31; www.restaurantlagare.com

Once a train station, La Gare is now a trendy bar and favored hang-out spot of the wealthy young locals. Try the heated terrace seating over the old train platforms or warm up by the fire in the inner lounge. If you still have your youth, head out to cheaper, more fun places before midnight (or even 11pm).

▶ ⚲ ⓂLa Muette. Ⓢ Wine €5.50. Martinis €5.50. 🕐 Open daily noon-2am.

Duplex   CLUB

2 bis av. Foch

☎01 45 00 45 00; www.leduplex.com

Stories of this late-night disco make their way around Paris, and we mean that in an infamous way. The three-story subterranean club plays mostly R and B and hip hop and stays packed until dawn with young people looking to hook up.

▶ ⚲ ⓂCharles de Gaulle-Étoile. 𝒊 Women enter free before midnight on F. Ⓢ Cover (includes 1 drink) Tu-Th €15, F-Sa €20, Su €15. Drinks M €8, Tu-Th €9, F-Sa €11, Su €9. 🕐 Open Tu-Su midnight to dawn.

MONTMARTRE

As we've said, Pigalle is pretty sketchy. But that doesn't mean there aren't decent areas to go at night in Montmartre. The areas around **Place de Clichy** and Ⓜ**Abbesses** have fewer tourists at night, and therefore have fewer pickpockets hanging around. Still, if you go to Montmartre, don't make yourself a target: take a taxi or the Noctilien home.

🔇 Le Rendez-Vous des Amis   BAR

23 rue Gabrielle

☎01 46 06 01 60; www.rdvdesamis.com

You know you're in for a night of debauchery when the owners and bartenders drink more than the customers, pounding shots and beers at random. The customers have the advantage of drinking from "giraffes," which are 3 ft. tall, 3L cylinders from which you pour your own beer. Patrons rock out to house music and occasional live guitar jams. Cigarettes are sold out front on an informal basis, but don't bring your drink outside—the burly but friendly bouncer will have words for you. Don't arrive too drunk, either: the subsequent hike from Ⓜ Abbesses is slightly less challenging than Everest.

▶ ✝ Ⓜ Abbesses. Exit the Metro and walk up rue la Vieuville and follow it as it curves right and then left. Continue (literally) up rue Drevet until you reach rue Gabrielle. Ⓢ Beers €2.30-7; pitchers €7. Giraffes €20. Cocktails €6. Tapas and snacks €7. 🕐 Open daily 8am-2am.

🔇 L'Escale   BAR

32 bis rue des 3 Frères

☎01 46 06 12 38

Young folk cram around the small tables of this tiny bar, and the owner proudly proclaims on their Facebook page that L'Escale and its strong drinks—for example the pint-sized mojitos (€4.50)—are the number-one enemy of the police. There's generally a guest DJ playing house music on Sunday nights (and you thought Sunday was boring).

▶ ✝ Ⓜ Abbesses. Exit the Metro and walk up rue la Vieuville and follow it as it curves right and then left. The bar is straight ahead at the intersection with rue des 3 Frères. Ⓢ Cocktails €4.50. 🕐 Open daily 2pm-2am. Happy hour 4-10pm.

Hélice Bar   BAR

50 rue d'Orsel

☎01 46 06 24 70

This bar has more of an indie rock scene than most bars in Paris, and is famous for its super cheap beer. The bartenders provide snacks to keep patrons from falling over too fast as they jam to local bands on Thursday nights.

▶ ⚲ Ⓜ Abbesses. Walk downhill on rue des Abbesses until you get to rue des Martyrs. Though this is not a straight intersection, keep going as straight as you can onto rue d'Orsel. The bar is on the left. Ⓢ Beer pints €3.50-5. Cocktails €5. ⓒ Open Tu-Sa 6pm-2am.

EASTERN PARIS

Bars will try to lure you out here with cheap drinks, but you really shouldn't be wandering this area at night.

▨ Rosa Bonheur   BAR, GLBT

2 av. de la Cascade

☎01 42 00 00 45; www.rosabonheur.fr

If there is one place in the neighborhood that we recommend you start your night, it's Rosa Bonheur. This bistro bar is located within the confines of the Parc Buttes-Chaumont, and is right near the Metro. Now that we have security out of the way

A Whole New World Down There

Every street in Paris has an equivalent address in the underground sewer system, equipped with more than 1300 mi. of tunnels, pipelines, and waterways. All the corners within the sewers have street signs that mirror the ones on the surface—perhaps Parisians were preparing for a sunless, underground lifestyle on the off chance they all turned into vampires.

In actuality, the layout is thanks to architect Eugène Belgrand's efforts to reduce waste in the growing city. He enlarged the size of the drains, increased the sewer system, and built pipelines that, if stretched out, would run from Paris to Istanbul. Unfortunately, with one stinky problem solved, another arose. Since its construction, several robbers—affectionately nicknamed the "termite gangs"—have attempted to break into banks and shops after digging their way from the sewers into the buildings above.

(thank you, bouncers), it's also in an adorable, almost colonial-style building that emerges from the trees of the park. Rosa hosts lots of community service and charity events for GLBT rights and environmental awareness as well as Paris's *Silence de Danse,* where you put on headphones, dance, and look really funny.

▶ ♯ Ⓜ Botzaris. Ⓢ Shots €4. Beer €5. Cocktails €9. ⏰ Open W-Su noon-midnight. Last entry 11pm.

Ourcq   BAR, TEA HOUSE

68 quai de la Loire
☎01 42 40 12 26

Adjust your sense of "nightlife" to more of a "happy hour" and come here during the day (after a visit to the Cité des Sciences et de L'Industrie, for example). The drinks are cheap and the brasserie doubles as a tea house with books and board games.

▶ ♯ Ⓜ Laumière. Ⓢ Wine €2-3. Beer €2.50-4. Cocktails €5. ⏰ Open W-Th 3pm-midnight, F-Sa 3pm-2am, Su 3-10pm.

Arts and Culture

A trip to the Opéra Garnier, comic relief at the Odéon Théâtre, or late-night wining and dining at the Moulin Rouge are all possibilities for total cultural immersion, and will leave you with more memories than that one night on the Mouffetard. If this sounds boring to you (hopefully it doesn't, but we cater to all tastes), you'll be pleased to know that Paris's concerts get just as rowdy as its clubs. Whether you have a solid grasp of French or are a novice who just laughs because everyone else is, you'll definitely leave feeling a bit more *je ne sais quoi*.

Budget Arts and Culture

Paris oozes culture. And it's not all expensive. With ubiquitous free music, especially jazz, there's plenty to do for budget travelers. Check out Le Baiser Salé in Châtelet, or Le Pop-In, Les Disquaires, or Le China in Bastille. Published weekly, *Pariscope* lists many cheap theater, music, and film events over the next week in Paris—pick one up to see what's coming to an arrondissement near you.

THEATER

🏛 **Odéon Théâtre de l'Europe** LATIN QUARTER AND ST-GERMAIN
2 rue Corneille

☎01 44 85 40 40; www.theatre-odeon.fr

The Odéon is a classically beautiful theater: gold lines the mezzanine and muted red upholstery cover the chairs. Many plays are performed in foreign languages with French translation shown above on a screen. Despite the fact that this is the mecca of Parisian theater, the prices are stunningly reasonable and standing tickets are dirt cheap. The under-26 crowd can score the luxury of a seat for the same price, so save your young legs—watching foreign performances of *Measure for Measure* or *La Casa de Fuerza* takes enough energy already.

▶ ♯ ⓂOdéon. *i* Limited number of rush tickets available night of the show. Ⓢ Shows €10-32, under 26 €6-16. Rush tickets €6. ⓧ Performances generally M-Sa 8pm, Su 3pm.

🏛 **Théâtre de la Ville** CHÂTELET-LES HALLES
2 pl. du Châtelet

☎01 42 74 22 77; www.theatredelaville-paris.com

Since the '80s, the Théâtre de la Ville has become a major outlet for avant-garde dance, and it's been attracting art students ever since. One recent show was entitled "Walking next to our shoes… intoxicated by strawberries and cream, we enter continents without knocking." An open mind is a must.

▶ ♯ ⓂChâtelet. Walk down rue de Rivoli toward Hôtel de Ville. Ⓢ Tickets €24, under 30 €13. ⓧ Box office open M 11am-7pm, Tu-Sa 11am-8pm.

CABARET

🏛 **Le Lapin Agile** MONTMARTRE
22 rue des Saules

☎01 46 06 85 87; www.au-lapin-agile.com

Halfway up a steep, cobblestoned hill that American tourists describe as "just like San Francisco," Le Lapin Agile has been providing savvy Parisians and tourists with music, dance, and theater since the late 19th century. The tiny theater was a hotspot of the 20th-century bohemian art scene—Picasso and Max Jacob are on the list of people who cabareted here.

▶ ♯ ⓂLamarck-Coulaincourt. Follow rue St-Vincen to rue des Saules.

Arts and Culture

Ⓢ Tickets €24, students under 26 €17; includes 1 drink. Drinks €6-7. Ⓧ Shows Tu-Su 9pm-2am.

Bal du Moulin Rouge   MONTMARTRE

82 bd de Clichy

☎01 53 09 82 82; www.moulin-rouge.com

Ever since Christina and Co.'s music video, the only thing people associate with the Moulin Rouge is that universal question, *"Voulez-vous coucher avec moi?"* But the world-famous home of the can-can isn't just about sex; it's also about glam and glitz. Since its opening in 1889, the Moulin Rouge has hosted international superstars like Ella Fitzgerald and Johnny Rey, and it now welcomes a fair crowd of tourists for an evening of sequins, tassels, and skin. The shows remain risqué, and the tickets prohibitively expensive. The late show is cheaper, but be prepared to stand if it's a busy night.

▶ ✝ Ⓜ Blanche Sarl. *i* Elegant attire required; no shorts, sneakers, or sportswear. Ⓢ 9pm show €102, 11pm show €92; includes ½-bottle of champagne. 7pm dinner and 9pm show €150-180. Occasional lunch shows €100-130; call for more info. Ⓧ Dinner daily 7pm. Shows daily 9 and 11pm.

CINEMA

The French love movies. They go to the cinema almost every week, and conversations are peppered with references to local art films and box-office hits. Angolophone movie-goers should look for "VO" when selecting English-language films, as they are in *version originale.*

🖼 L'Arlequin   LATIN QUARTER AND ST-GERMAIN

76 rue de Rennes

☎01 45 44 28 80

A proud revival theater, L'Arlequin mixes modern French films with selections from a pool of international award-winners. Three films are featured each week, undoubtedly decreasing the prevalence of adolescent movie-hopping. Some films are in English, but the vast majority are in French.

▶ ✝ Ⓜ St-Sulpice. Ⓢ Full price €9.50; M-Th students, under 18, and over 60 €7; F-Su under 18 €7.

Cinémathèque Française   BASTILLE

51 rue de Bercy

☎01 71 19 33 33; www.cinematheque.fr

Though it's had some problems settling down (it's moved over five times, most recently in 2005), the Cinémathèque Française is committed to sustaining film culture. A must-see for film buffs, the theater screens four to five classics, near-classics, or soon-to-be classics per day; foreign selections are usually sub-titled. The cinema also features multiple movie-related exhibits, which include over 1000 costumes and objects from the past and present world of film.

▶ ♿ Ⓜ Bercy. Ⓢ €7, ages 18-26 and seniors €5, under 18 €4. 🕐 Ticket window open M from noon to last showing, W-Sa from noon to last showing, Su from 10am to last showing. Exhibits open M noon-7pm, W-Sa noon-7pm, Su 10am-8pm.

Arts and Culture

On Location

Many films have been shot on location in Paris over the years. If you're a movie buff, head to these locations to see in real life what you saw on screen:

- **The Louvre:** *Funny Face* (1957), *The Age of Innocence* (1993), *The Da Vinci Code* (2006)

- **Quai Saint Bernard:** *The Bourne Identity* (2002)

- **Montmartre:** *Amélie* (2001), *Moulin Rouge!* (2001)

- **Banks of the Seine:** *Everyone Says I Love You* (1996)

- **Pont de Bir-Hakeim:** *Last Tango in Paris* (1972)

- **122 avenue des Champs Elysées:** *The Accidental Tourist* (1988)

- **Theatre Vrai Guignolet:** *Charade* (1963)

- **Pont Neuf:** *An American in Paris* (1951)

- **Trocadéro:** *The Dreamers* (2003)

MUSIC

You can find live music in almost any bar, club, or boat on the Seine, but for true venues that make the House of Blues look tame, head to the party centers of Montmartre and Bastille.

🔲 Elysée Montmartre   MONTMARTRE

72 bd Rochechouart

☎ 01 44 92 45 36; www.elyseemontmartre.com

Following a worryingly common trend among Montmartre

venues, this concert hall burned down in March 2011. It plans to reopen in early 2012. Famous since 1807 and known to Anglophones for the Roots's song *You Got Me,* this concert hall has hosted the likes of David Bowie, Counting Crows (they recorded their debut album here), and Pendulum. Boxing matches are also held here when the rockers aren't around.

▶ ✢ ⓂAnvers. Ⓢ Tickets €14-45. ⏰ Opens at 11:30pm for all shows.

Le Bataclan   BASTILLE

50 bd Voltaire

☎01 43 14 00 30; www.le-bataclan.com

In French, *bataclan* is slang for "stuff" or "junk." In French music culture, Bataclan means a packed 1500-person Chinese pagoda that hosts alternative rock bands like Oasis, Blur, Jeff Buckley, and MGMT. The craziest venue in Bastille, Le Bataclan attracts a more local crowd since, for some reason, the French fall in love with more obscure bands (who are usually cheaper than those playing at Elysée Montmartre).

▶ ✢ ⓂOberkampf. Ⓢ Tickets start at €15. ⏰ Open Sept-July.

Shopping

"Shopping" and "Paris" are almost synonymous. But the excessive wealth of Champs-Élysées and Île St-Louis are not for the faint of heart—they're for the rich. The many antiques, rare books, and tempting tourist trappings you find across the city could easily empty pockets. No one likes credit card debt, so we recommend the vintage shops and quirky boutiques in the youthful Marais and Bastille.

BOOKS

The French love reading almost as much as they love film, museums, and art. Some of the best insight into why the French put autodidacts on a pedestal can be seen in these stores. Be sure to check out the most famous of the city's bookstores, **Shakespeare and Co.**

📓 Abbey Bookshop   LATIN QUARTER AND ST-GERMAIN
29 rue de la Parcheminerie
☎01 46 33 16 24; www.alevdesign.com/abbey

Clear your afternoon if you're going to Abbey Bookshop—you'll need the time. Set in a back alley, the sheer number of books is a bit overwhelming, whether they're shelved or stacked on the floor. This Canadian-owned shop probably has what you're looking for, and if not, they'll order it for you. Plus, they carry *Let's Go*—they've obviously got the right idea.

▶ ✜ Ⓜ Cluny-La Sorbonne. Follow rue Boutebrie and take a left onto rue de la Parcheminerie. *i* Books in English and other languages available. 🕐 Open M-Sa 10am-7pm.

📓 Gibert Jeune   LATIN QUARTER AND ST-GERMAIN
pl. St-Michel
☎01 56 81 22 22; www.gibertjeune.fr

If you're studying abroad in Paris, this is probably where you'll want to buy your textbooks—Gibert Jeune carries over 300,000 titles. By the time you're through shopping here, you'll look like a real *savant parisien*. And it's air-conditioned, which can be a welcome change during the Parisian summer.

▶ ✜ Ⓜ St-Michel. 🕐 Open M-Sa 9:30am-7:30pm.

Lady Long Solo   BASTILLE
38 rue Keller
☎09 52 73 81 53; www.ladylongsolo.com

Offering an assortment of counter-cultural books that range from anti-colonial diatribes to **The Communist Manifesto,** Lady Long Solo stocks all form of left-leaning print, including guides to the wonders of medical marijuana. Thank Marx and his ideas of price controls, since books here are some of the cheapest in the city.

▶ ✜ Ⓜ Bastille. Follow rue de la Roquette until rue Keller. Ⓢ Books as low as €2. 🕐 Open daily 2-7pm.

Les Mots à la Bouche
THE MARAIS

6 rue Ste-Croix de la Bretonnerie
☎01 42 78 88 30; www.motsbouche.com

Logically located in the Marais, this two-story bookstore offers mostly GLBT literature, photography, magazines, and art, with everything from Proust to guides on lesbian lovemaking. Straight guys could probably learn a few pointers from that last one, too. The international DVD collection is somewhat hidden in the corner of the bottom level (€7-25); titles range from the artistic to the pornographic.

▶ ⚑ ⓂHôtel de Ville. Take a left onto rue Vieille du Temple and a left onto rue Ste-Croix de la Bretonnerie. ⌚ Open M-Sa 11am-11pm, Su 1-9pm.

CLOTHING

Parisians know how to dress well. It's in their blood. If you want to dress like them, you don't have to drain your bank account, or as they say in French, *"fais chauffer ta carte bleu"* (heat up your credit card). **Galeries Lafayette** is the French equivalent of Macy's and will save you time and money, and for everything vintage, head to the Marais or Châtelet-Les Halles.

▨ Free 'P' Star
THE MARAIS

8 rue Ste-Croix de la Bretonnerie
☎01 42 76 03 72; www.freepstar.com

Enter as Plain Jane and leave a star—from the '80s or '90s, that is. Choose from a wide selection of vintage dresses (€20), velvet blazers (€40), boots (€30), and military-style jackets (€5) that all seem like a good idea when surrounded by other antiquated pieces but require some balls to be worn out in the open. Dig around the €10 jean pile and €3 bin for ripped jeans that died out with Kurt Cobain.

▶ ⚑ ⓂHôtel de Ville. Follow rue de Renard and turn right onto rue St-Merri, which becomes rue Ste-Croix de la Bretonnerie. *i* There are 2 other locations at 61 rue de la Verrerie (☎01 42 78 076) and 20 rue de Rivoli. Ⓢ Credit card min. €20. ⌚ Open daily noon-10pm.

▨ Mamie Blue
OPÉRA AND CANAL ST-MARTIN

69 rue de Rochechouart
☎01 42 81 10 42; www.mamie-vintage.com

This vintage store does more than sell old clothes at reduced prices—it transports shoppers back through the decades. Old French music plays in the background to keep you expecting

Six Ways to Dress French

Although Paris is known to be the world's most fashion-conscious city, individuality rarely rears its head. Blending in with the locals means keeping your day-glo American Apparel tights at home and doing as the Parisians do.

- **The fur coat.** The concept of animal cruelty seems to be ignored in Parisian fashion; practically everyone wears a woodland creature at some point during the winter season.

- **The scarf.** It's unclear whether Parisians use the *écharpe* as a mere fashion statement, or if they're just morbidly afraid of wind.

- **The wedge heels.** Called *escarpin,* the pump isn't just for 30-something cougars dressing too young for their age. High heels are a defining staple in a woman's daily outfit, and even prepubescent Parisian Lolitas sport them.

- **The nondescript leather bag.** If your forearm isn't raised and your fingers aren't ready to snap at a moment's notice, get out of town.

- **Oxford lace-up shoes.** In the city where Hemingway began *A Farewell to Arms,* it's not really surprising that the choice of footwear would be equally intellectual.

- **The perpetual frown.** Because being happy is *très* tacky.

a giant hug for liberating the city circa 1945. Mamie Blue specializes in clothing from the '20s-'70s, and we're thinking the prices might be a little over-adjusted for inflation.

▶ ✿ Ⓜ Anvers. Walk toward Ⓜ Barbès-Rochechouart and take the 1st left. The store is 2 blocks down on the right. Ⓢ Dresses €40-175. ⏰ Open M 2:30-7:30pm, Tu-Sa 11:30am-1:30pm and 2:30-7:30pm.

Galeries Lafayette MONTPARNASSE AND SOUTHERN PARIS

40 bd Haussmann

☎ 01 42 82 34 56; www.galerieslafayette.com

While Galeries Lafayette has your acronymic clothing brands for men and women, their own brand sells for nearly 60% of the price. For guys who can't quite rock deep V-necks and three-quarter length pants, come here for more subdued button-ups.

▶ ✿ Ⓜ Chaussée d'Antin-La Fayette. ⏰ Open M-W 9:30am-8pm, Th 9:30am-9pm, F-Sa 9:30am-8pm.

Printemps Haussmann OPÉRA AND CANAL ST-MARTIN

64 bd Haussmann

☎01 42 82 50 00; www.printemps.com

Founded in 1865, this *grand magasin* has over 44,000 sq. m of space and brands from bargain basement to luxury. While the prices are slightly higher than other malls, you get the added benefit of shopping in a historical site and being seen among semi-fashion conscious Parisians.

▶ ⚡ Ⓜ Havre-Caumartin. ⏰ Open M-W 9:35am-8pm, Th 9:35am-10pm, F-Sa 9:35am-8pm.

MUSIC

For vinyl collectors, there are two "Croco" music places in the Latin Quarter specializing in soul, rock, and jazz. We have listed CrocoDisc for all your soul and funk needs; CrocoJazz (64 rue de Montaigne Ste-Geneviève) has every type of jazz under the sun, but is probably too cool for you.

📷 Crocodisc LATIN QUARTER AND ST-GERMAIN

40/42 rue des Écoles

☎01 43 54 33 22; www.crocodisc.com

Specializing in soul and funk, with its second store next door selling contemporary rock and electro, Crocodisc has everything you might need on disc and vinyl. With the faint smell of slow-burning cigars and stacks of old records, Crocodisc sets the mood just right.

▶ ⚡ Ⓜ Maubert-Mutualité. Ⓢ CDs €1-15. Records €2-18. ⏰ Open Tu-Sa 11am-1pm and 2-7pm.

SPECIALTY

For everything else that you can't wear, read, or listen to, we give you this category. Buying these is more for the experience than for utility.

📷 Pylônes ÎLE DE LA CITÉ AND ÎLE ST-LOUIS

57 rue St-Louis en l'Île

☎01 46 34 05 02; www.pylones.com

A colorful collection of amorphous shapes and colors, Pylônes is the store version of the Pompidou. It sells things you'll impulsively buy, never need, but always marvel at, like cheese graters topped with doll heads (€18). More useful (but just as fun) items include cigarette cases (€12) and espresso cups (€6). The artful objects are fun to look at even if you don't buy anything.

▶ ✚ ⓂPont Marie. *i* 5 other locations around the city. Ⓢ Cups €6. Wallets €24. 🕐 Open daily 10:30am-7:30pm.

🖼 La Grande Épicerie de Paris   INVALIDES
38 rue de Sèvres
☎01 44 39 81 00; www.lagrandeepicerie.fr

If a Parisian supermodel took on the form of an *épicerie* (supermarket), she'd be this one. Snooty Invalides women saunter up and down the aisles for the best (or most expensive) cheeses, wines, and Nespresso coffee makers. There is an aisle of American candy and products, but it exists mainly for the locals to cluck their tongues as they walk down. La Grande Épicerie de Paris is better for picking up a bottle of wine and some chocolate than a whole list of groceries, as the prices are as out of reach as the model.

▶ ✚ ⓂVaneau. 🕐 Open M-Sa 8:30am-9pm.

Excursions

If you ever feel like the sweltering Metro, omnipresent tour buses, and mean club bouncers are getting you down, it may be time to get away from the city. Fortunately, a world of farmland, cooling breezes, and spectacular history is right outside the 20 arrondissements. If you didn't get enough royal history in the Louvre, Versailles has the mother of all palaces. It still serves as the place for wealthy Parisians to wind down and raise their kids (the Revolution could only change so much), and you can benefit from a glimpse of Parisians with their guards down. If you want to escape the tourists as well, head to Chartres to see the French countryside crammed into one little town and view the well-preserved, elusively blue Cathédrale de Chartres. So get your hungover self out of bed, stop by the market for some bread and cheese, and head to the train station—you have a date with some Nutella under the shade of a cathedral that even locals appreciate. You may even see a smile from one of them. Don't be frightened.

Budget Excursions

Only a €6 train ride away, Versailles can be a very inexpensive daytrip from Paris. The gardens are free, so, unless you're dying to see the Hall of Mirrors, you don't need to spend any money once you're there. And don't worry—the gardens are overwhelmingly beautiful by themselves. Chartres is more expensive to get to, but its main attraction, the cathedral, is free. For a truly satisfying budget day trip, grab a blanket and pack a picnic before departing from Paris.

VERSAILLES

Less than a 30min. train ride (or a 15min. death commute by scooter) from the center of Paris is a town famous for a single house. "House" might be an understatement. Your history books will tell you that this palace was hated just as much as the Bastille, but thankfully its beauty (and, we can only assume, massive tourism potential) saved it from the raging mob. Versailles is about as modest as the man who built it—the ultimate arrogant Frenchman, the "Sun King," Louis XIV. He had plenty of time to pimp his 580m-long crib, too, over his 72-year rule. The city surrounding the château mainly serves as another suburb for wealthy Parisian families. Some things never change.

Orientation

Versailles is a blessing for the navigationally challenged. In the middle of the **place d'Armes** sits the massive **Château de Versailles,** with **avenue de Paris** extending from the center. Crossing av. de Paris is **avenue de l'Europe,** which leads to the train stations Rive Droite and Rive Gauche (corresponding to the terminus locations in Paris). Av. de l'Europe also crosses through **place de Notre Dame,** where you can find banks, a large open air market, and cheaper creperies. For a daytrip, you won't go beyond the two avenues, whose intersection holds the tourist office.

Sights

🏛 Château

☎01 30 83 78 89; www.chateauversailles.fr

Though the Sun King's palace boasts a whopping 51,200 sq. m of floor space, the 10 million lowly serfs that visit the château every year are granted access to only a small percentage of it. After a walk through the **Musée de l'Histoire de France,** which—surprise!—briefly recounts French history, visitors are shepherded down the halls in a single direction. The museum's 21 rooms feature stunning depictions of the royal family, including a smaller copy of Rigaud's famous portrait of **Louis XIV** with those sexy red-heeled shoes that would have made Dorothy blush. (Louis was notoriously short and always wore heels like it was Friday night.) Up the main staircase to the right is the two-level chapel, built in 1710, where the king heard mass. Here God competed with the Sun King for attention, as the court came for the privilege of watching the king pray. It might have worked well for Louis XIV, but his grandson and selfish Austrian wife should have done a lot more praying.

The luxurious **State Apartments,** which include the king's bedroom, the **Room of Abundance,** the **Apollo Salon,** and the famed 🏛**Hall of Mirrors** are through the hallway. The bed, like the man, is incredibly short. Curtains encircle the bed, inspiring some interesting questions about his self-esteem in the boudoir. The Apollo Salon houses the Sun King's throne, 3m tall, which enabled the King to tower over his subjects and enjoy the view of the beautiful fresco of himself on the ceiling (we've made enough overcompensation jokes already). As if the Apollo Salon weren't narcissistic enough, the sumptuous Hall of Mirrors exemplifies the King's need to look at himself. Lined with the largest mirrors 17th-century technology could produce, and windows that overlook the grand gardens outside, the room served as a reception space for great ambassadors. Today, it can be rented out for a Napoleon-sized fortune (we mean small, as in his stature, not large, as in his coffers).

The **Queen's Bedchamber** (which cannot be rented out; keep holding out for the Lincoln Bedroom), where royal births were public events to prove the legitimacy of heirs, is much less ornate than the king's, but almost exactly as the queen left it on October 6, 1789. Not to worry though; from what we could tell, they changed the sheets.

▶ ⑤ €15, under 18 and EU residents 18-25 free; includes audio guide. "Passport" €18, under 18 and EU residents 18-25 free; allows entry to the château, Trianons Palace, and Marie Antoinette's estate. Nov-Mar 1st Su each month free. ⏰ Château open Tu-Su Apr-Oct 9am-6:30pm, last entry 5:30pm; Nov-Mar 9am-5:30pm, last entry 4:50pm.

Gardens

When you have a big-ass house, you need a big-ass garden to go with it—otherwise it just looks silly. The château gardens are an impressive 800 hectares (if you aren't fluent in hectares, just know that they're huge) and are filled with fountains and row upon row of hedges. The price of admission to the château includes this visit, so go look at the pretty shrubbery. During **Les Grandes Eaux Musicales,** almost all the fountains are turned on at the same time, and chamber music booms from among the groves—but you'll pay extra to experience that.

▶ ⑤ Free. Grandes Eaux Musicales €8, ages 6-17 €6, under 6 free. ⏰ Gardens open daily Apr-Oct 8am-8:30pm; Nov-Mar 8am-6pm. Grandes Eaux Musicales Apr-Oct Sa-Su 11am-noon and 3:30-5:30pm.

Trianons and Marie Antoinette's Estate

Contrary to what officials will tell you, the walk up to Trianons and Marie Antoinette's Estate does not take 25min. Less ambitious sightseers are overwhelmed by the prospect of leaving the main area, which makes for a quieter and infinitely more pleasant Versailles experience for those willing to make the trip. Within Marie Antoinette's house are numerous examples of her self-importance. Her bedroom had riggings that could raise mirrors to obscure the windows at the turn of a crank—a need for privacy rarely seen in modern France. Entrance to the compound was strictly forbidden; even the king had to ask for permission. The little Austrian was so secluded that the tables in the dining rooms were designed to be lowered and raised from the floor, since it must have been so annoying for her to have to actually *see* the servants. While the tables are no longer there, you can still see the lines in the marble where the plans used to be. In an apparent misread of Rousseau's ideas on the simple life of reclusion (heavy on reclusion, completely lacking in simple), Marie Antoinette had the gardens commissioned to include a 12-building compound with a dairy farm, gardener's house, mill, and swan-filled lake. Simplicity is relative when you're a queen.

If you're surprised by the unnecessary opulence of

Marie Antoinette's Estate, bear in mind that she was just following precedent. The **Grand Trianon** served as Louis XIV's château-away-from-château when the stress of Versailles became too much to bear. It also served as a nice place to house his mistress(es) and (up to) seven illegitimate children by Madame de Montespan alone. Still luxurious, but nowhere near the size of Versailles, this is the palace of the super-wealthy average Joe.

▶ Ⓢ €10, under 18 and EU residents 18-25 free. 🕑 Open Tu-Su Apr-Oct noon-6:30pm; Nov-Mar noon-5:30pm. Last entry 40min. before close.

Food

Eating in Versailles is less expensive than you would expect, considering the three million tourists that visit each year. Restaurants and vendors jack up the price about €1-2 for the privilege of eating where the kings once did, but prices outside the gilded gates are more reasonable. Packing a lunch is recommended, but if you don't want to schlep it from Paris, stop by a market or the deli below.

🔲 Maison Beaudet   DELI $

4 rue Maréchal Foch

This small gourmet deli supplies the cheapest of the cheap sandwiches as well as a selection of wines, cold self-serve pasta, deli meats, and pretty much anything you would need for a picnic.

▶ 🛉 Turn left facing the Mairie and it will be on your left. Ⓢ Sandwiches €3.50. Sandwich, dessert, and soda €6. 🕑 Open Tu-Su 9am-6pm.

Essentials

Practicalities

• **TOURIST OFFICES:** Get maps, hotel and market information, and a complete city guide (even though you're probably just going to the Château). Also provides travel advice for visitors with disabilities. (2 bis av. de Paris ☎01 39 24 88 88; www.versailles-tourimse.com 🛉 Corner of av. de Paris and av. de l'Europe. 🕑 Open Apr-Sept M 10am-6pm, Tu-Su 9am-7pm; Oct-Mar M 11am-5pm, Tu-Sa 9am-6pm, Su 11am-5pm.)

- **PHARMACIES:** English spoken with Dr. Elizabeth Kennedy. (rue de la Pourvoierie ☎01 39 50 09 23 ✚ Corner of rue Maréchal Foch and rue de la Pourvoierie ⏰ Open M 10am-8pm, Tu 8:30am-8pm, W-Th 9am-8pm, F 8:30am-8pm, Sa 9am-7:30pm.)

- **ATMS:** HSBC. (18 rue du Maréchal Foch ⏰ Open 24hr.)

Getting There

RER trains beginning with "V" run from St-Michel Notre Dame to **Versailles-Rive Gauche.** From **Gare Saint-Lazare,** trains run to **Gare de Versailles Rive Droite,** which is on the opposite side of the town, and equidistant from the Château as the other train station. From Montparnasse, trains arrive at **Versailles-Chantiers,** which is the farthest from the Château. Buy a round-trip ticket, as ticket lines in Versailles are long. Buy your RER ticket before going through the turnstile to the platform; when purchasing from a machine, look for the **Île-de-France ticket** option. While a Metro ticket will get you through these turnstiles, it won't get you through RER turnstiles at the other end and could ultimately result in a significant fine. (⑤ Round-trip €5.80. ⏰ 30-40min., every 20min. 4:50am-12:15am.)

Such Gaulle!

French leaders are renowned for their ambition and belief in the greatness of France. The most famous 20th-century French leader, Charles de Gaule, was not, however, always known for his elegance or subtlety of phrasing. Here are some of his more off-the-cuff remarks.

- **ON LEADERSHIP:** "Who honestly believes that, at age 67, I would start a career as a dictator?"

- **ON CHINA:** "China is a big country, inhabited by many Chinese."

- **ON FRENCH-SPEAKING CANADIANS:** "Vive le Québec libre!" We're sure the Canadian government was delighted.

- **ON FRANCE:** "How can anyone govern a nation that has 246 different kinds of cheese?"

Excursions

Getting Around

Versailles is entirely walkable for what you want to see; it's almost like they anticipated the tourists when they built it. Any bus that goes to the city center will stop next to the Château, but you can walk to and from most points of interest in 10min.

CHARTRES

Were it not for a holy scrap of fabric, Chartres might still be a sleepy hamlet. But the cloth that the Virgin Mary supposedly wore when she gave birth to Jesus somehow ended up here, making Chartres a major medieval pilgrimage center. The majestic cathedral that towers over the city isn't the only reason to visit; the *vieille ville* is also a masterpiece of medieval architecture, which almost makes you forget the zooming highways that have encroached upon it.

Orientation

To reach the **Cathédrale** from the train station, walk straight ahead down **avenue Jehan de Beauce** to **place de Châtelet** and look up. You'll see the cathedral and the **place de la Cathédrale** and quickly begin to comprehend that the church isn't the only show in town. Don't make the mistake of asking a local where the cathedral is; you'll get laughed at or severely snarked. The **Musée des Beaux-Arts** and other prominent sights are located behind the cathedral. **La Maison Picassiette** is a little farther away, about 10min. from the *vieille ville* by taxi. Chartres's medieval tangle of streets can be confusing, but getting lost is enjoyable.

Sights

Is the cathedral the best show in town? Obviously, yes. It even offers three attractions in one. It attracts the historical buffs with its crypt, the pilgrims with its relics, and the athletic with its giant I-dare-you-to-climb-me tower. Just try to break up your sightseeing with some non-cathedral attractions as well.

La Cathédrale Notre-Dame de Chartres

📱 La Cathédrale   CHURCH
18 cloître Notre-Dame
☎02 37 21 75 02

The Cathédrale de Chartres is quite possibly the best-preserved medieval church in Europe, having miraculously escaped any major damage during its nearly 1000 years of existence. While Notre Dame's statues were beheaded, this architectural wonder survived the French Revolution and two world wars unscathed. This was after earlier cathedrals on this site were destroyed by fire, though, so we guess it earned a bit of good luck. Most attribute the church's ability to escape revolutionaries and the Nazis to its housing of the **Sancta Camisa,** the cloth that the Virgin Mary wore while giving birth to Jesus. Donated by Charles the Bald, so named for his lack of hair (or his full head of it—historians still can't decide if the name was ironic), the Sancta Camisa attracts thousands of sick Catholics in the hopes that it will heal their ailments. It's on display in the back of the church, and alternates between the three chapels. If you're having trouble finding it, just look for the mob of non-praying tourists.

Other must-sees include the 176 stained-glass windows that date from the 13th century. They were preserved through both world wars by the heroic and extremely savvy town authorities, who carefully dismantled all the windows and stored them in Dordogne until the fighting was over. The glass designs are characterized by a stunning color known as "Chartres blue," which has not been successfully reproduced in modern times. The windows of Chartres often distract visitors from the treasure below their feet: a winding labyrinth pattern that is carved into the floor in the rear of the nave. The labyrinth originally served as a pilgrimage substitute—by following this pattern on their hands and knees, the devout would enact a symbolic voyage to Jerusalem, and then still have time to be home by dinner. Commitment loophole? Maybe.

▶ ⌗ In pl. de la Cathédrale. *i* English tours of the cathedral begin outside the gift shop in the cathedral. 1hr. English audio tours available at the gift shop require ID. ⑤ Free. English tours €10, students and children €5. Audio tours for cathedral €4.20; for choir loft €3.20; for both €6.20. ⌚ Open daily 8:30am-7:30pm. English tours M-Sa noon and 2:45pm.

Tour Jehan-de-Beauce   TOWER

Only the in-shape and non-claustrophobic can climb the narrow, 300-step staircase to the cathedral's north tower, but those who do shall receive wealth and fame—in reality, just a really stellar view of the city and the surrounding valley. If you can't make it all the way to the top, the first viewing platform offers a slightly obstructed but nonetheless impressive panorama.

▶ ⑤ €7, ages 18-25 €4.50, under 18 free. ⌚ Open May-Aug M-Sa 9:30am-noon and 2-5:30pm, Su 2-5:30pm; Sept-Apr M-Sa 9:30am-noon and 2-4:30pm, Su 2-4:30pm.

La Crypte   CRYPT

Visitors may enter the 110m subterranean crypt only as part of a guided tour. Chapels within the crypt alternate between Gothic and Romanesque styles and house the original statues from the facade. You are led to the foundation stone of the church, where two priests and the Sancta Camisa miraculously survived for three days during one of the most destructive fires to afflict the cathedral. Parts of the crypt, including the well in which Vikings tossed the bodies of their victims during raids, date back to the ninth century.

▶ *i* 30min. tours in French leave from the store opposite the cathedral's south entrance at 18 cloître Notre-Dame. English leaflets are available at La Crypte store. Ⓢ €2.70, students €2.10, under 7 free. Ⓩ Tours Apr-Oct M-Sa 11am, 2:15, 3:30, and 4:30pm; Su 2:15, 3:30, and 4:30pm. Tours Nov-Mar M-Sa 4:15pm, Su 11am. Additional tour 5:15pm June 22-Sept 21.

Other Sights

▨ Maison Picassiette   MUSEUM
22 rue du Repos
☎02 37 34 10 78

After buying this plot of land at 22 rue du Repos, the owner (in a fit of recycling savvy) decided to make intricate mosaics out of pieces of broken and discarded glass that he found. If you thought mosaics only come on floors and walls, think again. At Maison Picassiette, chairs, tables, lamps, stoves, and even the doghouse are covered with depictions of the cathedral and biblical scenes that could make good color blindness tests. Apart from a slight headache, you'll leave with a new understanding of hot glue that will shame every macaroni art project your mother ever put up on the fridge.

▶ ⚲ Well outside the city center, it is most accessible by taxi, which can be found in pl. de la Cathédrale or pl. Pierre Sémard. Ⓢ €5.20, students and under 26 €2.60, under 18 free. Ⓩ Open Jul-Aug M 10am-6pm, W-Sa 10am-6pm; Oct-Apr M 10am-noon and 2-6pm, W-Sa 10am-noon and 2-6pm.

Musée des Beaux-Arts   MUSEUM

29 cloître Notre-Dame

☎02 37 90 45 80

The former Bishops Palace, the beautiful and creaky building
that is now home to this museum, is a little more impressive
than the collection itself. The museum deals with the medieval
history of Chartres, including a temporary exhibit on ◤dragons
and their most famous slayer, St. George (sorry Buffy). It also
houses 15th- through 19th-century European paintings, suits of
armor, and a sword collection.

▶ ✝ Across the street from the cathedral. Ⓢ Permanent collection €3.10,
under 18 and seniors €1.60. Permanent collection and temporary exhibits
€5.10/2.60. Ⓩ Open May-Oct M 10am-noon and 2-6pm, W-Sa 10am-noon
and 2-6pm, Su 2-6pm; Nov-Apr M 10am-noon and 2-5pm, W-Sa 10am-
noon and 2-5pm, Su 2-5pm. Last entry 30min. before close.

Centre International du Vitrail   MUSEUM

5 rue du Cardinal Pie

☎02 37 21 65 72; www.centre-vitrail.org

The Centre International du Vitrail is strangely located in a
medieval tithe barn dating from the 12th century. It might
not be the ideal setting for a stained-glass museum, but it's
there nonetheless. Exhibits explain the process that creates the
windows and the evolution of the craft from the Middle Ages
until the modern day. Expect a lot of debate on why they can't
replicate that special blue in the cathedral.

▶ ✝ Across the street from the cathedral. Ⓢ €4, students and under 26 €3.
Ⓩ Open M-F 9:30am-12:30pm and 1:30-6pm, Sa 10am-12:30pm and 2:30-
6pm, Su 2:30-6pm.

Food

Food in Chartres really only caters to the tourist population, so
falling into a tourist trap is inevitable. While your cheapest option is always to picnic, there are some calmer joints that don't
attract the hordes of pilgrims.

Épicerie de la Place Billard   GROCERY STORE $

19 rue des Changes

☎02 37 21 00 25

Épicerie de la Place Billard is a friendly, inexpensive grocery
store that sells all the picnic basics, though there isn't much

green space in Chartres to eat it on. The store also sells over 40 flavors of *limonade* (€5).

▶ ⚡ 3 blocks southeast of the cathedral. 🕐 Open M-Sa 6:30am-7:30pm, Su 6am-6pm.

Le Pichet 3   RESTAURANT, GROCERY STORE $$
19 rue du Cheval Blanc
☎02 37 21 08 35; www.wix.com/francechartres/lepichet3

Combining a boutique and restaurant (to maximize buying impulses), this restaurant will have you torn between ordering stewed duck and buying colorful scarves, beads, and photos of the city. Or you could just give up and chill with a coffee on the second-floor terrace of this split-level establishment.

▶ ⚡ Exit pl. de la Cathédrale to the west (on rue de l'Horloge) then turn left onto rue du Cheval Blanc. Ⓢ Lunch menu €14. *Plats* €11-15. 🕐 Open daily 11am-6pm.

Le Moulin de Ponceau   TRADITIONAL $$$
21 rue de la Tannerie
☎02 37 35 30 05; www.moulindeponceau.fr

Le Moulin de Ponceau has about 20 tables that snake along the tranquil Eure River and up rue de la Tannerie, just 5min. from the cathedral. Think of your ideal farm-inspired countryside meal and you'll begin to imagine their lamb covered in rosemary gravy, sweetbreads, and olive polenta. While the prices are more Parisian than practical, the dining experience is entirely worth it.

▶ ⚡ From the cathedral, follow rue des Acacias down to the river. Once over the river, turn left onto rue de la Tannerie. Ⓢ *Entrées* €12. *Plats* €19. Desserts €10. *Prix-fixe* menus €29-39. 🕐 Open Tu-Sa noon-3:30 and 7-10:30pm, Su noon-3:30pm.

Nightlife

There's not much excitement in Chartres at night, especially during the week. Tourists are generally a bit older than the lively expat crowd in Paris, so don't expect much beyond a refreshing drink before your train ride back.

L'Académie de la Bière   BAR
8 rue du Cheval Blanc
☎02 37 36 90 07

L'Académie de la Bière is one of the only viable bars in

Chartres. With Guinness, Delerium, and the vintage "Bière de Chartres" signs hanging high, the bar's priorities are clear: beer, beer, and more beer. Summer sees the opening of the beer garden where you can chill out on comfy padded chairs under the awning. Unless you're coming here on a weekend, don't expect much of a party, as it's mostly older locals and some tourists throwing back a few before heading to bed or boarding the train.

▶ ⚓ On pl. de la Cathédrale, across the street from the cathedral. ⓢ Beers €4-6. ⏰ Open M-Th 6pm-1am, F-Sa 6pm-2am.

Essentials

Practicalities

- **TOURIST OFFICES:** The **Office de Tourisme de Chartres** provides maps and books accommodations. (pl. de la Cathédrale ☎02 37 18 26 26; www.chartres-tourisme.com ⏰ Open M-F 9am-1pm and 2-6pm, Sa 10am-1pm and 2-6pm.)

- **TOURS:** English-language walking tours are available at the tourist office. (ⓢ €6, under 12 €4. ⏰ 1hr., Jul-Aug Tu 2:30pm.) Audio tours of the *vieille ville* are also available. (ⓢ €5.50, 2 for €8.50. ⏰ 1hr.)

- **CURRENCY EXCHANGE: Currency Exchange Office.** (Parvis de la Cathédrale ☎02 37 36 42 33 ⏰ Open Mar-Oct M-Sa 9am-5pm.)

Emergency

- **POLICE: Hôtel de Police.** (57 rue du Docteur Maunoury ☎02 37 23 42 84 ⚓ Follow rue Collin d'Harleville to pl. des Épars and continue onto rue du Docteur Maunoury.)

- **LATE-NIGHT PHARMACIES: Pharmacie Desprez Buis.** (49 rue Soleil d'Or ☎02 37 36 02 63 ⏰ Open 24hr.)

- **HOSPITALS/MEDICAL SERVICES: Louis Pasteur Hospital.** (4 rue Claude Bernard ☎02 37 30 30 30 𝒊 English-speaking doctors.) For a closer but French-speaking hospital, go to 34 rue du Docteur Maunoury, near the police station.

Getting There

Chartres is accessible by frequent **trains** from Gare Montparnasse, on the Nogent-le-Rotrou line. There are two SNCF trains per hour during the summer; pick up a schedule ahead of time, as times are frequently irregular (thanks, striking workers). Trains take an hour and cost €30 (ages 12-24 and seniors €22, under 12 €5). The train station in Chartres is located at pl. Pierre Sémard. (☎02 37 84 61 50)

Getting Around

Chartres is a very walkable city, with most of its worthwhile sights clustered around the cathedral. The Maison Picassiette is the main exception and is most accessible by **taxi.** We suggest Taxi 2000. (pl. Pierre Sémard ☎02 37 36 00 00) If you ever get lost, look up—the cathedral is visible from almost everywhere in the town, so you can easily find your way back to the center.

Essentials

You don't have to be a rocket scientist to plan a good trip. (It might help, but it's not required.) You do, however, need to be well prepared, and that's what we can do for you. Essentials is the chapter that gives you all the nitty-gritty you need to know for your trip: the hard information gleaned from 50 years of collective wisdom and several months of furious fact-checking. Planning your trip? Check. Where to find Wi-Fi? Check. The dirt on public transportation? Check. We've also thrown in communications info, safety tips, and a phrasebook, just for good measure. Plus, for overall trip-planning advice from what to pack (money and as little underwear as possible) to how to take a good passport photo (it's physically impossible; consider airbrushing), you can also check out the Essentials section of www.letsgo.com.

So, flick through this chapter before you leave so you know what documents to bring, while you're on the plane so you know how you'll be getting from the airport to your accommodation, and when you're on the ground so you can find a laundromat to solve all your 3am stain-removal needs. This chapter may not always be the most scintillating read, but it just might save your life.

RED TAPE

> ## Entrance Requirements
>
> - **PASSPORT:** Required for citizens of all countries.
> - **VISA:** Required for non-Eu citizens for stays longer than 90 days.
> - **WORK PERMIT:** Required for all foreigners planning to work in France.

Documents and Formalities

We're going to fill you in on visas and work permits, but don't forget the most important one of all: your passport. **Don't forget your passport!**

Visas

Those lucky enough to be EU citizens do not need a visa to globetrot through France. You citizens of Australia, Canada, New Zealand, the US, and other non-EU countries do not need a visa for stays of up to 90 days, but this three-month period begins upon entry into any of the countries that belong to the EU's **freedom of movement** zone. For more information, see **One Europe** (below). Those staying longer than 90 days may apply for a longer-term visa; consult an embassy or consulate for more information.

Double-check entrance requirements at the nearest embassy or consulate of France (listed below) for up-to-date information before departure. US citizens can also consult http://travel.state.gov.

Entering France to study requires a special visa. For more information, see the **Beyond Tourism** chapter.

Work Permits

Admittance to a country as a traveler does not include the right to work, which is authorized only by a work permit. For more information, see the **Beyond Tourism** chapter.

Essentials

One Europe

The EU's policy of freedom of movement means that most border controls have been abolished and visa policies harmonized. Under this treaty, formally known as the Schengen Agreement, you're still required to carry a passport (or government-issued ID card for EU citizens) when crossing an internal border, but, once you've been admitted into one country, you're free to travel to other participating states. Most EU states (the UK is a notable exception) are already members of Schengen, as are Iceland and Norway. In recent times, fears over immigration have led to calls for suspension of this freedom of movement. Border controls are being strengthened, but the policy isn't really targeted against casual travelers, so unless you've been traveling so long that you look like an illegal immigrant, you should still be fine to travel with ease throughout Europe.

Embassies and Consulates

- **FRENCH CONSULAR SERVICES IN AUSTRALIA: Consulate General.** (31 Market St., Sydney, NSW 2000 ☎02 9268 2400; www.ambafrance-au.org ☒ Open M-Th 9am-1pm, F 9am-12:30pm.)

- **FRENCH CONSULAR SERVICES IN CANADA: Consulate General.** (1501 McGill College, Montréal, QC H3A 3M8 ☎514-878-4385; http://consulfrance-montreal.org ☒ Open M-F 8:30am-4:30pm.)

- **FRENCH CONSULAR SERVICES IN IRELAND: Embassy.** (36 Ailesbury Rd., Dublin 4 ☎1 277 50 00; www.ambafrance-ie.org ☒ Open for visa services M-Th 2-4pm, F 2-3pm.)

- **FRENCH CONSULAR SERVICES IN NEW ZEALAND: Embassy.** (34-42 Manners St., Wellington 6142, New Zealand ☎04 384 25 55; www.ambafrance-nz.org ☒ Open M-Th 9am-1pm and 2-6pm, F 9am-1pm and 2-4pm.)

- **FRENCH CONSULAR SERVICES IN THE UNITED KINGDOM: Embassy.** (21 Cromwell Rd., London SW7 2EN ☎020 7073 1250; www.ambafrance-uk.org)

- **FRENCH CONSULAR SERVICES IN THE UNITED STATES: Embassy.** (4101 Reservoir Rd. NW, Washington DC 20007 ☎202-944-6000; www.ambafrance-us.org)

- **AUSTRALIAN CONSULAR SERVICES IN PARIS: Embassy.** (4 rue Jean Rey ☎01 40 59 33 15; www.france.embassy.gov.au ☎ Open M-F 9am-5pm.)

- **CANADIAN CONSULAR SERVICES IN PARIS: Embassy.** (37 av. Montaigne ☎01 44 43 29 00; www.france.gc.ca ☎ Open M-F 9am-noon and 2-5pm.)

- **IRISH CONSULAR SERVICES IN PARIS: Embassy.** (4 rue Rude ☎01 44 17 67 00; www.embassyofireland.fr ☎ Open M-F 9:30am-noon.)

- **NEW ZEALAND CONSULAR SERVICES IN PARIS: Embassy.** (7 ter rue Léonard de Vinci ☎01 45 01 43 43; www.embassyofireland.fr ☎ Open July-Aug M-Th 9am-1pm and 2-4:30pm, F 9am-2pm; Sept-June M-Th 9am-1pm and 2-5:30pm, F 9am-1pm and 2-4pm.)

- **UNITED KINGDOM CONSULAR SERVICES IN PARIS: Embassy.** (35 rue du Faubourg St-Honoré ☎01 44 51 31 00; http://ukinfrance.fco.gov.uk ☎ Open M-F 9:30am-1pm and 2:30-6pm.)

- **UNITED STATES CONSULAR SERVICES IN PARIS: Embassy.** (2 av. Gabriel ☎01 43 12 22 22; http://france.usembassy.gov ☎ Open M-F 9am-3pm.)

MONEY

Getting Money from Home

Stuff happens. When stuff happens, you might need some money. When you need some money, the easiest and cheapest solution is to have someone back home make a deposit to your bank account. Otherwise, consider one of the following options.

Wiring Money

Arranging a **bank money transfer** means asking a bank back home to wire money to a bank in Paris. This is the cheapest way to transfer cash, but it's also the slowest and most agonizing, usually taking several days or more. Note that some banks may only release your funds in local currency, potentially sticking you with a poor exchange rate; inquire about this in advance. In general, bank transfers in Paris can be performed at post office banks *(La Banque Postale)*. **Banque de France** has some of the most competitive rates for international transfers in Paris; however, if your home bank has a relationship with a bank in France, make sure to use that bank, as the rate will often be better.

Money transfer services like **Western Union** are faster and more convenient than bank transfers—but also much pricier. Western Union has many locations worldwide. To find one, visit www.westernunion.com or call the appropriate number: in Australia }1800 173 833, in Canada 800-235-0000, in the UK 0808 234 9168, in the US 800-325-6000, or in France 08 00 90 04 07. Money transfer services are also available to **American Express** cardholders and at select **Thomas Cook** offices.

US State Department (US Citizens Only)

In serious emergencies only, the US State Department will help your family or friends forward money within hours to the nearest

The Euro

Despite what many dollar-possessing Americans might want to hear, the official currency of 16 members of the European Union—Austria, Belgium, Cyprus, Finland, France, Germany, Greece, Ireland, Italy, Luxembourg, Malta, the Netherlands, Portugal, Slovakia, Slovenia, and Spain—is the euro.

Still, the currency has some important—and positive—consequences for travelers hitting more than one eurozone country. For one thing, money-changers across the eurozone are obliged to exchange money at the official, fixed rate and at no commission (though they may still charge a small service fee). Second, euro-denominated traveler's checks allow you to pay for goods and services across the eurozone, again at the official rate and commission-free. For more info, check a currency converter (such as www.xe.com) or www.europa.eu.int.

consular office, which will then disburse it according to instructions for a US$30 fee. If you wish to use this service, you must contact the Overseas Citizens Services division of the US State Department. (☎+1-202-501-4444, from US 888-407-4747)

Withdrawing Money

To use a debit or credit card to withdraw money from a cash machine (ATM) in Europe, you must have a four-digit Personal Identification Number (PIN). If your PIN is longer than four digits, ask your bank whether you can just use the first four or whether you'll need a new one. Credit cards don't usually come with PINs, so if you intend to hit up ATMs in Europe with a credit card to get cash advances, call your credit card company before leaving to request one.

ATMs are readily available throughout Paris. They get the same wholesale exchange rate as credit cards, but there is often a limit on the amount of money you can withdraw per day. Depending on your domestic bank, there may be a surcharge of €1-5 per withdrawl. The most common banks are BNP Paribas, Crédit Agricole, HSBC France, and Société Générale, and many have relationships with other international banks that waive the surcharge if you withdraw from them. Check with your domestic bank to see if it has any such relationship before traveling to Paris.

Tipping

By law in France, a service charge, called *service compris,* is added to bills in bars and restaurants. Most people do, however, leave some change (up to €2) for sit-down services, and in nicer restaurants it is not uncommon to leave 5% of the bill. For other services, like taxis and hairdressers, a 10-15% tip is acceptable.

Taxes

As a member of the EU, France requires a **value added tax (VAT)** of 19.6%, which is applied to a variety of goods and services, though the rate is less for food (5.5%). Non-EU visitors to France who are taking these goods home may be refunded this tax for purchases totaling over €175 per store. When making purchases, request a VAT form and present it at the *détaxe* booth at the airport. Goods purchased this way must be carried at all times while traveling, and refunds must be claimed within six months.

Essentials

GETTING THERE

How you arrive in Paris will be dictated by where you come from. Those flying across the Atlantic will most likely end up in Paris-Charles de Gaulle, one of Europe's international hubs. If flying from within Europe, it will probably be cheaper for you to fly into Orly. Though it hardly counts as arriving in Paris, flying into Beauvais from other European cities will often save a lot of money. RER lines, buses, and shuttles run regularly from all three airports to Paris; however, time and price varies with the airport. With its confusingly endless amount of train stations, Paris offers options for both those coming from within France and those with pteromechanophobia traveling by train from the rest of Europe.

By Plane

Paris-Charles de Gaulle (CDG)
In Roissy-en-France, 23km northeast of Paris
☎01 48 62 22 80; www.adp.fr

Most transatlantic flights land at Aéroport Paris-CDG. The two cheapest and fastest ways to get into the city from Paris-CDG are by RER and by bus. The RER train leaves from Terminal 2. To get to the station from Terminal 1, take the Red Line of the Navette, a free shuttle bus that leaves every 6-10min. From there, the RER B (Ⓢ €8.70, which includes Metro transport when you get off the RER.) will transport you to central Paris. To transfer to the Metro, get off at Gare du Nord, Châtelet-Les Halles, or St-Michel. The **Roissybus** (☎01 49 25 61 87 Ⓢ €10. ⌚ 35min.; every 15min. during the day, every 20min. at night.) stops at every terminal. If you're taking the bus back to the airport, you can catch it at the corner of rue Scribe and rue Auber at pl. de l'Opéra.

ORLY (ORY)
In Orly, 18km south of Paris
☎01 49 75 15 15; www.adp.fr

Aéroport d'Orly is used by charters and many continental flights. From Orly Sud Gate G or Gate I, Platform 1, or Orly Ouest Level G, Gate F, take the **Orly-Rail** shuttle bus to the Pont de Rungis/Aéroport d'Orly train station, where you can board the RER C for a number of destinations in Paris, including St-Michel, Invalides, and Gare d'Austerlitz. Another option is the

RATP ▧**Orlybus** (☎08 36 68 77 14 ⑤ €6.90. ⌚ 30min., every 12-20min.), which runs from Metro and RER stop Denfert-Rochereau to Orly's south terminal. You can also board the Orlybus at Dareau-St-Jacques, Glacière-Tolbiac, and Porte de Gentilly. RATP also runs **Orlyval** (☎01 69 93 53 00 ⑤ VAL ticket €8.30, VAL-RER ticket €11.), a combination of Metro, RER, and VAL rail shuttle that is the fastest way to get to the city. The VAL shuttle goes from Antony (RER B) to Orly Ouest and Sud. Buy tickets at any RATP booth in the city, or from the Orlyval agencies at Orly Ouest, Orly Sud, and Antony.

Beauvais (BVA)

In Tillé, 85km north of Paris

☎08 92 68 20 66; www.aeroportbeauvais.com

Aéroport de Paris Beauvais serves **Ryanair, EasyJet,** and other budget airlines. The **Shuttle Bus** leaves from Paris-Beauvais and goes to Porte Maillot in Paris, where you can take the Metro to the city center (☎03 44 11 46 86; www.aeroportbeauvais. com ⑤ €15. Cash only. Must be purchased in arrival lounge. ⌚ Every 20min. after flight arrivals.) To get back to Beauvais, arrive 3¼hr. before flight time at bd Pershing, near the Hotel Concorde La Fayette at Porte Maillot, and purchase tickets on the bus.

By Train

SNCF (www.sncf.fr) sells train tickets for travel within France and offers *la Carte 12-25,* which, for a one-time €49 fee, guarantees reduced prices if you want to hop around France. If you're traveling to France from another country, check out **Rail Europe** (www. raileurope.com). **Gare du Nord** (112 rue de Maubeuge) is the arrival point for trains from northern France and Germany, as well as Amsterdam (⑤ €130. ⌚ 3½hr.), Brussels (⑤ €90. ⌚ 1hr.), and London. (⑤ €50-120. ⌚ 2½hr.) **Gare de l'Est** (78 bd de Strasbourg) receives trains from eastern France, southern Germany, Austria, Hungary, Munich (⑤ €125-163. ⌚ 9-10½hr.) and Prague. (⑤ €118-172. ⌚ 12-15hr.) **Gare de Lyon** (20 bd Diderot) has trains from: Florence (⑤ €135-170. ⌚ 9-12hr.); Lyon (⑤ €60-70. ⌚ 2hr.); Marseille (⑤ €45-70. ⌚ 3-4hr.); Nice (⑤ €100. ⌚ 5½hr.); Rome. (⑤ €177-200. ⌚ 12-15hr.). **Gare d'Austerlitz** (85 quai d'Austerlitz) services the Loire Valley and the Iberian peninsula, including Barcelona (⑤ €135-170. ⌚ 7-12hr.) and Madrid. (⑤ €220-300. ⌚ 12-13hr.) **Gare St-Lazare** (13 rue d'Amsterdam) will welcome you from northern France, while **Gare Montparnasse** (17 bd Vaugirard) is for trains from northeastern and southwestern France.

GETTING AROUND

By Metro

In general, the Metro is easy to navigate, and trains run swiftly and frequently. Pick up a colorful map at any station. Metro stations themselves are a distinctive part of the Paris landscape and are marked with an "M" or with the *"Métropolitain"* lettering designed by Art Nouveau legend Hector Guimard. The earliest trains start running around 5:30am, and the last ones leave the end-of-the-line stations (the *portes de Paris*) at about 12:15am during the week (2:15am on Friday and Saturday). Connections to other lines are indicated by orange *correspondance* signs, and exits indicated by blue *sortie* signs. Transfers are free if made within a station, but it's not always possible to reverse direction on the same line without exiting. Hold onto your ticket until you exit the Metro and pass the point marked *Limite de Validité des Billets;* a uniformed RATP *contrôleur* (inspector) may request to see it on any train. If you're caught without one, you must pay a €40 fine on the spot. Don't count on buying a ticket late at night, either—some ticket windows close as early as 10pm, and many close before the last train arrives. It's a good idea to carry one more ticket than you need, although large stations have ticket machines that accept coins. Tickets cost €1.70 per journey, although it's much more useful to but a *carnet* of 10 tickets for €12. Avoid the most dangerous stations (Barbès-Rochechouart, Pigalle, Anvers, Châtelet-Les Halles, Gare du Nord, Gare de l'Est) after dark. When in doubt, take a bus or taxi.

By RER

The RER *(Réseau Express Régional)* is the RATP's suburban train system, which passes through central Paris. The RER travels much faster than the Metro. There are five RER lines, marked A-E, with different branches designated by a number. The newest line, the E, is called the Eole *(Est-Ouest Liaison Express)* and links Gare Magenta to Gare St-Lazare. Within central Paris, the RER works exactly the same as the Metro, requiring the same ticket

How to Metro

You'll hear it a thousand times: keep your Metro ticket until you exit. If you don't, you may well be caught and, according to French punishment, be horribly shamed in public as well as having to pay a fine. Here are some other Metro tips to be aware of:

- **NO SMOKING:** But that doesn't mean people won't light up while on the exit escalator.

- **MONEY ISSUES:** Unless you have a European credit card, bring coins. Change machines are notoriously hard to find, and shops are not quick to change your €10 note. We've seen many a tear over this problem in the early morning when the red eye from JFK comes in.

- **CONNECTIONS:** The Metro is designed so you only need to make one transfer to get anywhere in the city. But don't be silly—following this rule might mean traveling halfway across the city in the wrong direction just to change just to change lines.. Instead, brush up on your pronunciation of *"correspondence,"* swallow your obsession with efficiency, and take the multiple connections in significantly less time.

at the same price. The principal stops within the city, which link the RER to the Metro, are Gare du Nord, Nation, Charles de Gaulle-Étoile, Gare de Lyon, Châtelet-Les Halles, St-Michel, and Denfert-Rochereau. The electric signboards next to each track list all the possible stops for trains running on that track. Be sure that the little square next to your destination is lit up. Trips to the suburbs require more expensive tickets, which can also be bought at the automatic booths where you buy Metro tickets. You must know what zone you're going to in order to buy the proper ticket. You'll need your ticket to exit the RER station. Insert your ticket just as you did to enter, and pass through. Like the Metro, the RER runs 5:30am-12:30am on weekdays and 5:30am-2:30am on weekends.

By Bus

Although slower than the Metro, a bus ride can be a cheap sightseeing tour and a helpful introduction to the city's layout. Bus tickets are the same as those used for the Metro and can be purchased in Metro stations or from the bus driver (€1.70). Enter the bus through the front door and punch your ticket by pushing it into the machine by the driver's seat. Inspectors may ask to see your ticket, so hold onto it until you get off. When you want to get off, press the red button so the *arrêt demandé* (stop requested) sign lights up. Most buses run daily 7am-8:30pm, although those marked **Autobus du nuit** continue until 1:30am. Still others, named **Noctilien,** run all night (🕐 M-Th approximately every 30min., F-Sa approximately every 15min., Su approximately every 30min.). Look for bus stops marked with a moon sign. Check out www.noctilien.fr or inquire at a major Metro station or at Gare de l'Est for more information on Noctilien buses. Bus map routes are posted at the bus stops, as individual lines only give out contorted maps of their own routes. Noctilien #2 runs to all the major train stations along the periphery of Paris, while #12 and #13 run between Châtelet and Gare de Montparnasse.

By Taxi

Traveling by taxi in Paris can be intimidating. Parisian taxis usually have three fares that change based on the time of day and day of the week. Rush hours and early morning hours on the weekends are the priciest, whereas morning until midday fares on weekdays are the cheapest. They are measured out by the kilometer, and only switch to waiting time if the trip is over an hour. A taxi ride lasting 20min. will typically cost €6-10, and a long ride of nearly 40min. will be as much as €20-30. Taxis are easily hailed from any major boulevard or avenue, but stands are often outside major Metro intersections. From the airport, prices skyrocket to around €80-100.

By Bike

If you happen to have a screw loose, hate gambling with timetables, or just don't feel like walking, bike rentals may be for you. There are many **Vélib'** stations around the city where you can rent a public bike for prices ranging from free (under 30min.) to €7 (up to 2hr.). You can return the bike at any Vélib' station, not just the one you rented it from. Before you leave, check to see if your destination has open spots, as machines will not feel bad for you if you're late and can't find somewhere to park. Those at the top of hills are generally open, and those at the bottom are typically not; near major tourist spots are generally safe, and the quais are often open. You must have a credit card with a chip on it to use the automatic booths where you rent. **Paris Bike Tour** also offers bike rentals for €20 for a 24hr. period; each extra day costs €10. (38 rue de Saintonge ☎01 42 74 22 14 🕗 Open 9:30am-6:30pm.) The bad news is they require a €250 deposit and a copy of photo ID.

PRACTICALITIES

For all the hostels, cafes, museums, and bars we list, we know some of the most important places you visit during your trip might actually be more mundane. Whether it's a tourist office, internet cafe, or post office, these practicalities are vital to a successful trip, and you'll find all you need right here.

- **TOURIST OFFICES: Bureau Central d'Accueil** provides maps and tour information and books accommodations. (25 rue des Pyramides ☎01 49 52 42 63; www.parisinfo.com ✚ ⓂPyramides. 🕗 Open daily May-Oct 9am-7pm; Nov-Apr 10am-7pm.) Other locations at Gare du Nord (☎01 45 26 94 82), Gare de Lyon (☎08 92 68 30 00), and Montmartre. (21 pl. du Tertre ☎01 42 62 21 21 🕗 Open daily 10am-7pm.)

- **TOURS: Bateaux-Mouches** offers boat tours along the Seine. (Port de la Conférence, Pont de l'Alma ☎01 42 25 02 28; www.bateaux-mouches.fr ✚ ⓂAlma-Marceau or Franklin Roosevelt. *i* Tours in English. Ⓢ €11, under 12 €5.50. 🕗 Apr-Sept every 20-45min. M-F 10:15am-11pm; Oct-Mar every 45-60min. M-F 11am-9pm, Sa-Su 10:15am-9pm.)

- **GLBT RESOURCES: Paris Gay Village.** (61/63 rue Beaubourg ☎01 43 57 21 47; www.parisgayvillage.com ✚ ⓂRambuteau. *i* English-speaking staff. 🕗 Open M 6-8pm, Tu 3-8pm, W 12:30-8pm, Th 3-8pm, F-Sa 12:30-8pm.)

- **STUDENT RESOURCES: Centre d'Information et de Documentation pour la Jeunesse** provides information on temporary work, job placement, tourism info, and housing for students studying in Paris. (101 quai Branly ☎01 44 49 12 00; www.cidj.com ✚ ⓂBir-Hakeim. 🕗 Open M-W 10am-6pm, Th 1-6pm, F 10am-6pm, Sa 9:30am-1pm.)

- **TICKET AGENCIES: FNAC.** (74 av. des Champs-Élysées ☎01 41 57 32 19; www.fnacspectacles.com ✚ ⓂFranklin D.

Roosevelt. *i* There are various other FNAC stores throughout Paris; check www.fnac.fr for more locations. ⏰ Open M-Sa 10am-11:45pm, Su noon-11:45pm.)

- **INTERNET: American Library in Paris** has computers and internet access for members or guests with day passes. (10 rue du Général Camou ☎01 53 59 12 60; www.americanlibraryinparis.org ⇄ ⓂÉcole Militaire. ⏰ Open Tu-Sa 10am-7pm.) There is also free Wi-Fi at **Centre Pompidou** and in its **Bibliothèque Publique d'Information.** (pl. Georges Pompidou, rue Beaubourg ⇄ ⓂRambuteau or Hôtel de Ville. ⏰ Center open M 11am-9pm, W-Su 11am-9pm. Library open M noon-10pm, W-F noon-10pm, Sa-Su 11am-10pm.)

- **POST OFFICES: La Poste** (www.laposte.fr) runs the French postal system. There are many post offices in Paris; the most centrally located are in St-Germain (118 bd St-Germain

Emergency

Practicalities are great, but some things are particularly important, and we present those to you here. Hopefully you never need any of these things, but if you do, it's best to be prepared.

- **EMERGENCY NUMBERS:** Ambulance (SAMU): ☎15. Fire: ☎18. Police: ☎17.
- **POLICE: Préfecture de Police.** (9 bd Palais ☎01 58 80 80 80 ⇄ ⓂCité. Across the street from the Palais de Justice. ⏰ Open 24hr.)
- **CRISIS LINES: SOS Help!** is an emergency hotline for English speakers. (☎01 46 21 46 46 ⏰ Open daily 3-11pm.)
- **LATE-NIGHT PHARMACIES: Pharmacie Les Champs.** (84 av. des Champs-Élysées ☎01 45 62 02 41 ⇄ ⓂFranklin Roosevelt.) **Grande Pharmacie Daumesnil.** (6 pl. Félix Eboué ☎01 43 43 19 03 ⇄ ⓂDaumesnil.) **Pharmacie européenne.** (6 pl. de Clichy ☎01 48 74 65 18 ⇄ ⓂPl. de Clichy.)
- **HOSPITALS/MEDICAL SERVICES: American Hospital of Paris.** (63 bd Victor Hugo ☎01 46 41 25 25; www.american-hospital.org ⇄ ⓂPort Maillot then bus #82, or take bus #82 from Jardin du Luxembourg to its terminus.) **Hôpital Bichat.** (46 rue Henri Huchard ☎01 40 25 80 80 ⇄ ⓂPorte de St-Ouen.)

♯ Ⓜ️Odéon. 🕐 Open M-F 8am-8pm, Sa 9am-5pm.) and Châtelet-Les Halles. (1 rue Pierre Lescot ♯ Ⓜ️Les-Halles. 🕐 Open M-F 8am-6:30pm, Sa 9am-1pm.)

SAFETY AND HEALTH

General Advice

In any type of crisis, the most important thing to do is **stay calm.** Your country's embassy abroad is usually your best resource in an emergency; registering with that embassy upon arrival in the country is a good idea. The government offices listed in the **Travel Advisories** feature at the end of this section can provide information on the services they offer their citizens in case of emergencies abroad.

Local Laws and Police

La Police Nationale is the branch of French law enforcement that is most often seen in urban areas like Paris. To reach the Parisian police, call ☎17.

Drugs and Alcohol

Although mention of France often conjures images of black-clad smokers in berets, **France no longer allows smoking in public as of 2008.** The government has no official policy on berets. Possession of illegal drugs (including marijuana) in France can result in a substantial jail sentence or fine. Police may arbitrarily stop and search anyone on the street.

There is no drinking age in Paris, but restaurants will not serve anyone under the age of 16, and to purchase alcohol you must be at least 18 years old. Though there is no law prohibiting open containers, drinking on the street is considered uncouth. The legal blood-alcohol level for driving in France is 0.05%, which is less than it is in the US, UK, New Zealand, and Ireland, so exercise appropriate caution if operating a vehicle in France.

Disabled and GLBT Travelers

Fear not—Paris loves you. **L'Association des Paralysés de France, Délégation de Paris** is an organization devoted to helping the disabled in Paris. In addition to promoting disabled individuals' fundamental rights to state compensation, public transportation, and handicapped-conscious jobs, the association also organizes international vacations. (17 bd Auguste Blanqui ♪01 53 80 92 97.)

Le Centre Lesbien, Gai, Bi et Trans de Paris et Île-de-France functions both as a counseling agency in and of itself, offering counseling and reception services for limited times during the week, and as the umbrella organization and formal location for many other GLBT resource organizations in Paris. (63 rue Beaubourg ♪01 43 57 21 47 ⚲ ⓜRambuteau or ⓜLes Halles. ☒ Administrative reception open M 1-8pm, Tu 10am-1pm and 2-6pm, W 1pm-7m, Th-F 1pm-6pm.)

Specific Concerns

Demonstrations and Political Gatherings

The French Revolution may have been in 1789, but the spirit of the revolution certainly hasn't died. Protests and strikes—or *grèves,* as the locals call them—are frequent in Paris, and can be over anything from the minimum wage to Sarkozy's wardrobe choices, but violence does not often occur (unless he wears white after Labor Day). You may find yourself stuck in the city on the day of a transit strike (as one *Let's Go* researcher did), but who hasn't always wanted to ride a Vespa?

Pre-Departure Health

Matching a prescription to a foreign equivalent is not always easy, safe, or possible, so if you take **prescription drugs,** carry up-to-date prescriptions or a statement from your doctor stating the medications' trade names, manufacturers, chemical names, and dosages. Be sure to keep all medication with you in your carry-on luggage. It is also a good idea to look up the French names of drugs you may need during your trip.

Immunizations and Precautions

Travelers over two years old should make sure that the following vaccines are up to date: MMR (for measles, mumps, and rubella); DTaP or Td (for diphtheria, tetanus, and pertussis); IPV (for polio); Hib (for *Haemophilus influenzae* B); and HepB (for Hepatitis

B). For recommendations on immunizations and prophylaxis, check with a doctor and consult the **Centers for Disease Control and Prevention (CDC)** in the US (☎+1-800-232-4636; www.cdc. gov/travel) or the equivalent in your home country.

Travel Advisories

The following government offices provide travel information and advisories:

- **AUSTRALIA: Department of Foreign Affairs and Trade.** (☎+61 2 6261 1111; www.smartraveller.gov.au)

- **CANADA: Department of Foreign Affairs and International Trade.** Call or visit the website for the free booklet *Bon Voyage, But...* (☎+1-800-267-6788; www.international.gc.ca)

- **NEW ZEALAND: Ministry of Foreign Affairs and Trade.** (☎+64 4 439 8000; www.safetravel.govt.nz)

- **UK: Foreign and Commonwealth Office.** (☎+44 845 850 2829; www.fco.gov.uk)

- **US: Department of State.** (☎888-407-4747 from the US, +1-202-501-4444 elsewhere; http://travel.state.gov)

KEEPING IN TOUCH

By Email and Internet

Hello and welcome to the 21st century, where you're rarely more than a 5min. walk from the nearest Wi-Fi hot spot, even if sometimes you'll have to pay a few bucks or buy a drink for the privilege of using it. **Internet cafes** and free internet terminals are listed in the **Practicalities** section above. Surprisingly, one of the best ways to access free Wi-Fi in Paris is to hit up a good ol' McDonald's. For lists of additional cybercafes in Paris, check out www.cybercaptive.com and www.cybercafes.com.

    Wireless hot spots make internet access possible in public and remote places. Unfortunately, they also pose security risks. Hot spots are public, open networks that use unencrypted, unsecured connections. They are susceptible to hacks and "packet sniffing"—the theft of passwords and other private information. To prevent problems, disable "ad hoc" mode, turn off file sharing and network discovery, encrypt your email, turn on your firewall, beware of phony networks, and watch for over-the-shoulder creeps.

By Telephone

Calling Home from Paris

If you have internet access, your best—i.e., cheapest, most convenient, and most tech-savvy—means of calling home is probably our good friend 🄢Skype (www.skype.com). You can even videochat if you have one of those new-fangled webcams. Calls to other Skype users are free; calls to landlines and mobiles worldwide start at US$0.023 per minute, depending on where you're calling.

For those still stuck in the 20th century, **prepaid phone cards** are a common and relatively inexpensive means of calling abroad. Each one comes with a Personal Identification Number (PIN) and a toll-free access number. You call the access number and then follow the directions for dialing your PIN. To purchase prepaid phone cards, check online for the best rates; www.callingcards.com is a good place to start. Online providers generally send your access number and PIN via email, with no actual "card" involved. You can also call home with prepaid phone cards purchased in Paris.

Another option is a **calling card,** linked to a major national telecommunications service in your home country. Calls are billed collect or to your account. Cards generally come with instructions for dialing both domestically and internationally.

Placing a collect call through an international operator can be expensive but may be necessary in case of an emergency. You can frequently call collect without even possessing a company's calling card just by calling its access number and following the instructions.

Cellular Phones

In France, mobile pay-as-you-go phones are the way to go. The two largest carriers are **SFR** and **Orange,** and they are so readily available that even supermarkets sell them. Cellphone calls and texts can be paid for without signing a contract with a **Mobicarte** prepaid card, available at Orange and SFR stores, as well as tabacs.

You can often buy phones for €20-40, which includes various amounts of minutes and 100 texts. Calling the US from one of these phones is around €0.80 a minute, with texts coming in at around €0.50.

International Calls

To call France from home or to call home from France, dial:

1. **THE INTERNATIONAL DIALING PREFIX.** To call from **France, Ireland, New Zealand,** or the **UK,** dial ☎00; from **Australia,** ☎0011; and from **Canada** or the **US,** ☎001.

2. **THE COUNTRY CODE OF THE COUNTRY YOU WANT TO CALL.** To call **France,** dial ☎33, for **Australia,** ☎61; **Canada** or the **US,** ☎1; **Ireland,** ☎353; **New Zealand,** ☎64; and for the **UK,** ☎44.

3. **THE LOCAL NUMBER.** If the area code begins with a zero, you can omit that number when dialing from abroad.

By Snail Mail

Sending Mail Home from Paris
Airmail is the best way to send mail home from Paris. Write "airmail" or *"par avion"* on the front. For simple letters or postcards, airmail tends to be surprisingly cheap, but the price will go up sharply for weighty packages. Surface mail is by far the cheapest, slowest, and most antiquated way to send mail. It takes one to two months to cross the Atlantic and one to three to cross the Pacific—good for heavy items you won't need for a while, like souvenirs that you've acquired along the way. Sending a postcard from France costs €0.56, while sending letters (up to 20g) to Australia, Canada, New Zealand, or the US costs €0.85.

Receiving Mail in Paris
In addition to the standard postage system, **Federal Express** handles express mail services from most countries to France (☎+1-800-463-3339; www.fedex.com).

There are several ways to arrange pickup of letters sent to you while you are in Paris, even if you do not have an address of your own. Mail can be sent via **Poste Restante** to Paris, but it is not very reliable. Address Poste Restante letters like so:

Nicolas SARKOZY
Poste Restante
Paris, France

The mail will go to a special desk in the central post office at 52 rue du Louvre, unless you specify a local post office by street address or postal code. It's best to use the largest post office, since mail may be sent there regardless. Bring your passport (or other photo ID) for pickup; there may be a small fee. If the clerks insist that there is nothing for you, ask them to check under your first name as well. *Let's Go* lists post offices in the **Practicalities** section (above). It is usually safer and quicker, though more expensive, to send mail express or registered. If you don't want to deal with Poste Restante, consider asking your hostel or accommodation if you can have things mailed to you there. Of course, if you have your own mailing address or a reliable friend to receive mail for you, that will be the easiest solution.

TIME DIFFERENCES

France is 1hr. ahead of Greenwich Mean Time (GMT) and observes Daylight Saving Time. This means that it is 6hr. ahead of New York City, 9hr. ahead of Los Angeles, 1hr. ahead of the British Isles, 9hr. behind Sydney, and 11hr. behind New Zealand. Don't accidentally call your mom at 5am!

CLIMATE

As pleasantly romantic as it is to think of springtime in Paris, *le printemps* doesn't last forever. Paris has a temperate climate with four seasons. The Northern Atlantic current keeps weather from approaching any extremes. Winters in Paris can be cold, but heavy snow is not characteristic of the City of Light. Springtime in Paris is definitely a lovely time of year, even if it does come kind of late. Flowers bloom, trees grow leaves—it's everything you've read about. Summers are comfortable for the most part, though some days in August will have you wishing you had picked a city closer to a beach. Fall is brisk but enjoyable as the city's foliage changes before your eyes.

MONTH	AVG. HIGH TEMP.		AVG. LOW TEMP.		AVG. RAINFALL		AVG. NUMBER OF WET DAYS
January	6°C	43°F	1°C	34°F	56mm	2.2 in.	17
February	7°C	45°F	1°C	34°F	46mm	1.8 in.	14
March	12°C	54°F	4°C	39°F	35mm	1.4 in.	12
April	16°C	61°F	6°C	43°F	42mm	1.7 in.	13
May	20°C	68°F	10°C	50°F	57mm	2.2 in.	12
June	23°C	73°F	13°C	55°F	54mm	2.1 in.	12
July	25°C	77°F	15°C	59°F	59mm	2.3 in.	12
August	24°C	76°F	14°C	57°F	64mm	2.5 in.	13
September	21°C	70°F	12°C	54°F	55mm	2.2 in.	13
October	16°C	61°F	8°C	46°F	50mm	1.9 in.	13
November	10°C	50°F	5°C	41°F	51mm	2.0 in.	15
December	7°C	45°F	2°C	36°F	50mm	1.9 in.	16

To convert from degrees Fahrenheit to degrees Celsius, subtract 32 and multiply by 5/9. To convert from Celsius to Fahrenheit, multiply by 9/5 and add 32. The mathematically challenged may use this handy chart:

°CELSIUS	-5	0	5	10	15	20	25	30	35	40
°FAHRENHEIT	23	32	41	50	59	68	77	86	95	104

MEASUREMENTS

Like the rest of the rational world, Paris uses the metric system. The basic unit of length is the meter (m), which is divided into 100 centimeters (cm) or 1000 millimeters (mm). One thousand meters make up one kilometer (km). Fluids are measured in liters (L), each divided into 1000 milliliters (mL). A liter of pure water weighs one kilogram (kg), the unit of mass that is divided into 1000 grams (g). One metric ton is 1000kg.

MEASUREMENT CONVERSIONS	
1 inch (in.) = 25.4mm	1 millimeter (mm) = 0.039 in.
1 foot (ft.) = 0.305m	1 meter (m) = 3.28 ft.
1 yard (yd.) = 0.914m	1 meter (m) = 1.094 yd.
1 mile (mi.) = 1.609km	1 kilometer (km) = 0.621 mi.
1 ounce (oz.) = 28.35g	1 gram (g) = 0.035 oz.
1 pound (lb.) = 0.454kg	1 kilogram (kg) = 2.205 lb.
1 fluid ounce (fl. oz.) = 29.57mL	1 milliliter (mL) = 0.034 fl. oz.
1 gallon (gal.) = 3.785L	1 liter (L) = 0.264 gal.

LANGUAGE

You hopefully won't be surprised to learn that the official language in Paris is French. English speakers will be happy to note that English is the most commonly taught foreign langauge in France, followed by Spanish and German. Although American tourists get a bad rap in Paris, many *parisiens*—especially the youngsters—are eager to speak English with foreigners. So when you start speaking French to a stranger on the street and they respond in English, don't take it personally. However, don't assume that everyone speaks English. Centuries of snootiness and making nasally sounds have made the French experts at turning their noses up at obnoxious monolingual tourists. The key is to try—*par politesse*—with whatever attempted French accent you can, some of the daily formalities of *"bonjour"* and *"merci"* if you want your *pain au chocolat*.

Pronunciation

Reading French can be tricky, but the table below should help you avoid some of the upturned noses.

PHONETIC UNIT	PRONUNCIATION	PHONETIC UNIT	PRONUNCIATION
au	o, as in "go"	ch	sh, as in "shoe"
oi	ua as in "guava"	ou	oo, as in "igloo"
ai	ay as in "lay"	å	ah, as in "menorah"

Phrasebook

ENGLISH	FRENCH	PRONUNCIATION
Hello!/Hi!	Bonjour!	bohn-jhoor
Goodbye!	Au revoir!	oh ruh-vwah
Yes.	Oui	wee
No.	Non	nohn
Sorry!	Désolé!	day-zoh-lay
EMERGENCY		
Go away!	Allez-vous en!	ah-lay vooz on
Help!	Au secours!	oh sek-oor
Call the police!	Appelez les flics!	apple-ay lay fleeks
Get a doctor!	Allez chercher un médecin!	ah-lay share-shay un mayd-sin
Police Station	Poste de Police	Exactly like you'd think.
Hospital	Hôpital	Ho-pee-tal
Liquor store	Magasin d'alcool	Maga-zahn dal-cool

FOOD		
Waiter/waitress	Serveur/serveuse	server/servers
I'd like...	Je voudrais	je voo-dray
Thank you!	Merci	mare-see
Check please!	L'addition, s'il-vous-plait!	Lah-dee-sion, seal-voo-play
Where is...	Où est...?	Oo ay

ENGLISH	FRENCH	ENGLISH	FRENCH
I am from the US/Europe.	Je suis des Etats-Unis/de l'Europe.	What's the problem, sir/madam?	Quelle est la problème, monsieur/madame?
I have a visa/ID.	J'ai un visa/une carte d'identité.	I lost my passport/luggage.	J'ai perdu mon passeport/baggage.
I will be here for less than three months.	Je serai ici pour de moins trois mois.	I have nothing to declare.	Je n'ai rien à déclarer.
You are the woman of my dreams.	Vous êtes la femme de mes rêves.	Perhaps I can help you with that?	Peut-être je peux vous aider avec ça?
Your hostel, or mine?	Votre hôtel, ou le mien?	Do you have protection?	Avez-vous un préservatif?
I would like a round-trip ticket.	Je voudrais un billet aller-retour.	Where is the train station?	Où est la gare?
Can I see a double room?	Puis-je voir un chambre pour deux?	How much does this cost?	Combien ça coûte?
Where is the bathroom?	Où sont les toilettes?	Is there a bar near here?	Est-ce qu'il y a un bar près d'ici?
What time is the next train?	À quelle heure est le prochain train?	Do you have this bathing suit in another size?	Avez-vous ce maillot de bain dans une autre taille?
Can I have another drink please?	Puis-je prendre un autre boisson s'il vous-plait?	Please don't arrest me!	S'il vous plait, ne m'arrêtez pas!
I'm in a committed relationship.	Je suis dans une relation engagée.	You talkin' to me?	Vous me parlez?
It was like this when I got here.	C'était comme ça quand je suis arrivé(e).	I don't speak much French.	Je ne parle pas beaucoup de français.
I feel sick.	Je me sens malade.	Leave me alone!	Laissez-moi tranquille!
What time does reception close?	À quelle heure est-ce que la réception ferme?	I don't understand.	Je ne comprends pas.
Actually, I'm from Canada.	En fait, je suis Canadien(ne).	I didn't vote for him, I swear.	Je n'ai pas voté pour lui, je le jure.
Of course not!	Bah, non!	Does it inconvenience you if I...?	Est-ce que ça vous dérange si je...?
Do you have a map? I'm lost in your eyes.	Est-ce que tu as un plan? Je me suis perdu dans tes yeux.	Excuse me, I lost my phone number. Can I borrow yours?	Excuse-moi, j'ai perdu mon numéro de téléphone. Est-ce que je peux emprunter le tien?

Essentials

Let's Go Online

Plan your next trip on our spiffy website, **www.letsgo.com.** It features full book content, the latest travel info on your favorite destinations, and tons of interactive features: make your own itinerary, read blogs from our trusty Researcher-Writers, browse our photo library, watch exclusive videos, check out our newsletter, find travel deals, follow us on Facebook, and buy new guides. Plus, if this Essentials wasn't enough for you, we've got even more online. We're always updating and adding new features, so check back often!

Paris 101

You don't need to understand French—or speak with an affected accent—to know that Paris is a big deal (and that Parisians think so too). The allure of visiting the City of Light will never fade. Whether it be for romance, food, or fashion, Paris is at the top of practically everyone's list of desired vacation spots. It's a fashionista's one true love and a culinary enthusiast's heaven, yes, but the city has more to offer than Coco Chanel and croissants. The history and environment of Paris's culture have influenced almost every aspect of Western life: politics, art, and rapidly growing obesity rates, to name a few. *C'est la vie* after all—when in Paris, Parisian life seems like the one most people want to live. But do you really want to be that tourist who gawks and fawns over every Parisian you see, adamantly proclaiming your wish to be one of them, when all you're really doing is screaming, "Look at me! I'm a foreigner!"? Didn't think so. Read on to see Paris's rises and falls over the years, because even this idealized European sanctuary has had its low points. Then sit back, pour yourself a glass of wine (or three), and peruse our advice on how to walk, talk, and act like you've lived in Paris all your life.

Facts and Figures

- **PERCENTAGE OF FRENCH POPULATION THAT LIVES IN PARIS:** 20%
- **STEPS TO THE TOP OF THE EIFFEL TOWER:** 1665
- **NUMBER OF HEADS THAT ROLLED DURING THE REIGN OF TERROR:** 2800
- **POUNDS OF CHEESE CONSUMED ANNUALLY PER PERSON:** 40
- **PERCENTAGE OF THE CITY'S POPULATION THAT DIED IN THE BLACK DEATH:** 50%
- **NUMBER OF DAYS IT TOOK TO BUILD NOTRE DAME:** 31,755

HISTORY

Très, Très Long Ago (250 BCE-52 CE)

Paris is more than 2000 years old; the first inhabitants of the area hit the scene around 250 BCE. *Au début* (that's fancy talk for "in the beginning"), a tribe called the **Parisii of Gaul** formed a small fishing village beside the Seine River, naming their town **Lutetia.** Besides its location, Lutetia shared little with modern Paris—it was established during the second Iron Age, so the first Parisians lacked the elegant city luxury and swagger that they have today. But not everything about the town has dissolved with time: while Lutetia was founded on the left bank of the Seine, the right was left abandoned due to a flourishing marsh, or *marais*—hence the neighborhood name today.

Roman Glory (52-250)

The people of Lutetia weren't walking around with clubs, though: they were civilized. They even created their own currency. But, alas, sovereignty was not to be. **Julius Caesar,** along with his army of overambitious Romans, set his sights on the city in 52 BCE. The Parisii put up a valiant fight under Vercingétorix, their determined leader, but were ultimately defeated at the Battle of Alesia, setting a trend that would later prove unbreakable. To honor the Gauls' effort, Napoleon III had a 7m statue of Vercingétorix built in Alesia in 1865. A French inscription on the larger-than-life statue reads, "The Gauls united, forming a single nation animated by the same spirit, can defy the universe." As history has shown, this is a lie.

Under Caesar, however, the city grew larger and became an important center of the Roman Empire. Paris's first churches were built in the third century as **Saint Denis,** the city's first bishop, attempted to Christianize the city. Although Christianization was a success, St. Denis was abruptly decapitated (another trend, perhaps?) in 250.

Hometown Heroes (451-1000)

Always a group of active people (especially in war), Parisians took a hands-on approach to protect their city from renowned sweetheart **Attila the Hun** in 451: they prayed. Remarkably the prayers led by Ste. Geneviève repelled Attila from the city, or so the story goes. Geneviève was then named a patron saint of the city for making Parisians believe they could defend themselves without really doing much at all.

In 800, the Pope crowned **Charlemagne,** King of the Frankish people, as Holy Roman Emperor after he expanded the empire from Spain to Italy. Around two centuries later, Hugh Capet, the Count of Paris, became King of France, and Paris was soon renamed the capital of the country, generating an eternity of Parisian pride.

French Toast (1000-1643)

Under the leader Étienne Marcel, Paris became an independent commune in 1358. With the Holy Roman Emperor out of their hair, Frenchmen were now left to sort out their own problems during times of great political and religious conflict. This was a daunting task, since dealing with issues was not exactly a Parisian fort*e*. Perhaps sensing a dangerous future for the country's capital, in 1180 King Phillipe Auguste built a highly protected castle known today as the Louvre. Later kings held significantly weaker grips on the city. In 1407, civil war swept Paris, and in 1430, the English won control of the city for the following six years of the Hundred Years' War. In 1537, around 10,000 Protestants were murdered in the Saint Bartholomew's Day Massacre—the worst moment of the long period of religious conflict brought on by the Reformation.

You Say You Want a Revolution (1643-1799)

Unfortunately for the French aristocracy, this was not the end of unrest in Paris. Perhaps due to **Louis XIV's** obscenely luxurious lifestyle during his rule from 1643-1715, and also to the suggestion of his grandson's wife (a young Austrian by the name of **Marie Antoinette**) that those short on bread should just eat cake, the dregs of French society decided it was time to do something. Storming the Bastille prison seemed like a good idea, and that's just what they did on July 14, 1789. Three years later, the monarchy crumbled. These would be seen as the calm years of the revolution, as **Robespierre** and his Committee of Public Safety decided in 1793 to ensure the safety of Louis XVI, Marie Antoinette, and around 3000 others by politely offing their heads.

Shorty Breaks It Down (1799-1914)

Fed up with Robespierre's unhealthy relationship with the guillotine and the ineffectiveness of those who followed him, **Napoleon Bonaparte** overthrew the revolutionary government in 1799. Rewriting the constitution and issuing his own standardized "Napoleonic Code," Napoleon had ambitions that were larger than he was. In 1804, he somehow managed to convince people that naming himself Emperor was totally consistent with the ideals of the revolution. Though his domain at one point stretched from Spain to Russia, the 1815 **Battle of Waterloo** put a damper on his plans. Defeated, Napoleon was exiled to the tropical island of Saint Helena, setting a precedent that the punishment for trying to take over the world is to be forced to chill out in paradise for the rest of your life.

The next hundred years witnessed steady growth in technology, infrastructure, and culture, as well as a healthy smattering of further revolutions. Napoleon's nephew even showed up for a while and defied both republicanism and the rules of counting by ruling for 18 years as **Napoleon III**.

Check Out These Guns (1914-Present)

While the stalemate on the Western Front prevented the German forces from reaching Paris in WWI, the second time around the French were not so lucky. Hitler's forces occupied the city from 1940-44. Most of Paris's historical buildings and monuments were spared from the destruction of the war, but over half a million French citizens were not as lucky.

In 1958, undaunted by the failure of the first four, France embarked on the Fifth Republic. This nearly fell in May 1968 when student demonstrations took over the streets of Paris and eventually escalated into a nationwide general strike. The crisis passed, however, and since then the French government has demonstrated an uncharacteristic stability.

Since taking office in 2007, President **Nicolas Sarkozy** has personally maintained the city's reputation for elegance through his refined eye for accessories, such as third wife Carla Bruni. In Paris, the position of mayor has been held since 2001 by **Bertrand Delanoë,** an openly gay socialist, proving once again that France is nothing like America.

CUSTOMS AND ETIQUETTE

To put it as simply as possible, Parisians are picky. Here's how to attempt to fit in:

How to Win Friends

Everyone knows the stereotype of the unfriendly, pretentious Parisian, but, if you exhibit basic manners, most will simply label you as a foreigner and remain civil. Of course, what's defined as basic manners is a little more extensive in this noble city. Here are the basics. It is important to greet everyone that you interact with as *monsieur* or *madame.* Meeting friends, it is common to kiss once on each cheek, but upon first introductions, a handshake is acceptable. Simply saying please (*s'il vous plaît*) and thank you (*merci,* optional *beaucoup*) will earn you respect. Along those lines, Parisians will appreciate any attempts at speaking French; *bonjour, bonsoir,* and *pardon* are your three favorite words starting now.

How to Get By

At a restaurant, waiters will not bring you the bill unless you ask for it, and, although **tips** are usually included in the check, most customers add an extra five percent to go directly to the waiters. A 2008 law bans smoking in restaurants and bars, so don't test your luck. Be aware of crazy driving in the capital. Even the childhood "look both ways" lesson may not always cut it in Paris. Most public restrooms are free, but beware: most self-clean after every use, so get out of there fast unless you also want a shower.

Table Manners for Dummies

Simply staying nourished in Paris may be the most difficult task of all. When repeating proper table manners for the third time, at the third meal of the day, your mother was just plain old annoying. "No one's going to terminate a friendship over the occasional elbow on the table," you thought. Well, in Paris they just might. At a meal, don't think about eating before someone says, *"Bon appétit!"* If invited to a dinner party, it's polite to send flowers to the host beforehand, and be prepared to clean your plate completely; it is bad form to leave any food uneaten, as it can be seen as an insult to the cook and not a reflection of your appetite. Resist the temptation to fill wine glasses up to the top, no matter how delicious the wine. Although knives and forks are used to eat almost everything (even fruit), don't think about touching a knife to your salad leaves, since it is inexcusably offensive. And while the French generally abhor finger food, do not cut a baguette on the table—tear it. You may (rightfully) insist that these customs are peculiar, prissy, or pompous, to which we can only bid thee good luck.

FOOD AND DRINK

Trying to lose weight? Fat chance. You may intend to splurge on calories once in a while, but one bite of the traditional French cuisine will leave you indulging whenever you have the chance. With restaurants and cafes on every corner, dieting in Paris is almost completely out of the question. But why would you ever want to do such a thing in the first place?

Filet Mignon with a Side of Snails, S'il Vous Plaît

Whether you sit down at a bistro, bar, or sidewalk cafe, you won't run out of different dishes to enjoy. The country's luxurious cuisine dates back to the 1800s, when extravagant meals were equated with aristocratic social status. For breakfast, try a croissant, or a chocolate-filled *pain au chocolat*. Parisians typically sit down to lunch anywhere from noon to 2pm. Meals typically consist of simple salads, sandwiches on baguettes, crepes, croques-monsieur (a fancy-pants version of a grilled ham and cheese), or heavier meat dishes. Dinner may include a few fishy options: *bouillabaisse* is a popular traditional soup made from many different types of fish, and *escargots* are available at elegant restaurants for those who dare to try cooked snails. Perhaps the best part of dinner is dessert—from eclairs to chocolate mousse to crème brûlée, you'll find you have much to gain, and some bigger clothes to buy.

Drink (Read: Wine)

Okay, the header is a slight exaggeration—Parisians appreciate a good espresso in the morning and the occasional coffee after dessert. But while in Paris, it may be worthwhile to do as the Parisians do, by which we mean drink wine and lots of it. You shouldn't have difficulty doing so, as nearly all restaurants serve plenty of *vin*. Just don't be intimidated by the inordinate selection; the wine menu might look more like a textbook. If worse comes to worst, ask the waiter for a cup of the house best.

ART AND ARCHITECTURE

If you're into the above, you've definitely come to the right place. A city immersed in art itself, Paris also inspires artists to create.

Just a Few Paintings

The **Louvre,** a little museum you may have heard of, holds over 35,000 works of art, one of which is the **Mona Lisa.** This is somewhat of a big deal, despite the fact that the world's most notable painting is five times smaller than all the others surrounding it, and its glass case means you might wind up with a nice high-res photo of your camera flash. Moving forward in time from Leonardo, many famous artists from more recent movements were born in or spent time in Paris, from Impressionists like **Édouard Manet** to Fauvist **Henri Matisse.** If you're interested in modern and contemporary art, the **Centre Pompidou** is devoted to just that—even the building itself is a stunning work of modern art.

A History in the Streets

Paris's history is laid out on its streets, with buildings and monuments still standing from various architectural periods. Back in ancient times, Roman rulers built various religious buildings, like monasteries, in their favorite style: their own. During the Medieval period, the Gothic style developed, with flying buttresses suspending intricate stained glass windows and pointed arches. For examples of this, look no further than the cathedrals of **Notre Dame** and **Chartres.** During the Renaissance, proportion and balance were all the rage. This developed into the Baroque period and culminated in the flamboyance of **Versailles,** an exorbitant spectacle which the poor of Paris were rumored to have had issues with. In the 19th century, Napoleon III had Baron Georges-Eugène Haussmann renovate the streets of Paris: the wider boulevards and balconied apartment buildings that make up the city are all his work. The Industrial Revolution sparked a new form of Art Nouveau architecture that took its designs from patterns in the natural world. For an example, look up and wave hello to the **Eiffel Tower.**

FASHION

Style comes naturally to those who live in a fashion capital of Europe. Parisians, even when dressed casually, are very put together, and dressing fashionably does not always mean showing it all off—keep it classy. Remember that the gods of Chanel, Louis Vuitton, Dior, Hermès, Jean-Paul Gaultier, and Yves-St. Laurent, to name a few, reside in the area and are judging you. You can always stroll down the Champs-Elysées or hit up fashion week for inspiration, but you don't have to completely trash your current wardrobe. Jeans are acceptable in most places, but never wear sneakers to a nice restaurant.

HOLIDAYS AND FESTIVALS

With its eclectic history, Paris seems to have more obscure dates and events to celebrate than most cities. Aside from the standard Christmas, New Year's Day, and Easter, the city's festivals are unique. Keep in mind that museums and other monuments usually close on these dates.

HOLIDAY OR FESTIVAL	DESCRIPTION	DATE
Fashion Week	A week of fashion shows, complete with new styles by the world's most famous designer labels.	usually late January
Carnaval de Paris	Over 500 years old, this city carnival gives residents an excuse (as if you need one) to wear masks and parade through the streets.	March 4
VE Day	A celebration of the Allied victory over Germany in WWII. Festivities include a parade on the Champs-Elysées.	May 8

Fête de la Musique	This is pretty self-explanatory; free concerts and performances are given throughout the entire city. All types of music are performed.	June 21
Gay Pride Parade	Parades and presentations celebrate Paris's GLBT life.	mid-June
Bastille Day	This national holiday commemorates the storming of the Bastille in 1789. Kick it off with the *Bal du 14 Juillet*, a giant dance party the previous evening, and end with fireworks over the Eiffel Tower.	July 14
Beaujolais Nouveau Wine Festival	A nationwide celebration of the release of Beaujolais Nouveau wine; bar-hopping and drinking ensue.	November 15

Paris 101

Beyond Tourism

If you are reading this, then you are a member of an elite group—and we don't mean "the literate." You're a student preparing for a semester abroad. You're taking a gap year to save the trees, the whales, or the dates. You're an 80-year-old woman who has devoted her life to egg-laying platypuses and what the hell is up with that. In short, you're a traveler, not a tourist; like any good spy, you don't just observe your surroundings—you become an active part of them.

Your mission, should you choose to accept it, is to study, volunteer, or work abroad as laid out in the dossier—er, chapter—below. We leave the rest (when to go, whom to bring, and how many *Arrested Development* DVDs to pack) in your hands. This message will self-destruct in five seconds. Good luck.

STUDYING

We know, we know, it's become a cliché: the American college student heading off to France to discover Proust, Parisian men, and the perfect croissant. But there's a reason more than 15,000 students study abroad in France each year. Paris, the most popular destination, provides a mecca for the art- and architecture-inclined with its world-famous cultural landmarks. If you're already well-versed in the local tongue (and we don't mean that sexy man you met along the Seine), don't be afraid to enroll directly in the French university system. Navigating the course enrollment bureaucracy can be a nightmare, and that first *exposé oral* may be terrifying, but there's no better way to immerse yourself in Parisian life. Dozens of American-run study-abroad programs still give you an authentic French experience, but you can make your *fautes* and faux-pas in the company of fellow foreigners.

Visa Information

If you're lucky enough to have an EU passport, stop reading and count your blessings. Non-EU citizens intending to study abroad in France will need a **student visa** in order to study for more than three months. Most student visas are only valid for 90 days. Visas can be obtained at a French consulate or embassy, and will be automatically renewed for the duration of your studies. To apply for a visa, you'll need your passport, two additional passport photos, proof of enrollment, a letter from your home university certifying current enrollment, proof of financial resources, proof of insurance coverage, parental authorization if a minor, and all required vaccinations.

The visa fees are €60 for a short-term visa and €99 for a long-term student visa. Once in France, students with long-term visas must obtain a **carte de séjour** from the police proving their residency.

Universities

Students that manage to pass the *Baccalaureate* are able to enroll in a university. French universities are heavily subsidized, with students attending the Sorbonne for a mere €400 per year (and to think, American students pay upwards of US$35,000 for tuition alone). Most French students choose to live at home, rent free.

American Institute for Foreign Study (AIFS)

19 rue de Babylone

☎01 44 39 04 24; www.aifs.com

AIFS operates two programs in Paris. Students can focus on a variety of electives at the Sorbonne, or opt to concentrate primarily on French language at the Catholic University of Paris. The program includes extracurricular wine tastings, cooking classes, museum visits, and trips to national monuments.

▶ ⑤ Semester US$13,695-16,495; summer US$6495-8495. *i* Fall, spring, and summer terms available. 2-week orientation in Cannes required.

Council on International Educational Exchange (CIEE)

300 Fore St., Portland, ME, USA

☎+1-800-407-8839; www.ciee.org

CIEE hosts three programs in Paris: a semester-long course in critical studies as well as a semester or summer program in contemporary French studies. The French studies classes are intended for students who have had at least two semesters of French and are looking to improve their language skills. Students may also enroll in electives ranging from anthropology to religion.

▶ Ⓢ Semester US$13,800-16,800; 3-week summer US$3375, 6-week summer US$6550.

Arcadia University

450 S. Easton Road, Glenside, PA, USA

☎+1-866-927-2234; www.arcadia.edu/abroad

An interdisciplinary seminar entitled "History, Politics, and Diplomacy of France and Europe" forms the basis of Arcadia's semester study-abroad program in Paris. The six-week summer program has a similar focus with "Intensive French and Politics: Economics, Diplomacy, and the European Union."

▶ *i* Accommodation in dorms. Ⓢ Semester US$16,900; summer US$5990.

Institute for the International Education of Students (IES)

33 N. LaSalle Street, Chicago, IL, USA

☎+1-800-995-2300; www.iesabroad.org

IES provides a summer program in Arles; a semester- or year-long program in Nantes; and summer, semester, and year-long programs in Paris. Business students can earn a Certificate in International Management by enrolling in a full-time master's program with French and international students. Students take some of their classes on-site at the IES Abroad Center but are encouraged to take one or two courses at one of IES's French partner institutions.

▶ Ⓢ Semester US$16,700-18,215; summer US$6500-6675.

Experimental Learning International (CEA)

☎+1-800-266-4441; www.gowithcea.com

CEA instructs in English at its Global Campus in Paris, offering courses in liberal arts, social sciences, international business, art, and French culture and society.

▶ ⑤ Semester US$4945-7895. *i* Program provides shared apartments, homestays, or allows students to make individual arrangements.

Language Schools

As renowned novelist Gustave Flaubert once said, "Language is a cracked kettle on which we beat out tunes for bears to dance to." While we at *Let's Go* have absolutely no clue what he is talking about, we do know that the following are good resources for learning *la langue française.*

Alliance Française

101 bd Raspail

☎01 42 84 90 00; www.alliancefr.org

Alliance Française teaches courses for all levels of proficiency as well as evening workshops on pronunciation or writing. For those looking to work long-term in a Francophone country, professional courses on business French, legal French, tourism French, and medical French are also offered. Private and group lessons, as well as self-guided learning courses, are also available.

▶ ⑤ €50-234 per week. *i* Classes 4-20hr. per week. Personalized plans available.

Cours de Civilisation Française de la Sorbonne

47 rue des Écoles

☎01 44 10 77 00; www.ccfs-sorbonne.fr

Cours de Civilisation Française de la Sorbonne is a popular option for Americans looking for an excuse to be eligible for a student visa.

▶ ⑤ Semester courses €250-3000. *i* Regular language and civilization classes meet 12hr. per week, intensive courses meet 25hr. per week. Sessions range from 3 to 12 weeks.

Eurocentres

☎+41 44 485 5040; www.eurocentres.com

With sites in Paris, La Rochelle, and Amboise, Eurocentres offers French classes mostly in the mornings, with an option for business French. The program provides recreation rooms and internet access and organizes a variety of outings and social activities.

▶ ⑤ Courses €630-5368.

Culinary Schools

Maybe foie gras, frog legs, and *escargot* aren't on your menu back home, but you are sure to encounter these delicacies (and many more) on your travels through Paris. The city's restaurants serve all kinds of regional cuisine, and the adventurous traveler may be inspired to learn how to make some himself. We can't promise your creations will be as delicious as those of Paul Bocuse, but your friends probably won't be able to tell the difference anyway.

Cordon Bleu Paris Culinary Arts Institute

8 rue Léon Delhomme

☎01 53 68 22 50; www.cordonbleu.edu

There's no more prestigious training academy for the serious aspiring chef than the original Paris branch of the Cordon Bleu. More tourist-friendly options include 2-4hr. workshops and short week-long courses. Price of a one-day taste of Provence workshop: €175. Bragging rights: priceless.

▶ Ⓢ 1-day cooking class €175. *i* Certificate and degree programs available.

Promenades Gourmandes

41 rue de l'Échiquier

☎01 48 04 56 84; www.fmeunier.com

If the corporate Cordon Bleu is too impersonal for you, Paule Caillat's cooking classes and market tours are just the opposite. Capped at eight students, classes are scheduled on request and take place in a home kitchen in the Marais in either French or English. Every class includes a cheese tasting and three-course lunch that you prepare yourselves.

▶ Ⓢ Half-day cooking classes €270 per person.

Art Schools and Courses

Sick of just looking at the *Mona Lisa* and *Venus de Milo* in museums, or wondering how everyday items at the Centre Pompidou are art? It's easy to look at art while listening to your audio tour, but getting your hands dirty in an art class is a whole different painting.

L'École du Louvre

pl. du Carrousel, Porte Jaujard

☎01 55 35 18 35; www.ecoledulouvre.fr

Installed in the Louvre in 1882, the École du Louvre, dedicated to "making the Louvre into a living center of study," teaches undergraduate, graduate, and post-graduate classes in art history and museum studies as well as an 🎨**art auctioneer** training program. Looking for less of a time commitment? Every Monday, Tuesday, and Thursday evening, the École organizes free lectures by academics, curators, and other museum professionals.

▶ Ⓢ Undergraduate tuition €350.

Musée des Arts Décoratifs

107 rue de Rivoli

☎01 44 55 59 02; www.lesartsdecoratifs.fr

The Musée des Arts Décoratifs affords students the opportunity to take year-long day and evening classes and intensive holiday workshops in studio art. Topics range from the conventional (oil painting, sculpture, figure drawing) to the more esoteric (*trompe-l'œil* painting, engraving, and comic book making).

▶ Ⓢ €2000-4950; registration fee €300.

VOLUNTEERING

Oscar Wilde once famously said, "When good Americans die, they go to Paris." We're here to help you earn your place in French heaven by being a "good" American tourist and leaving the country in better shape than you found it.

Lavish palaces and châteaux like Versailles and Fontainbleu may leave you wondering how the world's fifth wealthiest nation could need any volunteers. But behind the gilded gates and expansive gardens, the country faces an abundance of social issues. Whether it's wildlife conservation, AIDS awareness, or archaeological restoration, there is no shortage of organizations eager to accept volunteers.

Youth and Community

Groupement Étudiant National d'Enseignment aux Personnes Incerées

12 rue Charles Fourier

☎01 45 88 37 00; www.genepi.fr

Founded by students after the violent riots over the prison system in the early '70s, GENEPI pairs student volunteers with inmates in French prisons to promote social rehabilitation through teaching and cultural activities.

Beyond Tourism

Secours Populaire Français

9/11 rue Froissart

☎01 44 78 21 00; www.secourspopulaire.asso.fr

A humanitarian organization created in 1945, Secours Populaire Français helps combat poverty by providing food, clothing, health care, and temporary shelter. It also organizes sporting and cultural activities to further brighten the lives of poor children and their families.

Conservation and Ecology

Club du Vieux Manoir

☎01 44 72 33 98; www.clubduvieuxmanoir.asso.fr

Club du Vieux Manoir arranges projects of various lengths to restore castles and churches and to teach young people the importance of protecting the *patrimoine national.*

▶ Ⓢ Membership and insurance fee €16 per year. Program fee €14 per day; includes food and lodging.

Ministry of Culture, Sous-Direction de l'Archéologie

3 rue de Valois

☎01 40 15 77 81; www.culture.gouv.fr

This government department oversees archaeological digs on French soil and, luckily for the archaeology nerds out there, publishes a list of summer excavations that accept volunteers in May. If you're lucky you might just dig up some buried treasure!

Rempart

☎01 40 15 77 81; www.culture.gouv.fr

Rempart is a union of nearly 170 nonprofit organizations throughout France that accept volunteers to restore historic sites and monuments, including military, religious, civic, industrial, and natural heritage sites and monuments.

▶ *i* 18+. Basic French knowledge recommended. Ⓢ Room and board vary by camp. Registration fee covers accident insurance.

Orange Rockcorps

www.orangerockcorps.fr

Sure, volunteering out of the goodness of your heart is admirable and does this world a whole lot of good. But what if you could benefit too? With Orange Rockcorps you can. For every four hours you spend volunteering, the organization gives you one

Beyond Tourism

ticket to a concert in Paris. And not just any concert. Tickets in the past have been for N.E.R.D, Damian Marley, Nas, and Akon. The Orange Rockcorps blog makes it even easier for you to connect to volunteer projects in your area.

WORKING

The City of Love isn't cheap. Whether you're spending your money on beignets, berets, or Beaujolais, you're bound to run out eventually. Now that your stomach is full, you look like a tourist, and your thirst is quenched, it's time to replenish that wallet. No one wants to call home and ask their parents to mail some traveler's checks, so take a peek at the listings below and save yourself the embarrassment.

Unfortunately we do have some bad news: travelers without EU citizenship face a particular challenge when searching for a job in France. Only employers who cannot find qualified workers in the EU may petition to bring in a long-term non-EU employee. If you're undeterred by the less-than-welcoming attitude toward foreign workers, you may want to try a job that requires English-language skills, since bilingual candidates have a better chance of finding work. Working as an au pair or teaching English are both popular long-term options. If you're in the market for a short-term stint, be on the lookout for a service or agricultural job. Classified advertisements in newspapers and online are good resources for international job-seekers.

Long-Term Work

As we mentioned, it can be tricky finding long-term work in France. American firms are a better bet. A listing of American firms in France is available for purchase from the **American Chamber of Commerce** in France (www.amchamfrance.org).

Teaching English

Teaching in French public schools and universities is largely restricted to French citizens. One of the only exceptions is the French government's foreign language assistants program, coordinated by the French embassy in your home country. Teaching assistants commit to teaching for seven to nine months in public schools throughout metropolitan France, or overseas in Guadeloupe, Martinique, French Guiana, and Réunion. Assistants work 12hr. per week in an elementary school (ages eight-11) or secondary school (ages 11-18). The salary is approximately €780 per month, which includes mandatory health insurance and French social security. No prior teaching experience is necessary, but some background in French language is required. Applicants must be 20-29 years of age and have completed a bachelor's degree. Interested American citizens and permanent residents should contact the embassy in Washington at least six months prior to the start of the academic year. For more information, visit **www.ambafrance-us.org.**

It is also sometimes possible to find jobs independently, but in most cases you'll need a Teaching English as a Foreign Language (TEFL) certificate. **ESL Base** (www.eslbase.com) posts notices for schools seeking native English speakers as teachers you then contact the school directly for information about full- and part-time opportunities. University fellowship programs can be a great way to find a teaching job. If you want to try your luck, the best time to do so is several weeks before the start of the academic year.

Au Pair Work

If you love people—especially the ones that barely reach your waist, can't speak in full sentences, and drink out of sippy cups—then this job is for you. Au pairs take care of children and work with parents, often becoming integral members of the family. They get some vacation time, room and board, and even a stipend.

Apitu

4 rue du Roquet

☎02 99 73 22 36; www.apitu.com

APITU is an au pair organization located in Paris that places foreign travelers with families looking for help. The company provides classes and training courses to acquaint you with the relevant job skills and to teach you the language (if you don't already speak French, that is).

▶ *i* Must be age 18-27 and work 1-12 months. Ⓢ Au pairs work 30hr. per week in exchange for room, board, and €80.

Europair

17 rue de Buci

☎01 43 29 80 01; www.europairservices.com

EUROPAIR's au pair program targets students traveling in France, with a preference for females. The organization offers

More Visa Information

EU citizens have the right to work in France without a visa, and can easily obtain a **carte de séjour** (residency permit) by presenting a passport, proof of employment, and other identification documents. Visit www.infomobil.org for a complete list of requirements.

Non-EU citizens hoping to work in France for fewer than 90 days must apply for an **Autorisation Provisoire de Travail** at a local branch of Direction Départementale du Travail, de l'Emploi et de la Formation Professionnelle (DDTEFP). A short-term, or Schengen, visa (US$82) may also be required. Non-EU citizens wishing to work in France for more than 90 days must have an offer of employment authorized by the French Ministry of Labor before applying for a **long-stay visa** (US$136) through their local French consulate. Within eight days of arrival in France, holders of long-stay visas must apply for a *carte de séjour*. International students hoping to secure a job must possess a **carte de séjour d'étudiant** (student residency card) and apply for an Autorisation Provisoire de Travail at a DDTEFP office. Students in France are permitted to work up to 19½hr. per week during the academic year, and full time during summer and holidays. Special rules apply for au pairs and teaching assistants; see www.consulfrance-washington.org for more info.

language classes to all its au pairs to promote bilingualism, and can place applicants in summer (two to three months) or longer (six to 12 months) jobs.

▶ *i* Au pairs work 30hr. per week. Must be 18-27, have a driver's license, and have experience with children. Ⓢ Au pairs receive room and board, at least 1 day off per week, and a small stipend.

Solution Au Pair

158 rue de Lannoy

☎09 70 449 377; www.solutionaupair.com

This agency was one of the first in France and has been placing young foreigners with families in Paris for decades. Solution Au Pair encourages its employees to discover new lifestyles, manners, and culture by spending time in the city and with French families.

▶ *i* Placements last 1-12 months. Ⓢ Au pairs work for room and board as well as a €70-90-per-week stipend.

Internships

Global Experiences
☎+1-877-GE-ABROAD; www.globalexperiencesabroad.com/
internships

If you have your eyes set on a certain field, or even just a passing interest in things like journalism, video production, and fashion, Global Experiences can help you find a placement. Though the cost is high, their listings are comprehensive.

▶ Ⓢ 10-week internships US$7990.

Short-Term Work

If you're looking for a quick and easy way to put some money in your pocket, consider a short-term job. Short-term work requires little commitment, and you can make enough to keep the party rockin'. Scouting the flyers at the famed English-language bookstore Shakespeare and Co. (see **Sights: Latin Quarter and St-Germain**) can be a great way for English speakers to find short-term jobs like tutoring or babysitting.

Easy Expat
www.easyexpat.com

As its name suggests, Easy Expat has an easy-to-navigate website that lists summer, seasonal, and short-term jobs as well as volunteer opportunities and internships. Options range from teaching ski lessons to working at Disneyland Paris—haven't you always wanted to dress up as Mickey Mouse?

Fédération Unie des Auberges de Jeunesse
☎01 40 15 77 81; www.fuaj.org

This organization helps you find short-term work in member youth hostels. Employees perform various tasks, such as catering or working the reception desk.

▶ *i* Submit applications to individual hostels.

Bombard Balloon Adventures
605 Belvedere Rd., West Palm Beach, FL, USA
☎+1-800-862-8537; www.bombardsociety.org

Are you ready to pull a *Wizard of Oz* and see where a balloon can take you? This seasonal job will give you the opportunity to do just that. The company hires pilots, ground crew, guides, and chefs for its hot-air balloon excursions.

Tell the World

If your friends are tired of hearing about that time you saved a baby orangutan in Indonesia, there's clearly only one thing to do: get new friends. Find them at our website, www.letsgo.com, where you can post your study-, volunteer-, or work-abroad stories for other, more appreciative community members to read.

Index

Index

Restaurants Index

Nightlife Index

Shopping Index

PARIS ACKNOWLEDGMENTS

MICHAEL THANKS: Billy, for being a phenomenal RM and spotting all the French mistakes I would have surely missed (and for his sass). Linda, because you and The Cause made every day an adventure—спасибо большой, товарищ. Leah, for being my Editor and Quad buddy, and for being one with the earth. Amy, for bringing the word "y'all" into my vocabulary and being an awesome hostess (TT shall continue). Chris, for fielding thousands of nitpicky questions, and for settling Catan with me. Everyone in LGHQ, for always bringing laughs and lots of food. Taylor, for conquering monstrous Paris in only seven weeks, and for the entertaining chat sessions. Al's, for feeding me. My awesome parents, who drove back and forth to bring me home for the weekend. Miranda and Kristin, for being the best friends in the world. And Bryan, for absolutely everything.

BILLY THANKS: Taylor for his quip for everything. Michael for his sass and his sassy editing. Chris for keeping to his schedules and for the Tanjore train. The Soviet/Snuggle Pod for its love, laughs, and coffee (JTR). Google Maps for all its enlightening wisdom. The Format Manual for its insistence on the Oxford comma. NPR for my walks to work. The RLL department for their tutelage. SJJ for exploring the streets of Paris with me. CUPA et mes amis français pour avoir été mes guides en France. Joe for being a #bestie. The residents of 300 Western for laughs, Vinho Verde, and the EBW. Rachel for her coffee breaks. Brandi for being a bee charmer. John for being a beeb. The fam for good ol' support. And Cambridge for a great four years.

ABOUT LET'S GO

The Student Travel Guide

Let's Go publishes the world's favorite student travel guides, written entirely by Harvard students. Armed with pens, notebooks, and a few changes of clothes stuffed into their backpacks, our student researchers go across continents, through time zones, and above expectations to seek out invaluable travel experiences for our readers. Because we are a completely student-run company, we have a unique perspective on how students travel, where they want to go, and what they're looking to do when they get there. If your dream is to grab a machete and forge through the jungles of Costa Rica, we can take you there. If you'd rather bask in the Riviera sun at a beachside cafe, we'll set you a table. In short, we write for readers who know that there's more to travel than tour buses. To keep up, visit our website, www.letsgo.com, where you can sign up to blog, post photos from your trips, and connect with the Let's Go community.

Traveling Beyond Tourism

We're on a mission to provide our readers with sharp, fresh coverage packed with socially responsible opportunities to go beyond tourism. Each guide's Beyond Tourism chapter shares ideas about responsible travel, study abroad, and how to give back to the places you visit while on the road. To help you gain a deeper connection with the places you travel, our fearless researchers scour the globe to give you the heads-up on both world-renowned and off-the-beaten-track opportunities. We've also opened our pages to respected writers and scholars to hear their takes on the countries and regions we cover, and asked travelers who have worked, studied, or volunteered abroad to contribute first-person accounts of their experiences.

Fifty-Two Years of Wisdom

Let's Go has been on the road for 52 years and counting. We've grown a lot since publishing our first 20-page pamphlet to Europe in 1960, but five decades and 60 titles later, our witty, candid guides are still researched and written entirely by students on shoestring budgets who know that train strikes, stolen luggage, food poisoning, and marriage proposals are all part of a day's work. Meanwhile, we're still bringing readers fresh new features, such as a student-life section with advice on how and where to meet students from around the world; a revamped, user-friendly layout for our listings; and greater emphasis on the experiences that make travel abroad a rite of passage for readers of all ages. And, of course, this year's 16 titles—including five brand-new guides—are still brimming with editorial honesty, a commitment to students, and our irreverent style.

The Let's Go Community

More than just a travel guide company, Let's Go is a community that reaches from our headquarters in Cambridge, MA, all across the globe. Our small staff of dedicated student editors, writers, and tech nerds comes together because of our shared passion for travel and our desire to help other travelers get the most out of their experience. We love it when our readers become part of the Let's Go community as well—when you travel, drop us a postcard (67 Mt. Auburn St., Cambridge, MA 02138, USA), send us an email (feedback@letsgo.com), or sign up on our website (www.letsgo.com) to tell us about your adventures and discoveries.

For more information, updated travel coverage, and news from our researcher team, visit us online at www.letsgo.com.

LET'S GO BUDGET

TAKE A LET'S GO BUDGET GUIDE TO EUROPE

LET'S GO BUDGET AMSTERDAM
978-1-61237-015-6

LET'S GO BUDGET ATHENS
978-1-61237-005-7

LET'S GO BUDGET BARCELONA
978-1-61237-014-9

LET'S GO BUDGET BERLIN
978-1-61237-006-4

LET'S GO BUDGET FLORENCE
978-1-61237-007-1

LET'S GO BUDGET ISTANBUL
978-1-61237-008-8

LET'S GO BUDGET LONDON
978-1-61237-013-2

LET'S GO BUDGET MADRID
978-1-61237-009-5

LET'S GO BUDGET PARIS
978-1-61237-011-8

LET'S GO BUDGET PRAGUE
978-1-61237-010-1

LET'S GO BUDGET ROME
978-1-61237-012-5

ALL LET'S GO BUDGET GUIDEBOOKS ARE $9.99.
*Let's Go also publishes guides to individual countries
that are available at bookstores and online retailers.*

For more information: visit **LETSGO.COM**
JOIN THE DISCUSSION WITH LET'S GO ON **FACEBOOK** AND **TWITTER**

HELPING LET'S GO. If you want to share your discoveries, suggestions, or corrections, please drop us a line. We appreciate every piece of correspondence, whether a postcard, a 10-page email, or a coconut. Visit Let's Go at www.letsgo.com or send an email to:

feedback@letsgo.com, subject: "Let's Go Budget Paris"

Address mail to:

Let's Go Budget Paris, 67 Mount Auburn St., Cambridge, MA 02138, USA

In addition to the invaluable travel advice our readers share with us, many are kind enough to offer their services as researchers or editors. Unfortunately, our charter enables us to employ only currently enrolled Harvard students.
Maps © Let's Go and Avalon Travel
Interior design by Darren Alessi
Production by Amber Pirker
Photos © Let's Go; Taylor Nickel and Ama Francis, photographers

Distributed by Publishers Group West.
Printed in Canada by Friesens Corp.

ISBN-13: 978-1-61237-011-8
ISBN-10: 1-61237-011-X
First edition
10 9 8 7 6 5 4 3 2 1

Let's Go Budget Paris is written by Let's Go Publications, 67 Mt. Auburn St., Cambridge, MA 02138, USA.

Let's Go® and the LG logo are trademarks of Let's Go, Inc.

LEGAL DISCLAIMER. For 50 years, Let's Go has published the world's favorite budget travel guides, written entirely by students and updated periodically based on the personal anecdotes and travel experiences of our student writers. Although every effort was made to ensure that the information was correct at the time of going to press, the author and publisher do not assume and hereby disclaim any liability to any party for any loss or damage caused by errors, omissions, or any potential travel disruption due to labor or financial difficulty, whether such errors or omissions result from negligence, accident, or any other cause.

ADVERTISING DISCLAIMER. All advertisements appearing in Let's Go publications are sold by an independent agency not affiliated with the editorial production of the guides. Advertisers are never given preferential treatment, and the guides are researched, written, and published independent of advertising. Advertisements do not imply endorsement of products or services by Let's Go, and Let's Go does not vouch for the accuracy of information provided in advertisements.

If you are interested in purchasing advertising space in a Let's Go publication, contact Edman & Company at 1-203-656-1000.

QUICK REFERENCE

YOUR GUIDE TO LET'S GO ICONS

	Let's Go recommends	☎	Phone numbers	⚐	Directions
i	Other hard info	⑤	Prices	⏰	Hours

IMPORTANT PHONE NUMBERS

EMERGENCY: ☎112			
Amsterdam	☎911	London	☎999
Barcelona	☎092	Madrid	☎092
Berlin	☎110	Paris	☎17
Florence	☎113	Prague	☎158
Istanbul	☎155	Rome	☎113

USEFUL PHRASES

ENGLISH	FRENCH	GERMAN	ITALIAN	SPANISH
Hello/Hi	Bonjour/Salut	Hallo/Tag	Ciao	Hola
Goodbye/Bye	Au revoir	Auf Wiedersehen/ Tschüss	Arrivederci/Ciao	Adios/Chao
Yes	Oui	Ja	Sì	Sí
No	Non	Nein	No	No
Excuse me!	Pardon!	Entschuldigen Sie!	Scusa!	Perdón!
Thank you	Merci	Danke	Grazie	Gracias
Go away!	Va t'en!	Geh weg!	Vattene via!	Vete!
Help!	Au secours!	Hilfe!	Aiuto!	Ayuda!
Call the police!	Appelez la police!	Ruf die Polizei!	Chiamare la polizia!	Llame a la policía!
Get a doctor!	Cherchez un médecin!	Hol einen Arzt!	Avere un medico!	Llame a un médico!
I don't understand	Je ne comprends pas	Ich verstehe nicht	Non capisco	No comprendo
Do you speak English?	Parlez-vous anglais?	Sprechen Sie Englisch?	Parli inglese?	¿Habla inglés?
Where is...?	Où est...?	Wo ist...?	Dove...?	¿Dónde está...?

TEMPERATURE CONVERSIONS

°CELSIUS	-5	0	5	10	15	20	25	30	35	40
°FAHRENHEIT	23	32	41	50	59	68	77	86	95	104

MEASUREMENT CONVERSIONS

1 inch (in.) = 25.4mm	1 millimeter (mm) = 0.039 in.
1 foot (ft.) = 0.305m	1 meter (m) = 3.28 ft.
1 mile (mi.) = 1.609km	1 kilometer (km) = 0.621 mi.
1 pound (lb.) = 0.454kg	1 kilogram (kg) = 2.205 lb.
1 gallon (gal.) = 3.785L	1 liter (L) = 0.264 gal.